THE BASS FISHERMAN'S BIBLE

Erwin A. Bauer

DOUBLEDAY & COMPANY, INC.
Garden City, N.Y.
1961

THE
BASS FISHERMAN'S
BIBLE

Contents

THE
BASS FISHERMAN'S
BIBLE

Largemouths are grand jumpers. A hooked bass will often make several exciting leaps and cartwheels.

Chapter 1

THE BLACK BASS "FAMILY"

It must have been a warm and wonderful day in June when Dr. James Henshall, a Cincinnati physician, snuffed out the gas light in his office for the last time and hurried to a nearby livery stable for his buggy. That was more than fifty years ago. He carried an umbrella, to conceal a fly rod, and his black valise contained hooks and rooster hackles rather than a stethoscope and other tools of his trade. He was starting on a fishing trip from which he never really returned.

For several decades Doc Henshall traveled up and down the Ohio Valley, fishing with an enthusiasm that was uncommon in his time. Sport fishing around the turn of the century was confined almost entirely to eastern trout and salmon, but this pio-

neering doctor had "discovered" another fish—a black bass—which was abundant in local waters.

Henshall not only caught bass wholesale with hook and line, but he devised new and better tackle to take them. He studied their habits and their physiology with a scientist's eyes and skills. He seined, netted, collected, autopsied, and kept valuable records, meanwhile swatting mosquitoes, losing sleep, and sometimes falling into chilly rivers. He wandered down into Kentucky's blue-grass country and later north through Michigan. During the periods when he returned to Cincinnati, he wrote about his experiences and with his frequently printed and reprinted *Book of the Black Bass* became the father or the founder of bass fishing as American fish-

ermen know it today. He was the bass fisherman's Boone and Audubon rolled into one.

It was Henshall who claimed that "inch for inch and pound for pound" the bass was the gamest fish of all. There's much room for argument there because, with times and transportation methods being what they were, Henshall never really knew such fish as the dolphin or the dorado, the tarpon or the bonefish. But still he had a point. All characteristics considered, the black basses easily rank among the great game fishes in the world today, just as they did in Henshall's day.

Bass are easy to catch, but not too easy, and that's an asset. They're strong and fast and pretty fair jumpers. They're far from the best on the table, but still here is good, robust fare. But best of all they're available. They're the most widely distributed freshwater game species in the Western Hemisphere and, except for the brown trout, in the whole world.

A wandering angler nowadays can stow bass fishing tackle in his car trunk or station wagon and hit the highways optimistically. No matter where he's going, and often no matter when, he can probably put the tackle to good use because the black basses—either largemouths, smallmouths, spotteds, or any combination of the three—are living and thriving in every corner of the country. Except in Alaska, there's no state in the Union where an angler can't find them and no month during the year when, some-

where on the map, they won't be striking.

Bass fishing wasn't always this convenient. For Henshall it was a day's trip to the next county and a week to west Kentucky. Now turnpikes, toll roads, new automobiles, modern outboard motors, and assorted flying machines from pontoon-equipped Cubs to giant Boeing jets place any fishing hole within one day's reach of almost any sportsman anywhere. Even the ranges of the basses have been expanded from what was a rather limited section of North America in primitive times.

Early records are so incomplete that no two fisheries authorities agree on the exact original ranges of the basses. But all that really matters, generally, is that largemouths were natives of the Southeast, the Midwest, and the fringes of the Great Lakes. Smallmouths shared certain sections of the Midwest and lived in all the Great Lakes except Superior. Spotted bass existed in certain streams of the Ohio and lower Mississippi drainage areas. Curiously, spotted bass weren't even identified as separate species until the twenties. None of the three existed in the western half of the United States, or specifically west of 100 degrees west longitude which runs from near Laredo, Texas, to Pierre, South Dakota. But no matter where you find them today, bass aren't bass at all. Instead they're sunfish, the largest members of a purely North American family that includes crappies, bluegills, warmouths, shell-

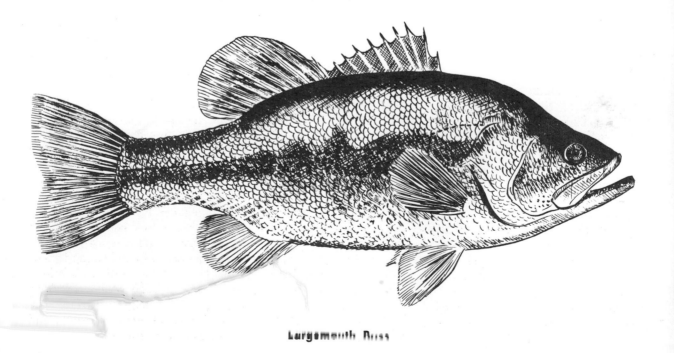

Largemouth Bass

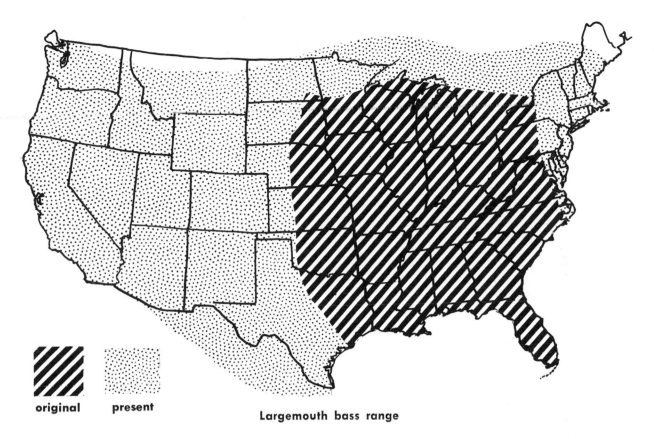

original   present

Largemouth bass range

crackers, punkinseeds, rock bass, Sacramento perch, and more than a dozen other smaller sunfishes. The only true fresh-water bass are the white and yellow bass, but common names aren't too important, as we will see.

The Largemouth Bass

The largemouth bass, *Micropterus salmoides* (Lacépède), is the most adaptable and widely distributed of his clan. They're still plentiful in nearly all of their original haunts, and they've followed wherever humans have seen fit to provide new waters. The odds are great that largemouths will never again be as abundant as in pre-Henshall times, when commercial netting for them was possible. In the 1880s the commercial catch (largemouths and smallmouths together) in southwestern Lake Erie alone ran to 599,000 pounds a year. Modern outdoorsmen are surprised to learn that largemouths were also netted in such old Ohio canal reservoirs as Buckeye, St. Marys, and Indian lakes. This happened in other states too. Changing habitats and the gradual introduction of carp (which devoured vegetation and completely changed the ecology of water-

sheds) which began in 1880 has made these concentrations impossible. Just the same, while trout and salmon have suffered with the advance of civilization, bass have adapted to it.

Largemouths thrive today in all the water-supply reservoirs of the East and Midwest which are still abuilding. Fishermen find them behind the high hydroelectric dams of the South and in the giant desert reservoirs of the West. Bigmouths have found almost two million new homes in farm ponds across our landscape—just as they've become naturalized in tepid Texas "water tanks," in *resacas* of the Rio Grande, and in old mill ponds of New England. They've even occupied many a trout pond where they are completely unwelcome and eventually must be poisoned out. They like the slow rivers, clear or slightly roily, of the Mississippi watershed as well as the tea-tinted jungle streams of Florida; and they've found northern flood-control reservoirs as suitable as the swamps, sloughs, oxbows, and bayous of Dixie. They grow firm and strong in pine and birch-rimmed lakes as far north as southern Canada. And they grow stronger still in brackish, tidal waters at many points along the Atlantic Seaboard. Of course, they've invaded California and have negotiated the Pacific to Hawaii.

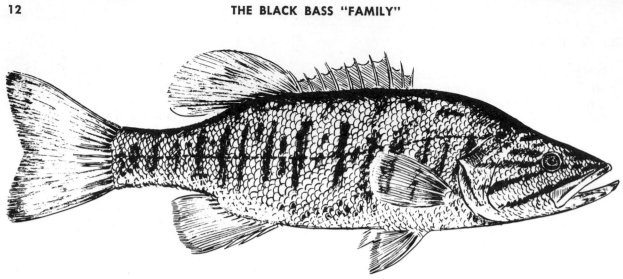

The smallmouth bass

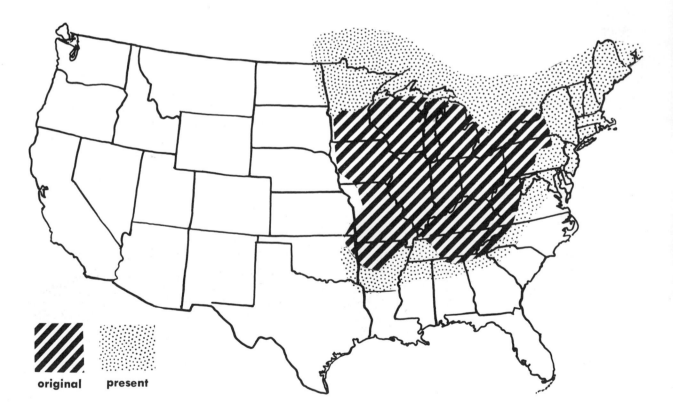

original   present

Smallmouth bass range

The Smallmouth Bass

Smallmouths *Micropterus dolomieu* (Lacépède) haven't been quite so adaptable as their more numerous, more adaptable cousins, and that's easy to explain. There just aren't so many available waters without vegetation and without earth bottoms. Generally smallmouths need cool, moving streams where the oxygen content is high, or cool and rock-bound lakes where there is a "current" or where the wind gives a wave action something like the tumbling of a stream.

Milton B. Trautman, whose book *Fishes of Ohio* is one of the most astounding volumes on fish ever compiled, has pretty well pinpointed the requirements of river smallmouths. The largest populations occurred in streams which consisted of about 40 per cent riffles flowing over clean gravel, boulder, or bedrock bottom; where the pools had a noticeable current; where there was considerable water willow; and where the stream dropped from 4 to 25 feet per mile. The last can be determined for any stream by consulting a topo map. And Trautman's is good reference material for any prospecting bass fisherman.

Today smallmouths are at home in Maine and New Brunswick as well as the four lower Great Lakes. They're the fish of Kentucky's moonshine country, of lonely Ozark waterways, and of Eastern rivers like the upper Potomac, the Shenandoah, Susquehanna, and the Delaware. They grow fat and bronze colored and wild in many lakes across southern Canada. In many of these they were only released in recent years.

The Spotted Bass

The spotted or Kentucky bass, *Micropterus punctulatus*, has nine rows of scales between the lateral line and the forepart of the dorsal fin. The upper jaw does not extend beyond a vertical line projected through the eye, and most individuals have a large black (or dark) spot on the point of the gill cover. A spotted bass also has a small patch of teeth on the tongue. Neither the smallmouth nor the largemouth has these teeth.

Any history of how basses were distributed would be fascinating, and it would sound almost fictional. Actually it has been so haphazard and so unplanned that to compile an accurate history is no longer impossible. Just for example, one early unofficial shipment of smallmouths was carried across the Virginia mountains in the tender of a Chesapeake and Ohio coal train. Years ago the state of Ohio, as well as neighboring states (Pennsylvania, Indiana, New York), operated a railway "fish car" that transported bass from Lake Erie to streams statewide. More than once, in the early years of this widespread fish transplanting, a local politician won an election when he just happened to show up at the moment a load of fish arrived to stock his constituents' lake.

Bass have been transported by hand, in milk cans by game wardens, on muleback, and via canal barge. Eastern states have traded bass eggs to western states for wild turkeys, and there's even a record of shipping bass to Mexico in exchange for quail. In recent years aerated tank trucks have been doing the job, but the newest innovation is to ship them in polyethylene bags into which enough oxygen has

The spotted bass

Spotted bass range

been pumped to last for a week! No wonder it's now possible to fish for bass in such widely scattered places as Bavaria, Austria, South Africa, Australia, Cuba, and in scattered parts of South America.

Bass have as many names and nicknames as there are regions in the country. Besides largemouth, the critter is commonly called bigmouth and even wide-mouth. In the South he's a trout or a green trout. Elsewhere you'll hear linesides, jumper, Oswego, or green bass. It isn't true, though, as one angler told his nonfishing wife, that largemouths are the fe-males of the breed, and smallmouths the males.

Smallmouths have fewer names, and bronzeback is the most popular because that is an apt descrip-tion of the fish in many waters. But he's also known as trout, brownie, or bronze bass and occasionally as striper or striped bass for the vertical bars on his flanks.

Spotted bass are also called Kentuckies, Kentucky bass, or Kentucky spotted bass.

Identification

Distinguishing among the basses is a popular pas-time wherever anglers gather, and it isn't always too accurately done. The most obvious physical characteristics are sometimes similar enough to allow margin for mistake. For instance, all three species have a wide variation in color from silvery through green to bronze or solid black, depending, it's con-ceded, on the color and chemical content of the waters they inhabit. Perhaps there is also a slight variation in color from season to season in individual fish—as between spawning season and fall or when the murky waters of early spring become alcohol-clear in autumn.

Still . . . largemouths generally tend to shades of green or green-black, while smallmouths are almost always tinged in shades of tarnished brass or bronze. A brown coloration isn't unusual. Largemouths may have a horizontal dark stripe along the side; small-mouths never do. Smallmouths may (but not al-ways) have several vertical dark stripes or blotches; largemouths never have them. Spotted bass usually have a distinct dark spot on the edge of the gill cover, but sometimes largemouths also have such a mark—which makes it evident that to depend on markings and color alone is unwise.

Actually the basses are easy to identify positively, and it's only necessary to do a little counting. On all species there is a fine, lateral line that curves all the way from the gill cover at about eye level to the tail. If there are eleven rows of scales between that line and the front of the dorsal fin, it's a smallmouth. If there are seven rows, it's a largemouth. If there are nine rows, it's a spotted bass. Following this scale-row count, you just can't miss.

Since spotted bass are the hardest to identify, and since they have actually been called (erroneously) a cross between a largemouth and a smallmouth, try an extra check if the scale-row count measures nine. Run your finger over the tongue and if you feel a small patch of teeth there, it's a spotted for sure. No other bass have them.

There's still another hasty method to make an identification, but it isn't so positive as the scale-row count. Project a straight line vertically through the eye of the bass. If the jaw of the fish extends beyond the eye, or your line, it's a largemouth. If not, it's a smallmouth or a spotted.

Size

Largemouths invariably average heavier than smallmouths. An exception occurs in waters where both species exist and where the water "type" is most suited to smallmouths. Then the smallmouths will grow larger faster. The world's record largemouth is a 22 1/4 pounder taken by G. W. Perry in Montgomery Pond near Valdosta, Georgia, in 1932. Anything is possible in fishing, but this is one world's record that is likely to last a long time. The largest fish taken every year in Florida, where largemouths grow biggest of all, usually run about 15 or 16 pounds, and even these are mighty rare. The best chance for a new largemouth record would result from stocking them in a new, fertile water somewhere, perhaps in Latin America, where there is a year-around growing season.

The smallmouth world record, an 11-pound-15-ounce trophy taken in Dale Hollow Lake, Kentucky, stands a slightly better chance of being broken. It was caught by D. H. Hayes of Leitchfield, Kentucky, in 1951. Paul Richardson, Jr. of Carthage, Missouri, caught what is probably the record spotted bass in the nearby Spring River on March 9, 1958. The fish weighed 7 pounds 2 ounces, and it was taken on a live minnow.

Nationwide, largemouths taken by anglers will average between one and two pounds. Smallmouths will average a pound. Generally both species run larger the farther south they're found, and the main reason is a longer active feeding and growing season. North of the Ohio River, a six-pound largemouth is bragging size. South of there it takes a larger fish, say an eight- or ten-pounder, to raise a serious bass fisherman's eyebrows.

The bass of each individual lake and stream have different rate of growth and development. Although a largemouth might reach a pound or more after only six months under ideal conditions, the national average largemouth needs two years to reach ten inches and from one half to three quarters of a pound. Smallmouths need three years to reach comparable growth.

Together, bass and bass fishing are an important economic factor in our lives whether we fish for them or not. The best estimates available reveal that 85 per cent (or 25 million) of all fishermen fish for bass or fish in waters that contain bass. Figuring that they spend an everage of $500 a year for their sport—and maybe that figure is conservative—bass fishermen pick up an annual check that runs into billions of dollars—more than is spent on baseball and football put together. That expenditure includes travel expenses, gas, lodging, boats, motors, special clothing, and meals, as well as tackle, bait, license, guides, and the like.

Black bass are important game fish no matter how you look at them.

Life Histories

Along about the end of April in a belt that would stretch from New York to Nebraska, any careful observer can detect a restlessness among the smallmouth bass in any stream in which they live. It might even resemble a migration. But actually it's the beginning of spring spawning—the beginning of life for the species.

As water temperatures soar above 55 degrees Fahrenheit, the male bronzebacks spend more time in shallow water, continually searching for a suitable nest site. Then as if on signal these same males begin to scoop out nests, or redds, on gravel, coarse sand, or rocky bottoms just as the mercury passes 60 degrees. It's almost as if spawning is triggered by the thermometer. These male-built nests, incidentally, are saucer-shaped depressions from 14 to 30 inches in diameter which are "fanned out" by vigorous movements of the tail fin. This "fanning" causes the deformed or reddened tails which anglers often find on bass in early spring.

When the nest is completed the male selects a "ripe" female and drives her to the nest by nudging her with his snout—or by actually biting her on the

Playing a largemouth close to shore. Fish was hooked in area of sunken brush.

flank or gill flap. In typically feminine fashion she usually refuses to remain on the nest the first time; instead she retreats to deeper water. But male bass are always persistent, and after several such attempts from a hundred to several thousand eggs are deposited.

Female bass have been found to carry as many as 15,000 eggs, but 7000 is much nearer the average. However, all of these are not deposited at once, nor do all of the deposited eggs mature at the same time. This is a safety mechanism which permits re-nesting in case predatory fish or spring freshets destroy the first nest. In any case, after egg laying is finished the female either retires or is driven to deeper water by the male, who takes over caring for the eggs and the young.

Smallmouth eggs hatch in from 3 to 5 days, and at first the young fish sink into crevices in the rocks. From one to two weeks after the eggs are deposited

the fry rise and hover over the nest in a school, meanwhile being guarded by the male parent, who will attack any other fish—or fisherman's lure—which passes close to them. The fry are nearly black in color at this time. They move about rather slowly until all the nourishment in the yolk sac is absorbed and until they're a little more than an inch long. This is usually the most critical period in a bass's life, because by now the male parent has grown hungry enough to eat as many of them as he can catch. The lucky ones escape to feed on tiny water animals called crustaceans and perhaps to grow to catchable size.

About the same time that things are stirring in smallmouth streams and lakes, there's activity in largemouth waters too. Depending on the latitude, this species will spawn sometime between April and June—although largemouth spawning has actually been observed in Florida and points south during every month of the year. In any case, the restlessness in largemouths begins somewhat later than with smallmouths, and serious spawning occurs somewhere between 63 and 68 degrees.

Largemouths' nests are seldom as elaborate as those of smallmouths, and sometimes a male will select a site and nothing more. Largemouths prefer to deposit eggs on rootlets of submerged plants or grass, on aquatic vegetation, on either a mud or soft sand bottom. An average bass nest will be about 3 or 4 feet deep, but the extremes run from a few inches to 10 or 12 feet, which is the case in some clear, glacial lakes of Michigan. Eggs hatch in from 3 to 6 days and are cared for by the male parent—until his appetite gets the better of him. Young largemouths which survive feed on tiny water animals called Cyclops and Daphnia. As they grow older they add larger and larger insects to the menu.

It's obvious that the entire procedure of spawning is a precarious business. Weather is a factor because a sudden cold spell can interrupt everything. Rains and floods can take a toll; conceivably they can wipe out an entire year's "hatch" in one lake or in one region. Turbidity—the presence of silt or earth in suspension—can interfere with spawning, too, because it filters rays of sunlight which are necessary to hatch eggs by slowly heating the water. In lakes smallmouths sometimes like to spawn in fairly deep water—perhaps in 8 or 10 feet. If the sun cannot penetrate that far the eggs simply will not hatch.

Beginning the minute the original egg is deposited, a bass's life is one of eating and being eaten. It's an aquatic rat race to survive. Crayfish and an endless host of formidable water insects and amphibians compete to eat the eggs as soon as they're dropped. After they hatch, larger fish are always seeking them. Even when a bass reaches several pounds there's no escape; it's then that fishermen are his problem, but it's only fair to add that anglers are probably the least serious problem in the entire life cycle.

Just as bass are always hunted in the cruel underwater world, so are they always hunting. They'll eat anything they can swallow, and there have been many cases of tackling critters they *couldn't* swallow. All this is fine for fishermen who show up at streamside with many strange lures. For the record, though, the following have been found in largemouth bass stomachs: an adult red-winged blackbird, muskrats, common water snakes, ducklings, a bottle cap, mice, a Micronite cigarette filter, a sora rail, and a shoehorn. But the truth is that once they have passed 12″ in length, 95 per cent of any bass's food consists of crayfish and smaller fishes with a few of the larger insects thrown in. In some waters

the entire diet might consist of crayfish; in others it might consist of gizzard shad. Those are the staples, but they will feed on anything alive and moving.

Because bass often live in weedy fresh waters which are never as clear as ocean salt waters and therefore not available to observation by divers, all that is known of bass movements after spawning is what can be determined by netting from the surface, from what fishermen can find, from stomach analysis, and by circumstantial deduction. That doesn't give a biologist as complete a picture, say, as it does a game biologist of pheasants and white-tailed deer, which live where anyone can watch them.

The point that's being made here is that, in large lakes and reservoirs especially, virtually nothing is known about the habits, activities, and movements of bass after they desert shallow water after spawning. As we'll see later, some topnotch fishermen suspect that even largemouths of medium size school up and concentrate in "packs" (at least for certain periods in the year) far more than anyone believes. But no one knows for sure. It has been definitely established by trawling experiments that small-

An 8-pound largemouth from Cumberland Lake, Kentucky. Angler here is widely traveled, outdoor writer, George Laycock.

mouths in Lake Erie gather in vast schools and travel aimlessly about. The word aimlessly is used here only because no one has been able to find a pattern to these travels.

On the other hand there's evidence that largemouths particularly are sedentary—that they establish "territories" which they defend against trespass by all other fishes. This trait has been evident among bass in captivity. One smallmouth which has appeared in news features was a resident of the Ohio Division of Wildlife's aquarium in its Columbus headquarters for several years. This fish shared his tank with several rock bass, but the rock bass (which were eaten one by one) were invariably driven from one corner of the tank which the smallmouth reserved for himself. This bass defended his territory to the extent of attacking the red fingernails of pretty secretaries when tapped against the glass during coffee breaks. He thumped his head hard many times before he learned the futility of it.

There are exceptions to this, of course, as we've pointed out with the wandering smallmouths of Erie, but generally bass are not "cruising" fish. They commute from shallow to deep water and they even migrate in streams, but this is not a continual movement such as that which white bass make in fresh water and which tuna, mackerel, and other species make in the salt. Nine tenths of a bass's life will be spent relatively motionless near the bottom—no matter whether the bottom is only inches deep or a hundred feet straight down.

One other point is most evident to most observers of bass. Largemouths especially like "edge"—or in a sense, cover. The "edge" may be a sunken log or a stump, a channel or opening in a weed bed, a point of land or a shoal, an old car body, a bar, a flooded fence row, a drop-off, or the edge of the lake itself. To repeat, there are exceptions, but the "rule of edge" is a valuable one to remember.

Of the three basses, the least known of all is the spotted. In *Fishes of Ohio*, however, Dr. Trautman does point out that they usually inhabit moderate or large-sized streams having gradients of less than 3 feet per mile with long, sluggish, rather deep pools.

Spotted bass spawn in the shallows when water temperatures reach the low sixties, and they appear to be more tolerant of turbid waters than either smallmouths or largemouths.

Trautman reports that about the time water temperatures reach 50 degrees, there is a pronounced upsteam migration into smaller streams, but that by early summer most adults as well as the young of the year retreat again to larger streams and to deeper holes. It isn't unusual for the spotted bass to share some water with other bass. Except in a few southern reservoirs, though, it isn't a dweller of lakes.

These are the facts fisheries biologists know about bass today, and they sadly admit that it isn't a very complete dossier. It's complete enough, however, to gradually liberalize the open seasons on bass in recent years. A generation ago every state had a closed season, usually during the spawning period, a legal limit of from 4 to 12 bass per day and a legal size limit from 10 to 12 inches each. Nowadays many states have no restrictions at all, except to buy a fishing license, and still others have eliminated at least part of the restrictions.

The reason for closed seasons and limits on bass in the first place was to protect them during spawning and to assure that the waters would never be fished out. Right after World War II it became evident to many biologists, and especially to the late, brilliant Dr. R. W. Eschmeyer, that legal fishing methods in use had little or no effect on fish populations—rod-and-reel angling simply couldn't fish out a lake—so why close seasons and limit catches at precisely the period when fishing might prove best? The number of bass in a lake, these biologists realized, was determined by factors other than sport fishing. That meant that an angler could fish for bass during the spawning season, and even catch them right off the spawning beds, with a clear conscience.

Only one thing is certain about bass and bass fishing, though: both are entirely unpredictable. But still the fisherman who knows the most about them and what makes them tick has a better chance of ending the day with a heavy stringer.

Casting rocky shoreline of large reservoir. Bass remain close to "edges" like this.

Chapter 2

BASIC BASS FISHING

Typical smallmouth stream. It's late summer and the water is low. The angler is fishing a deep pocket which is the most likely place for smallmouths. Scene is Big Walnut Creek in central Ohio.

Bill Madden, a young man who manages Indiana's Willow Slough State Fish and Game Area near Morocco, has checked enough fishermen there to make an astounding discovery. He figures that 12 men of the 22,000 who fished there in 1958 accounted for 90 per cent of all bass caught!

This isn't exactly an isolated case. Similar creel checks elsewhere across America have revealed that from 5 per cent to 10 per cent of all anglers catch from 80 per cent to 90 per cent of the bass. On a Michigan lake 4 men among hundreds of summer residents caught an estimated 85 per cent of all smallmouths caught. For years at Jackson Lake, Ohio, one man landed more bass than any 10 men thereabouts combined, and he didn't spend too much time at it.

It isn't possible to explain fully this lopsided success story because there isn't any secret formula, no one has yet invented a "never fail" lure, and no miracle methods are involved. It is simply a matter of finding bass and then of presenting a bait or lure in a manner which will cause them to strike. This combination may be an entirely different technique in every individual lake or stream in the country. But still it is possible to suggest some basic information which can help anyone to catch bass or, perhaps, to catch *more* bass no matter what the locality.

Where to Find Bass

First it's necessary to find the fish. Sometimes it's easy, but sometimes it isn't. We do know that bass invariably will be on the bottom no matter whether the water is shallow or thirty feet deep. They seldom stay "suspended" in mid-depth. We also believe that they prefer "edge" and a water temperature in the vicinity of 70 degrees. So let's put these three concepts together.

On a typical midwestern lake in May, an average largemouth bass will probably spend most of his time on the bottom in shallow waters (because the water there has just reached 70 degrees) and near some kind of edge (which may be around a newly emerging weed bed or along a strip of shore line). The odds are good he'll linger in this same area as long as all conditions are "right"—as long as the water doesn't become too warm, the vegetation too dense, or food fishes too scarce.

Two months later, on this same lake, this same largemouth will have moved, but he will be in the same sort of position—on the bottom, in water of approximately 70 degrees, and near some sort of edge. The only difference is that the edge will be deeper, possibly as deep as 50 feet, but usually wherever the 70-degree water layer exists. The availability of food or of suitable edge may alter the exact position somewhat, but—an angler must remember this—bass will never be too far away.

Largemouth bass like cover, either a weed bed, a sunken log, a shoal, or the edge of a lake, and prefer to remain at a temperature level of 70°.

Of course, there are exceptions to this 70-degree layer theory, and the most obvious occurs in all-shallow lakes where the temperature soars well above 70 in the summer and where no cooler patches of water exist. Largemouths have managed to survive in 85-degree water in Ohio and in 89 degrees in Florida.

But back to the typical midwestern lake. Although the largemouths will spend most of midsummer in deep water, they often will make regular migrations into shallow water to forage heavily. These migrations may occur in morning or evening or both, but as water temperatures continue to climb through August, they will tend to occur most often at night. Of course, bass are easier to reach with bait or lures when they are in shallow water because they are more accessible, and the odds on catching them are better because they're actually feeding at the time. Still they will strike just as readily while in the depths—if a suitable presentation of a bait is made.

A largemouth bass feeds most frequently, consumes the most food, and grows most rapidly when water temperatures are between 70 and 75. Beginning in midwinter when the water is just above freezing, the basal metabolism of a bass, or of most fresh-water fish, increases steadily as the water warms up. This means that a bass requires more and more food to live—until a critical point is reached. Beyond that point, or that temperature which cannot be pinpointed, the metabolic rate diminishes rapidly until the fish can no longer survive. Among northern "strains" of largemouths that critical point is somewhere between 75 and 80. In the South it's slightly higher.

Still another point is worth making, although it is not a hard or fast rule. The larger bass become, the more likely they are to prefer deeper water. On the average they will spawn in deeper water than smaller bass. And if the 70-degree layer of water is very thick they'll tend toward the deepest part of it.

The deeper the bass, the harder it is for a fisherman to find them. It's a matter of probing a strange, unseen underwater world—of working in the dark. Except for a few veteran bass fishermen with experience and an "instinct" to quickly find bass in deep water, locating them is a case of trial and error. There's little choice except to present baits or lures over widely scattered areas until the proper depth and "climate" are located. Once these places are found, they'll produce for a long time to come, and even when bass eventually move away from

In their search for cover at 70° bass may go as deep as 50 feet.

them it will be a gradual move. Also, these places will be productive year after year at approximately the same period.

Since many of these hot spots will be located beneath "open" water rather than close to shore, it's a wise fisherman who marks the spot by triangulation, by carefully orienting with landmarks on shore. It's always a good idea to make more than a mental note. Instead, put it in chart or written form.

Frequently it's necessary to be absolutely accurate in the matter of marking a bass area, because it may be no more than a sharp drop-off that curves

at night they move out onto nearby riffles and runs where hellgrammites, crayfish, and minnows are most plentiful and available.

Smallmouths are a little less inclined to strike in deep water than are largemouths, but here again is a fish which can be caught at any time—by someone and by some specific method.

The failure to catch bass has been blamed on the weather more than any other single factor, and I myself have been inclined to consider certain weather conditions much better or worse than others. Still it's scientific fact rather than suspicion that

When you have located a hot spot for bass, mark it by triangulation, with permanent landmarks on shore, for future reference.

for any distance from a few yards to several hundred feet along an underwater contour. It's not an easy matter to find such a thin target. But to be able to locate it precisely the first time will save much unnecessary exploration later on.

As a fisherman gains experience in exploring for bass, he learns that finding abrupt drop-offs or "reefs" is like finding pay dirt. They're worth plenty of concentration, even if he doesn't start catching bass immediately. Underwater weed beds or sunken "islands" are worth investigating, too, because all the bass in a vast area or maybe even in an entire lake might be concentrating there. Many, many limits of trophy fish have been taken without moving from such spots as these.

Finding bass in rivers—and most often these will be smallmouths—is similar to finding them in lakes except that the angler seldom has to deal with great depths. Once spawning is finished and streams begin to warm, the bronzebacks leave the shallows and retire to deep pools and pockets, at least during midday. Briefly at daybreak, on some evenings, and

weather has far more effect on fishermen than on fish anywhere. This does not refer to water temperatures, which are important, or to floods and droughts which could make fishing impossible. It's still true that if you can find bass it's also possible to catch them whether it's raining and windy or calm with bright sunshine. This becomes more evident all the time as newer, more effective tackle is designed and as biologists learn more about fishes.

Still, finding bass is only half of successful bass fishing, because it's possible to fish all day in water that's full of them and yet never have a strike. Here again it's important to understand several important bass characteristics.

Important Bass Characteristics

It's known that bass will strike moving objects when they're neither hungry nor actively feeding. Every experienced angler has taken them with full stomachs and even with forage fish only partly swallowed. But bass probably cannot see or "feel" an object that is moving or passing them too far away. And since they are not stalkers or followers as are northern pike and muskies, they will not strike a bait or lure very far away unless they're busily feeding—and bass do seem to feed in "periods." The bigger bass become, the more lazy they become and the less inclined they are to pursue a lure. It's like a middle-aged man with a middle-aged spread who isn't quite so active any more.

There is also the matter of color. Many tests have been made which prove that bass are both color-blind and, on the other hand, color-conscious. The odds are best that still no one really knows. In either case it still remains that, at times and in places, bass show a preference for certain colors, or at least for certain shades, and for shiny finishes rather than dull ones or vice versa. Therefore this color factor also enters into what a bass will strike.

The correct presentation of a bait or lure is a factor too. Should it be presented quickly and briefly—or slowly, in a tantalizing manner? Should it fall in the water heavily? Or softly? Just what kind of action, if any, should it have? Considering that there are thousands of artificial lures on the market today and that hundreds of kinds of live bait are available, a bass fisherman's dilemma is obviously only partly solved when he finds his fish.

This will seem fundamental to experienced bass fishermen, but there are two main methods to deliver a lure or bait—by casting or by fly-rodding. Trolling, drifting, and a vintage method called skittering are possible too. But with just a few local exceptions casting and fly-rodding are the most important, and the latter is effective only in shallow water—usually in water less than 6 feet deep and seldom in water over 10 feet deep. Casting (and this category includes use of bait casting, spin-bait

Finding bass is only half the problem. Here Bob Ketchum of Mountain Home, Arkansas, still has to pick the right lure and then make the right retrieve.

Another typical river in central Ohio in midsummer.

casting, and spinning, because all of them are essentially the same; only operation of the reel is any different) is adaptable to both deep and shallow water.

Casting is delivering a lure and then retrieving it either in a lifelike manner or some other manner designed to cause fish to strike it. A better bass fisherman, then, is a man who casts his lure more often into productive water—into water of about 70 degrees, along the bottom and near some kind of edge. But the best bass fisherman of all will also retrieve slowly, and he will experiment with lures of various designs, actions, and finishes until he finds the one that does the job.

But remember that there are no absolute rules to bass fishing. Although nine times in ten the slow retrieve will be best, there will be days when a fast one is more effective.

The importance of retrieving a lure close to the bottom, or rather right along the bottom, simply can't be overemphasized. The lures will snag and cause delays and inconvenience, but the trouble is worth it. A retrieve that occasionally touches bottom along the way will often catch two or three times as many bass as the same lure retrieved at the same speed just 12 inches higher.

By distinct contrast there is the technique of surface or top-water fishing. In this a floating lure is cast (by any tackle) and retrieved in a lifelike manner or a manner calculated to tease bass into striking it. This is a most exciting method as well as a deadly method, but it has limitations because it's confined to use over shallow water. Since bass, except those in shallow swamp and marsh ponds, are only present in the shallows in springtime and for very brief morning, night, and evening periods later on, top-water fishing is practical only a fraction of each fishing season.

The more quickly a bass fisherman learns the tricks of the sport—and then practices them unconsciously—the better the odds will build up in his favor. For example, there is the matter of noise. The more quietly an angler behaves, the better his chances. It has been written often that banging a tackle box against the bottom of the boat or knocking the ashes from a pipe against a gunwale are to be avoided because they frighten bass. Well, that's true. I'm convinced that if it doesn't frighten them completely out of the vicinity, it will surely make them uneasy—on guard.

It has also been claimed that the "sound" or disturbance of an outboard motor will not frighten fish, and in fairly deep water this is true. But an outboard motor running through shallow water will scatter any bass nearby as quickly as an exploding hand grenade. I've seen it happen. Creaky or loose oarlocks will do the job just as well.

It's possible to multiply the chances of scoring just by making certain types of deliveries. For instance, cast so that the retrieve passes close to and parallel to a sunken log rather than across the log. This simple maneuver puts the lure within reach of lurking bass for a longer period of time—and for a longer distance. Similarly, a cast parallel to the edge of a weed bed or along a drop-off will be better than casts at right angles.

Except when surface fishing, there is no better advice than always to keep "feeling" for the bottom. It doesn't make any difference which lure is being used, because some will be snagged completely and lost anyway. But this technique not only reaches more bass, it also gives a fisherman a picture of the lake's bottom, of the underwater topography. By constantly feeling the bottom he will find edge features that cannot be found in any other way.

There is one way to eliminate much exploring of the bottom in a few states. As new lakes and reservoirs are built in these states, fisheries workers have accurately mapped the lake bed and have recorded it on charts or maps which are available to the public. These maps show the precise locations of sunken forests, fence rows, springs, shoals, bars, everything. It's a wise angler who obtains these maps beforehand when they're available.

It is more than just a homespun saying in the Deep South that the laziest fishermen catch the most and the biggest bass. There *is* some basis for this philosophy. To fish slowly and deliberately is to improve the odds as surely as feeling for the bottom. Put the two together and it's a deadly combination hard to match by any means.

A good, all-round bass fisherman is flexible and persistent. He maintains his tackle in good shape and religiously sharpens his hooks. He tries new methods and new lures, new retrieves and new places; he explores and experiments constantly. And he has the time of his life when he's fishing.

Chapter 3

CASTING TECHNIQUES

Buck Rogers, who lives out in Missouri but has fished everywhere and now makes a living advising others where to fish, has his own theories about catching bass. "You don't have to be able to knock out a gnat's eye at forty paces in order to catch them consistently," he'll tell you. "But it helps."

The Four Steps to Casting

Accurate casting certainly is important. In many situations it isn't possible to deliver a bait or lure, without snagging it, in any other way. And with today's new rods and reels it's an easy matter for anyone to do after a minimum of back-yard basic training, plus plenty of practice on the water. According to Rogers, "Casting is as easy as aim, back cast, forward cast, stop."

These four steps, correctly performed, tell the whole story of casting. First aim your rod almost as you would a rifle and concentrate on the target. Using your elbow as a pivot, bring the rod back smoothly and halt it when almost vertical. Then snap it forward with a firm downstroke, applying extra wrist power.

When the rod reaches a point halfway between the vertical and horizontal position, ease off with your thumb or forefinger to permit the line to pay out. Exactly how this is done will depend on the type of reel—bait casting, spin-bait casting, or spinning. When the lure approaches the target, feather or thumb it to a stop. It would be hard to describe the technique in any more simple form. But it wasn't always that easy.

Bait Casting

Bait casting is an all-American technique. It was born when a couple of fishing watchmakers in Frankfort, Kentucky, developed a precision-multi-plying reel—a reel that would permit smooth and effortless casting of a bait and with which, during both casting and retrieve, the spool would make several turns for each turn of the reel handle. Bait casting received it's biggest boost when the famous old Dowagiac, Rush Tango, and Pfleuger Tandem Spinner lures were developed and widely distributed. The next great development after that was the level-wind mechanism, which automatically spooled line evenly on the retrieve. Other developments came in the form of steady, continual improvements in bait-casting line—and these are still being made.

Bait casting is largely a matter of co-ordination between wrist and thumb. The rod is held so that the reel handles are up and slightly pointed toward the caster at the beginning and end of each cast. The grip on the rod handle should be firm but not tight. The thumb should be placed so that it can control revolving of the reel spool.

The caster should lower the rod in front of himself to a position of about ten o'clock, pointing the tip at the target. When the target is lined up, the caster should bring the rod upright with a snap of the wrist—plus a very little bit of arm movement. The upward motion should be fast, and it must be stopped at no farther back than the one o'clock position. It's better still to stop it at twelve o'clock.

Without a second's hesitation the rod must be snapped forward again to about the ten o'clock position and the pressure on the reel released so that line can run out. The forward thrust of the rod must be fast enough to put a fairly deep bend in the rod, because it is mostly the straightening out of this bend which delivers the lure to its target.

The thumb is the key to every cast. The thumb should rest on some stationary part of the reel as well as on the spool, because this steadies the thumb —just as a heel on the floorboard steadies a foot on a car accelerator.

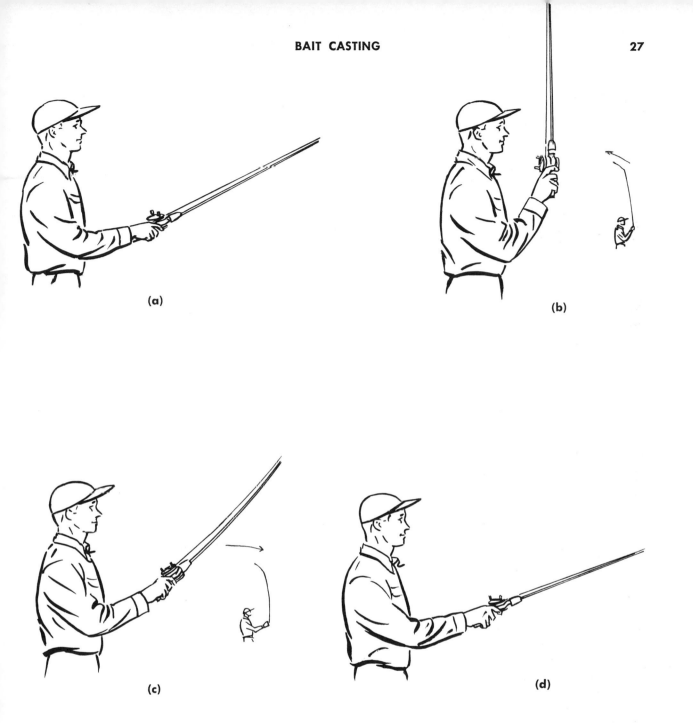

(a)

(b)

(c)

(d)

THE FOUR STEPS TO BAIT CASTING

(a.) Aim your rod and concentrate on the target, holding your thumb firmly on the spool. (b.) Using your elbow as a pivot, bring the rod back smoothly and half it when almost vertical. (c.) Snap the rod forward with a firm downstroke, applying extra wrist power. (d.) When the rod reaches a point halfway between the vertical and horizontal position, ease off with your thumb to permit the line to pay out.

When thumb pressure on the spool is removed at the proper instant, the lure will travel to its target. But while it is traveling the caster must maintain contact with the whirling reel spool with the tip or side of his thumb. Too little pressure allows the line to overrun and backlash into a "bird's nest." Too much pressure shortens and stops the cast. This controlling of pressure with the thumb is the most difficult part of bait casting. It comes quickly to anyone, though, with practice.

When properly done, bait casting is beautiful to see. A good bait caster can literally knock out a gnat's eye at forty feet. Because of its delicate method of control it is the most accurate bass-fishing method of all, and it is *the* method to be used in tight places—in flooded jungles in heavy vegetation, through stump "fields," in many of the forgotten places where every cast must virtually thread a needle or become hopelessly tangled.

Bait casting is versatile, too. Besides the standard overhand cast described here, it's possible to make a sidearm cast, or sideswipe, to place a lure beneath overhanging vegetation. It's even possible to cast underhand or to cast backhanded into difficult spots. And the same thumb control of the reel spool when casting also gives the most positive control over a fighting fish. This is valuable when it's necessary to stop the run of a big fish—immediately—to keep it from getting into a sunken treetop or tangle of smartweed.

What is a good basic casting outfit? Simply, it's a matched rod, reel, and line that "feels" good to a fisherman and one which he can use with good accuracy. For bass fishing alone it's a fairly light outfit, but if it's to be used for other fishes—for pike, muskies, and maybe even in salt water—a concession can be made to the heavy side.

The best bait-casting reels will have lightweight spools, usually of aluminum, which stop revolving soon after the reel handles are spun. This is a good test. Otherwise a serviceable reel is sturdy in construction, smooth of operation, easy to lubricate and service. That last is important, for a bait-casting reel can be kept in hard service year after year if the fisherman will only grease the gears at regular intervals, oil bearings after every day's fishing, and with an old toothbrush keep sand or similar gritty materials from moving parts. For major overhauling, most manufacturers do a good job on their own reels quickly and inexpensively. It's best to mail reels in to them before the busiest season begins to assure prompt service, though.

The most frequently used bait-casting lines nowadays—and generally they're the best—are the braided monofilaments. They're soft and of fine diameter for their tested strength. They come in solid colors and in multiple colors, such as Cortland's Cam-o-flage; which of these is best is a matter of personal preference. Now many casters are beginning to use the new, pliable monofilaments for bait casting.

It's seldom necessary to use line of more than 10-pound test in bait casting, and for most situations 6 or 8 pounds is sufficient. The lighter lines help make it possible to use lighter lures.

There have been as many different trends in casting rods as there have been in ladies' fashions during the past quarter century. There has even been a revolution in rod building materials—from greenheart and solid steel to split bamboo or tubular steel and finally to the fine Fiberglas models of today. The last are handsome, durable; and the best ones have an action that makes casting pure pleasure.

Just after World War II, rods were built with a constant steady taper from butt to tip, and this was a considerable advancement over prewar models. Probably the bulk of casting rods on the market still have this design—and it isn't a bad one, either, because good accurate casting is possible with them. A few years later, though, around 1950, reinforcing was added to the butt end of some rods to produce a livelier tip action. This made for greater casting ease, it "felt better" to some fishermen, and it was made-to-order for casting smaller lures. Now there's still a newer trend. From a wider diameter butt section, the greatest taper occurs just past the center of the rod, and this levels out near the tip end. The result is a very sensitive wand that casts a wide variety of lure weights. A light or medium rod 5 to 5 1/2 feet long of this design is a splendid choice for average bass fishing.

Spin-Bait Casting

A spin-bait casting reel combines the fixed-spool principle of spinning with the thumb control of bait casting. The reel is top-mounted on the rod, and it can be used with either a bait-casting rod or a spinning rod, although the bait-casting rod with its standard offset reel seat is by far the best. It features a right-hand wind, and the reel can be "palmed" in the left hand exactly in the manner of regular bait-casting reel during the retrieve. The chief virtue of spin-bait casting is that it has eliminated backlashes, and it is possible for anyone with normal co-ordination to master with just a little practice. In effect, it has made bass fishing easily possible for everyone.

Line peels off the end of the spool of a spin-bait casting reel, and an internal pickup device controls its release and engagement. As in other types of casting, the size of lure which can be used depends on rod action and diameter of the line. Most spin-bait casting reels of bass size operate best with monofilament lines of about 6-pound test. A good balanced spin-bait casting outfit will deliver lures from 1/4 to 1/2 ounce, although the latter is slightly on the heavy side.

One objection to spin-bait casting reels is commonly heard; that the protective housing is such a great source of friction to the outgoing line that it reduces casting distance as compared to bait-casting reels handling lures of equal weight. Maybe that's true at extreme distances, but for all practical purposes, the range of these reels is adequate for any but the most unusual bass fishing. These reels constitute a great advancement in fishing tackle, and now it seems they're here to stay.

Casting with the spin-bait casting reel is almost the same as when using a standard bait-casting reel. The same principles apply to all casts—overhand, sidearm, and underhand. The main difference is that there is a push button for thumb control. On some models you press the lever to disengage the line, and on others you press and then release the lever to accomplish the same purpose. With some reels it's possible to "feather" the outgoing line and thereby to slow it down. Re-engaging the line is accomplished either by turning the reel handles or touching the lever a second time. No matter, the actual motion of casting is always the same.

Nearly all new spin-bait casting reels now have antireverse mechanisms and smooth-running, jerk-free brakes.

Spinning

Before World War II only a handful of anglers believed that European spinning with its fixed-spool, open-faced reels and their radically different appearances would ever be popular in America. But ten years after the war ended, spinning had had an astounding effect. Nearly every angler owned a spinning outfit, and its ease of operation had made it

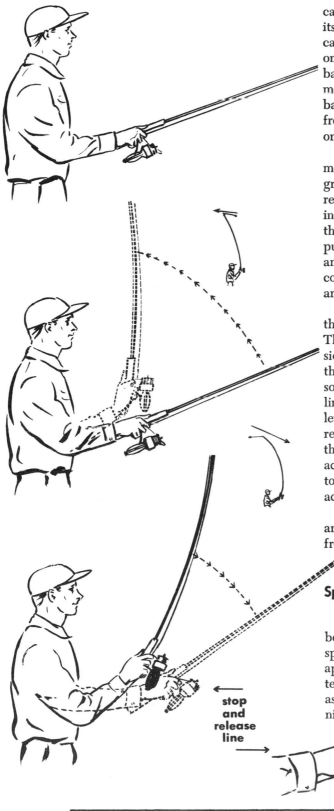

stop
and
release
line →

Casting with a spinning rod and reel

possible for many more citizens to take up a fascinating sport. Spinning was simple, trouble-free, and easy to learn. It eliminated the backlash, and that was to fishing history what inventing the wheel was to world history.

But already today, spinning with the standard open-faced reels is fading. It is slowly being replaced in popularity by spin-bait casting and the closed-faced reels which are even *more* trouble-free and easy to use.

No doubt the "old" original type of spinning will have its fans for many years to come. It has an important place in bass fishing because of its ability to deliver the very small lures—of 1/4 ounce and even smaller—which are so necessary to take bass at certain times and in certain places. It isn't so accurate a method as bait casting, but it's accurate enough for most situations. Because monofilament is never so limp as braided bait-casting lines and because of the various line-gathering devices on spinning reels, it isn't quite so suitable for using surface lures. But still the ability to cast tiny lures alone makes the method invaluable—especially in waters where fishing pressure is extra-heavy and bass are extra-sophisticated.

There are dozens of models of spinning reels on the market today, and selecting a good one is more a matter of budget than anything else. Nearly all are entirely serviceable for much hard fishing. Since line capacity isn't a factor in bass fishing, a small reel will do. But if the reel must double for bigger fish, maybe in the salt, why not pick a bigger one?

The number of rods on tackle shelves, it sometimes seems, is even greater than the number of reels. Since most of them look alike, roughly, they must be purchased largely on trust, on reputation, or on recommendation of another angler. Little is to be gained from standing in the store and checking the rod for "whip."

Here, however, are some qualities to consider in a spinning rod for bass. It should be about 6 to 6 1/2 feet in length with hard and wear-resistant gathering guides. Usually it's wise to avoid "bargain" rods. Most rods today are made of hollow Fiberglas, and although some split-bamboo models are available and are indeed beautiful to own and use, Fiberglas must be rated highest because of its extreme durability. These rods will take a great amount of abuse.

A good bet is to settle for a rod made by a reputable manufacturer in a light or medium action. And better still, if the salesman permits, try several rods all rigged up outside the store. See how they cast. See how they feel. Then buy the one that seems to "belong" in your casting hand.

The size of line to use is the size with which you feel you can safely handle big bass. In water free of vegetation, 6-pound test or even 4-pound could do the job. In water full of snags or weeds 8- or 10-pound test will do. In small-stream fishing it isn't strange to use 2- or 3-pound line on the lightest kinds of outfits.

One other word about spinning lines; they're available in nylon monofilament (single strand) and in braided monofilaments. But for the writer at least, there is no comparison. For day-in, day-out heavy fishing the monofilament is far more dependable and far easier to use.

The actual act of spinning is virtually the same as bait and spin-bait casting. You aim, back cast, forward cast, and stop. The back cast should stop at the vertical or one o'clock, and the forward cast should follow without even a split second's pause to about ten o'clock. Only the use of thumb and fingers is different. And retrieving (for a right-handed caster) is done with the left hand.

Just before aiming, the caster picks up the line with his right forefinger and holds it away from the bail. Meanwhile with the left hand the "bail" is turned or flipped over to the open position. Then midway of the forward cast the line is allowed to slip off the forefinger and to peel off the fixed spool of the reel. It can be feathered by the forefinger as it peels off, and it can be stopped on target by placing the forefinger on the spool or by a quick forward turn of the reel handle which also closes the bail.

Some delicate timing is involved in releasing line at the proper instant, but usually this comes quickly with practice—back-yard practice if no water is readily available. Otherwise, spinning is as easy—and as pleasant—as that.

Chapter 4

LESSONS FOR BASS CASTERS

My friend George Laycock isn't an easy man to discourage, but there was a morning at Ouachita Lake, Arkansas, several summers ago when he came very near to tossing in the sponge. He—or rather we —had fished that picturesque Ozark lake diligently for a day and a half with practically nothing to show for it. Then we met John Bono, who operates a dock near the dam.

"The place is full of bass," Bono said. "Anyone can catch them."

"O.K.," George answered. "Suppose you show us how *you* can do it."

Bono wasn't jesting. He could and did catch bass beginning within a hundred feet of his dock. So did George and I, because we copied his technique —a method I had used successfully a dozen times before in a dozen different places. Jigging—with lead-head jigs, or bucktails, or doll flies—just didn't seem like the right medicine for a large southern reservoir with a shore line that was mostly a sunken hardwood forest. But it was and that's the way bass fishing goes.

Jigs are probably the oldest artificial lures in the world, and until recent years their use has been confined to salt water. A jig is nothing more than a weighted head, usually of molded lead, with a tail composed of hair, hackles, feathers, yarn, or nylon. Probably bucktail is the most popular tail material. Compact and easy to cast, a jig is strictly a bottom lure.

John Bono used his jig in the prescribed manner. He cast it, allowed it to sink to the bottom, and then retrieved it slowly in short, sharp jerks along the bottom. On every second or third cast he was snagged to a tree limb or some other underwater obstacle, and the toll in lost lures was considerable. But still he hooked enough good bass to make it

The buctkail jig

more than worthwhile. Fact is, he hooked some largemouths that would be betting size in any tap-room anywhere.

With a brand-new supply of jigs, George and I left Ouachita and traveled north to Norfork Lake for a session of fishing with Bob Ketchum of Mountain Home. Norfork Lake has been a red-hot bass lake in recent years, and that's fine with Ketchum because he's a red-hot bass fisherman. Bob, George, and I started out at daybreak the first morning, and from the beginning there were few dull moments. We started using our jigs on those steep and rocky shore lines right away, and we also started catching fish.

One of my first casts fell near the water's edge, and after allowing it to settle I began my slow retrieve, twitching the rod tip at intervals. Halfway to the boat I had a sharp strike, and just about the time I caught up with my reel handles a smallmouth lurched out of the water. Two more times the fish jumped before I had him in the net—at which time George also hooked a bass. In the next couple of minutes he proceeded to land a largemouth. Here is one of the few places where you find the two cousins side by side, and here also was evidence that both were suckers for jigs properly manipulated.

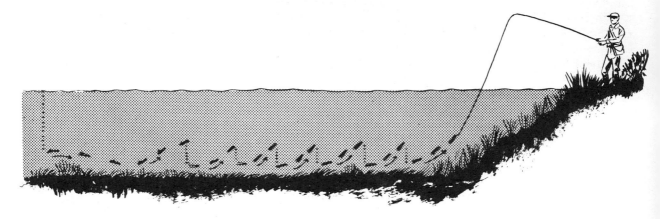

The jigging technique

I had taken smallmouths on jigs before. The place was the channel between Sugar and Middle Bass islands (in the Bass Islands archipelago in western Lake Erie) and the time was June 1951. Ed Kinney, a topnotch fisheries biologist, had just introduced light spinning tackle to the splendid smallmouth fishing around the Bass Islands, and with it he had made catches that astonished even those old-timers who spent too much time remembering the good old days. But our catch this day wouldn't sell anyone on spinning. It consisted of one medium-size sheepshead.

I'd just been fishing in the Florida salt with Phil Francis of Clewiston, and I happened to have several 1/4-ounce bucktails left over from the trip. Idly I knotted one of these to the line and cast it in the general direction of Pelee Island over in Canada. Then I gave it the deep, quick retrieve I'd used in salt water. In ten casts or so I hooked a 2-pound bass and ten casts after that, a walleye. Then nothing.

"Why don't you slow down that retrieve?" Ed suggested. And that turned out to be the ticket.

We filled a stringer with fish that day, and in fishing the Bass Islands almost every summer since then, this has been the most consistent method of all. It has worked wonderfully well on smallmouths elsewhere too.

These successful sessions with jigs do not mean that here is *the* bait—*the* lure which will kill bass anytime, anywhere—but to a wise angler it should point out the value of deep fishing, of keeping a lure right on or very near the bottom. There are other deep lures which do the job just as well as jigs in some situations, better in other situations, but less effectively in still others. A serious bass fisherman will always keep in mind that bass stay

on the bottom in any depth; there he can try them with a selection of lures and retrieves until he finds the right combination.

The lure can be either an artificial or a live bait. Before we left Ketchum at Norfork he demonstrated how the jigging technique could be applied to live crayfish. He merely hooked them through the tails and allowed them to sink to the bottom. Next step was the slow, jerky retrieve. Both spinning and spincasting are made-to-order for live-bait fishing because both can easily cast a lure as light as a small crayfish or minnow or lamprey.

Every fishing trip can be a valuable fishing lesson, and I've had quite a few of them at vast, shallow, weedy and mysterious Okeechobee at the northern edge of Florida's Everglades. This lake is so weedy in places that such celebrated bass haunts as Moonshine Bay, Turner's Cove, and Blue Hole sometimes resemble a flooded, half-cut hayfield. There are thousands of acres of this sort of cover, and enough bass thrive in it to make Okeechobee one of the finest fishing holes in the land.

The first time I fished Okeechobee many years ago, there was a "standard" local method of catching the bass, and my guide, Bud Fountain, was an expert at the game. He would run the boat into the center of a vast hayfield, cut the motor, and allow the boat to drift freely with the breeze while he cast continuously ahead of the drifting boat.

Bud's bait was a spinner with large blades which he retrieved rapidly on the surface. It was hard work to pump the reel handle fast enough to keep that spinner on top, but he didn't mind. He was used to it.

"You got to make it chatter," was the way Bud explained it.

We caught our share of bass using Bud's noisy,

churning surface retrieve. I remember a day we caught 6 of them over 6 pounds apiece and one weighed 7 1/4. The day before Bud had taken an 8-pounder. When strikes came they were savage strikes which made the bristles stand up on the back of your neck, because a bass had to shift into high gear just to catch the bait. Often the strike of a large fish was telegraphed ahead by the huge V-wake it made behind the spinner. It was exciting, suspenseful fishing, and there are no two ways about it, but . . . eventually my arm gave out. I put the top-water spinner away and exchanged it for a weedless, rubber-skirted spoon which could be retrieved slowly and leisurely.

I will never forget the next two days of fishing on Okeechobee. The weedless spoon slowly retrieved caught 7 or 8 bass for each one taken by the high-speed method. They were bigger fish too. But that's only part of the story, because the ratio remained the same when I changed again to casting a pork-frog lure and finally to popping bugs used on a fly rod. The slower the retrieve, the more bass were hooked. Nine days in ten that has been my experience wherever I found bass and fished for them. It's a most important principle for a bass fisherman to keep in mind.

Many years later at Okeechobee I learned another valuable technique that might be applicable to other waters elsewhere. Okeechobee is shallow (the best bass water is between 3 and 4 feet deep) and subjected to high winds around midday, so instead of allowing the boat to drift with the wind, my fishing companion, Ross LaByer, hit the water and tied the boat to his belt. Then he simply waded across the shallows, which he was able to cast more thoroughly by wading. In addition, it was much cooler sport on hot days, because Ross wore tennis shoes and swimming trunks rather than waders to plow through the weeds.

Every bass fisherman eventually must learn to cope with weeds—because many bass waters are filled with them and *few* bass waters are completely

This angler, Louis Bohley, is using a light spinning outfit and a weedless lure to catch a largemouth in a Medina County, Ohio, pond.

without them. Although some weeds grow in medium-depth water, most vegetation usually designates shallow areas and so much of this is potential surface-fishing water.

Vegetation begins to appear in springtime as soon as a combination of warming waters and sunshine stimulate their growth. There is a period then—sometimes for several weeks—when the stems extend upward but do not quite reach the surface and emerge. In many states this is also the period when bass spend the most time in the shallows, when water temperatures are in the vicinity of 70 degrees. It is a pregnant time to be fishing.

An angler has three choices just before vegetation has reached the surface. He can use surface lures, he can drop down to just above the tips of the vegetation, or he can fish bottom and try to make his retrieves between heaviest patches of vegetation. All three work very well at different times, and during *some* periods either method will produce. Except to say that the surface lures are usually best very early and late in the day, it's necessary to try all of them to find the best combination for any given day.

East Harbor is a shallow, protected bay along the southwestern shore of Lake Erie. Most of the season it is so choked with weeds that fishing of any type is all but impossible. The state of Ohio keeps a mechanical weed cutter on the job full-time, but still it's a losing proposition—except for that brief period in spring before the vegetation has consumed the place.

Al Staffan, a Columbus, Ohio, wildlife artist, and I were weekending at East Harbor during this period in May. Already the vegetation had reached within a foot of the surface, and in places there was only a few inches to go. The bass, if any were present, must have been in small pockets which couldn't be seen until the boat drifted right on top of them. We tried surface plugs in the beginning but didn't have the first strike. Then we tried weedless lures, but even the most weedless models in both of our tackle boxes couldn't weave a patch through that cabbage.

"It's thicker than sauerkraut," Al said.

By trying lures and then discarding them, Al finally found the combination. It was a small plug he hadn't used for years which floated on the surface when motionless but was a "busy" action when reeled very slowly just under the surface. Occasionally it would foul up on the weeds, but as long as Al could keep it just above the tips and moving at a snail's pace, he had steady action until dark—when the bass began to hit noisy surface lures.

This slow, just-under-the-surface retrieve is a fine technique for many springtime situations. It's a good one for bass fans to file away in memory.

More than any other kind of underwater cover, vegetation is a test of a caster's skill. And extra heavy vegetation demands accurate, pinpoint casting just to avoid it. A typical test occurred in July recently at Ghost Lake near Hayward, Wisconsin. This is a beautiful body of water; in fact it's one of my favorites in that whole northern vacationland, but large areas of it are full of vegetation. And the vegetation contains big muskies as well as bass.

The water was quite warm when I arrived, and my host, Dick Scheer, told me that momentarily even the pan fish seemed to be on strike. But again by trial and error we found a way to catch all the bass we could eat and plenty more besides.

Each evening the bass would gather in close to the shore—not simply in the weedy shallows along shore, but right in tight against the cattails. Here and there at intervals were tiny pockets of open water, and most of them contained bass. A cast into the pocket was worth a strike; an inch on either side only meant fouling in the weeds. This was the first time I'd found them in such tight, confined places—but it wasn't the last time.

It was late April the next year, and Eddie Finlay, who is secretary of South Carolina's conservation commission, and I were sampling some of the bass waters in the moss-draped lowland country around Georgetown. We'd had a fast session on the Cooper River, had tried casting the abandoned rice fields without too much luck, and finally had located a lonely, isolated pond within sight and sound of the Atlantic surf. It even had a slightly salty taste. And the weeds were so thick it resembled a 100-acre salad bowl.

This was certainly a forgotten pond, and except for a couple of alligators dozing in the sun and clouds of mosquitoes, nothing stirred . . . at least not until we launched a car-top boat and poled our way through a dense patch of pond weed. We flushed bass from the patch like quail from a pea patch. And after that, instead of poling carelessly through the weed beds, we cast *into* them.

Here was another case where casting skill paid off. To hit the tiny openings was to have a chance at bass—big bass—but otherwise it was just a nightmare of reeling in long strings of weeds and stems. Once a bass was hooked, though, the excitement was over because the fish invariably bored down into the weeds and we simple rowed to the spot and dug the bass out of the weeds manually. It was interesting digging, though, because, among others, we dug out a six-pounder and an eight-pounder.

This acrobatic bass was hooked while spin-bait casting along shoreline of Ouachita Lake, Arkansas.

Typical bait-casting situation on larger lakes is for two men to fish from one boat. These anglers hooked bass casting toward brushy shoreline.

We also made a note to return to that pond again, but this time about a month or so earlier. That way, we figured, we'd be on even terms with the vegetation.

It's an unwise fisherman who doesn't explore for new places to catch bass no matter where he lives. Perhaps only a few are as full of largemouths as that South Carolina seashore pond, but still some of them yield amazing catches. Many are located right in the middle of large metropolitan areas.

I've caught fine bass in a cemetery pond near the center of a large Ohio city. Another time I found them in a lagoon inside the infield of a race track and again in the canoe pond of an amusement park. During the day this latter place was bedlam—a beehive of activity—but after the park closed around midnight, it was no trick at all to catch bass just by casting from shore.

America's more than two million farm ponds are also worth exploring, and no bass fisherman anywhere is very far from one of them. Chances are there are many farm ponds within a short drive of his doorstep, whether that's in Pittsburgh or Paducah. Usually the ticket to fishing a farm pond is just a courteous request for permission from the landowner.

An average farm pond is a 1/2- to 2- or 3-acre impoundment built as a farm water supply. More often than not it is built on relatively fertile land, and the crop of bass it "raises" or "grows" is a little larger than in a pond of similar size elsewhere. Sometimes these ponds quickly fill with weeds, but every one is worth investigation.

There's no trick to finding farm ponds; you can see a good percentage of them from the road. Since the U. S. Soil Conservation Service has supervised the building of most agricultural ponds, a check at the local office will easily reveal the location of all others nearby. And just to cruise the back roads— the county and township roads—during evenings of the off season is a good way to get acquainted with pond owners as well as to locate ponds.

But besides the farm ponds, there are still other "forgotten" places which an angler can "find." Resthaven, a watery, state-owned parcel of real estate near Castalia and just off the Ohio Turnpike, is an interesting example which too few bass fishermen have bothered to "discover." I happened to be in on the creation of this area as a good fishing spot, and the story is worth telling.

Resthaven is a swampy area from which a shallow layer of marl was strip-mined more than a decade ago. The spoil banks that remained formed long and narrow fingers of water separated only by a whole maze of dikes and thin earth fills. Since these banks are covered with a dense mat of gray dogwood, birch, and similar second growth, it is a genuine nightmare to penetrate in a small boat or canoe. It's even worse to fish—but it's chock-full of bass and some of them are lunkers.

The bass in Resthaven are no accident. Delmar Handley, who once managed the vast 3000-acre area for the state of Ohio, and I often speculated on how good the fishing would be if we had the brood stock. Then one day Delmar, Al Staffan, Bill Kah, and I were fishing at East Harbor and before we knew it, fourteen good largemouths were on two stringers.

"Why not take these over to Resthaven?" Delmar asked.

"Why not?" Al echoed.

"Because we haven't any tank to carry them— that's why," Bill answered.

Then in a sudden burst of inspiration I mentioned that we had a rowboat. Why not mount it right side up in Delmar's pickup, fill it with water, and use it to carry the fish over the short trip? That's what we did, and that was the first and only stocking of bass at Resthaven, now an extraordinary fishing hole.

Fishing at Resthaven is an acid test for any caster in the world. It's nothing more than a jungle with its roots in the water. But for the man who can make short, accurate back casts, bow-and-arrow casts, and other tricky deliveries it's a promised land. I've known an angler to catch as many as 20 good largemouths in a morning's time, and I've almost matched that mark myself on several occasions. Still, Resthaven is only a sample of the "undiscovered" places which exist all across the country. They're waiting for fishermen to find them.

I have fished only one time apiece with Joe Krieger and Ed Hutchins—and the day with Ed I never had a strike. Yet these two anglers are pioneers in a type of bass fishing that has a great future—and which just may be revolutionizing the entire tackle or lure-making industry. Joe, by the way, is a tackle salesman, and his outdoor TV program in Tulsa, Oklahoma, is among the most popular in the whole Southwest. Ed has a Dodge-Plymouth auto agency in Columbus and is one of central Ohio's most serious sportsmen.

I teamed up with Krieger on a bass-fishing expedition to Oklahoma's beautiful Tenkiller Reservoir. Mac McClure of Tulsa had arranged the trip, and besides Mac it also included Dick Simpson and Charley Powell. Charley manages the Cookson Bend resort at Tenkiller. Our combined mission was to specially concentrate on catching some of the giant bass which have given Tenkiller plenty of space in the news in recent years.

No doubt Tulsa TV viewers may have doubted Joe Krieger and the great catches of bass he has exhibited on his program, sometimes still alive and flopping. That skepticism is easy to understand, because he has shown "impossible" limit strings with no fish under 6 pounds and with several over 8 pounds. But Krieger is just an unusually astute student of bass fishing. His formula for success consists of persistence plus hard and continuous casting, plus fishing very deep and using a type of plastic bait which has been sensational recently.

Krieger and I fished together at Tenkiller only for parts of two days, and although bass fishing had been extremely poor for almost a week we wound up with a dozen bass in the 4- to 6-pound class. We also had a 7 1/2-pounder and then lost another just like it when the fish wrapped my line around a branch and snapped it. It was pretty much the standard bottom-jigging technique which Krieger and I used in Burnt Cabin Creek, for example. This is one of many bays adjoining Tenkiller and is nothing more than a forest submerged in water as deep as 30 feet. Instead of standard jigs, though, we used plastic night crawlers with lead heads. The latter are designed to sink them more quickly and to serve

Resthaven in northern Ohio, a spot that's typical of many brushy, difficult-to-fish places that exist everywhere.

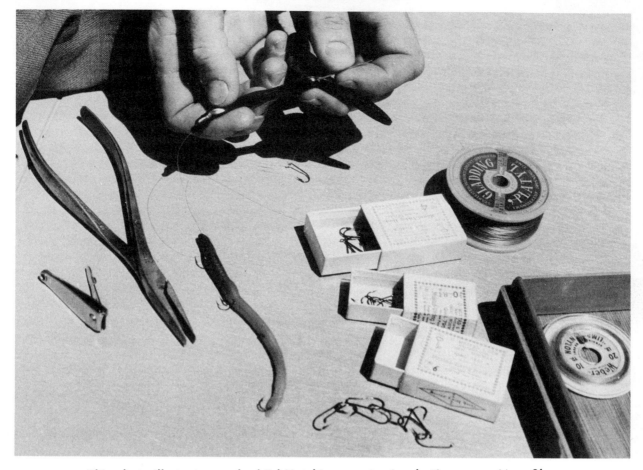

This photo illustrates method Ed Hutchins uses to rig plastic worms. Monofilament is inserted full length inside the worm with a standard sewing needle, and then three hooks are attached as shown.

as casting weights. The fishing was tedious sometimes because of the constant snagging, but it was suspenseful too. And it caught big bass when other anglers weren't even catching small ones.

Of course, Krieger depends on more than just plastic worms to catch bass. He's a good caster, he has much patience, and he capitalizes on the weaknesses of largemouth bass. Each time we hooked or caught a good bass Joe made a clear mental note of some land- or watermark which would locate that exact place for us again. Then, later on, we'd return there and cast the place thoroughly. More often than not it worked. The theory here is that if a specific spot is good enough for one lunker, others should like it, too, and for the same reasons. Actually, if there were ten commandments to bass fishing this would have to be one of them: keep going back to places where you caught big bass before. This is not only true from day to day, but it's also true from week to week and even from year to year. Krieger, for instance, has been fishing the same holes

in southwestern reservoirs like Tenkiller, Lake of the Cherokees, and Texoma for as long as a decade.

But back to the worms. It may sound strange to eastern fishermen, but probably 50 per cent of all bass over 4 pounds taken on artificials in the South and Southwest in 1958 and 1959 were taken on the plastic counterfeits. Boat-dock managers and concessionaires at Tenkiller and at Bull Shoals Lake, Missouri, estimate that 85 per cent of *all* bass there were taken that way. These lures have been so successful on so many species, in fact, that the soft and lifelike imitations of genuine bait critters may be permanently replacing the "hard" plastic or wooden plugs. Some tackle manufacturers predict a complete revolution in bass-fishing lures.

These plastic worms (as well as plastic eels, tadpoles, crayfish, hellgrammites) are now produced by many companies which harness or "rig" them in many different ways. Some have spinners; some haven't. Some have lead heads; others have nothing. All are good, and even deadly at times, but if bass are in medium to shallow water, Ed Hutchins has developed the best method of all to rig and use them. It's surely worth describing here.

Ed buys the plastic worms in bulk. Then with a sewing needle he runs a section of 7- or 8-pound monofilament longways through the center of the worm—and to this monofilament he ties sharpened #6 hooks. One is located in the tail, one in the head, and one just forward of the middle. The hooks are placed so as to be facing forward, and only the curved parts are exposed. The shanks are hidden inside the worm, which has accounted for amazing catches in waters where the bass become sophisticated by heavy fishing pressure early in life.

Recently my son Park and I were visiting the studio of an old friend and motion-picture producer, Karl Maslowski. The studio is perched precariously on a hillside just above a picturesque pond which is pounded steadily and daily by Karl's fishing friends and neighbors. As a result every resident bass in the pond knows every lure ever made by its catalogue number, and to catch just one in an evening's fishing nowadays is worth plenty of post mortems. But on this occasion Park had one of Ed Hutchins' worms in his kit, and just after lunch he proceeded to catch five bass in 45 minutes before a sixth fish half-hitched his line around an old dock piling and then escaped, lure and all.

Since that day, Park and I have made a game of using the worm in heavily fished or so-called "fished out" places. Let's just say we've had uncommonly good luck with it, including a 5 1/2-pound largemouth on a hot day in July. That bass was living in a quarry pond which thousands of Columbus citizens pass every day enroute from the suburbs to downtown.

On another occasion we asked permission to try a farm pond. The landowner said we were welcome to fish any time, but that it was useless. He said the pond contained a few small bluegills, but he assured us there wasn't a bass left in the place. We almost took his word for it—but now we know that it contains at least three 3-pounders, because we caught them and released them again.

One point cannot be overemphasized, though: *any of these plastic night crawlers or dew worms is next to worthless unless it's used properly. And properly, in this case, means very, very slowly.*

Try it this way. Cast the worm, preferably on a light spinning outfit, and let it settle to within a couple of feet of the bottom. Now start turning the reel handle slowly, making just about one complete turn every two seconds. A slight variation or speed-up may be necessary to avoid snags or vegetation, but keep it absolutely as slow as the type of water permits. On every third or fourth turn of the reel, give a slight—a very slight—twitch of the rod tip. The whole technique is like playing with dynamite around a bonfire.

Still, deadly lures and using them correctly are not all of bass fishing—nor even nearly all of it. I've already mentioned accurate casting. Persistence is important too. Every outdoorsman who has ever devoted much time to bass knows how they often feed in flurries. For a while they'll be active; then suddenly all goes dead. They seem to evaporate, and I've seen it countless times in countless places. But the persistent angler is most often on hand when these wild sprees happen.

Once Fred Scheer and I had dragged a canoe and our tackle through a mile or more of Sawyer County, Wisconsin, birch woods and then we slogged through a balsam swamp before we reached a pond Fred had "discovered" during a deer season some seasons before. It had looked like a forgotten bass pond at the time, but now, in July, it looked like the gathering place for all the mosquitoes in North America. And it didn't look any better after two hours of completely fruitless casting.

"The place *could* have frozen out last winter," Fred suggested. "Ice was pretty deep up here."

We had just decided to call it a wild-goose chase, and we were even unloading the canoe when there was a familiar roll on the surface nearby.

"You see that?" Fred asked.

"I did," I said, "and there's another." All at once, as if someone had thrown a switch, fish were rolling all over the lake.

Hastily we set up rods again, and for the next twenty minutes or so we had the brand of bass fishing that doesn't happen nearly often enough. It was incredible. I was using a darting surface plug, and it was only necessary to place it near a surface swirl where a coal-colored largemouth would inhale it. The bass, we found, were feeding on small yellow perch. Then abruptly it was all over. The bass seemed to dissolve in the cool, tea-colored water, because we never did get another strike.

The only certain thing about bass fishing, in the long run, is that it's completely uncertain. I've discussed slow retrieves, fishing the bottom, and being persistent. But none of this advice is valid when bass unaccountably school and cavort on the top in open water, as they do occasionally at Dix Dam and Dale Hollow in Kentucky, at Norris Lake and Watts Bar in Tennessee.

Maybe the finest advice of all to a bass caster is just to be flexible.

Chapter 5

FLY-RODDING FOR BASS

This photo shows technique of Andy McIntyre when fishing Cumberland Lake. He maneuvers best with the paddle in one hand while casting with the other hand.

Andy McIntyre is a solid citizen of his community, which is Monticello, Kentucky. But he is also looked upon as "slightly different" from his fellow men who are mostly anglers of an older school. This is to say that they're plug casters and their natural habitat is nearby Cumberland Lake, one of the longest and best fishing holes in the Southeast.

As long as bass stay shallow enough in springtime, Andy is a fly caster—a bass bugger. He uses a combination of the long rod and small floating bugs so effectively that every year he manages to raise the eyebrows of local and visiting bass fishermen alike around the Beaver Lodge dock at Cumberland. And he has great sport doing it, because of all forms of bass fishing, bugging is among the most exciting, in my book.

Let me repeat: bass bugging is the most *exciting*. That isn't to say it's the most effective, although that is sometimes the case. But when bass are in shallow water, say less then 6 feet deep, it's a fascinating sport that's hard to match.

To describe how Andy fishes at Cumberland is to pretty well describe the correct technique of bass bugging. The lake is serpentine in shape with 300 miles of rocky, steep, and irregular shore lines. Fishing from a small boat, he can maneuver with a paddle in his left hand, and he travels slowly parallel to the shore line—and just a short cast away from it. He then casts *in* toward shore and places his bug as near the water line as possible. Sometimes he even casts *onto* the shore and then pulls his bug gently into the water.

Except to say that Andy fishes extremely slowly— he always allows his bug to remain motionless for a long time before he twitches it the first time—that just about describes the McIntyre technique. Like Oklahoma spin caster Joe Krieger, he also returns over and over to places where he has taken big bass before, and it was from one of these spots that I once coaxed a 7 1/4-pounder from beside a sunken tree trunk. Until that day it was my largest bass on a fly rod.

This is a good point to summarize again. The way to fish a surface bug (or *any* surface lure or plug) is to concentrate on edges and to fish them very, very slowly. Cast and let the lure rest motionless for a long time, then move it only slightly, and after that leave it motionless once more. Often only a flick of the rod tip is enough. And there are days when the best results of all come from "dead bug" fishing— from giving the bug no action at all. Just cast and leave it; cast and leave it.

Too many bass fishermen never know the thrill of bugging, because the very technique of fly casting has been described to them as difficult or formidable. But that isn't the case at all. Except for spin-bait casting nowadays, it's probably the easiest method to learn; and once it *is* learned, fly casting becomes a rhythmic, pleasant way to deliver a lure.

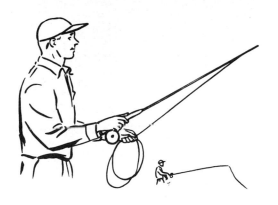

(1)

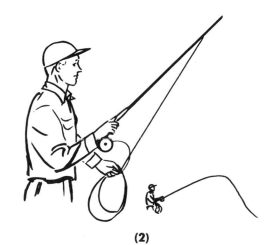

(2)

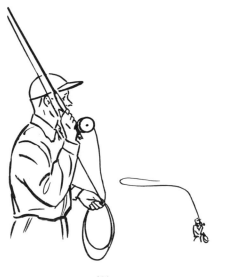

(3)

(4)

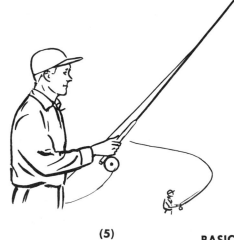

(5)

(6)

BASIC FLY-CASTING

(a.) Grasp 25 or 30 feet of coiled line in your left hand. (b.) With a smooth, but brisk upward motion bring the rod to a near vertical position. (c.) Pause, laying out the line behind you. (d.) When the line is fully out, there will be a slight tug. Begin the forward cast immediately. (e.) Stop the rod between a one o'clock and two o'clock position. (f.) As the line pays out in front, feed the slack from your left hand.

Fly casting differs from all other methods in that the line, which is heavy, rather than the lure, is cast. The fly reel acts as a storage device for the line and nothing more. On larger, stronger game fish the reel may be used in actually playing the fish, but in bass fishing this is hardly ever necessary. An angler controls, pays out, and picks up line with his left hand, if he is a right-hand caster, and vice versa.

Whereas bait casting is largely a matter of co-ordination between wrist and thumb, fly casting is a case of timing—of the proper interval between back and forward casts. Since fly casting can be practiced anywhere, on land or water, a fisherman can become quite efficient and accurate before he actually goes fishing the first time.

Try making the basic cast this way. Strip off 25 or 30 feet of line and lay it out in a straight line before you. Point the rod almost straight ahead, or toward a target, and grasp a coil or two of loose line in your left hand (assuming you're right-handed). Now, with a smooth, but brisk upward motion—and while keeping your right elbow fairly close against your body—bring the rod to the vertical or twelve o'clock position. This upward motion should be one of trying to throw the line high behind you. *Now*, pause until you feel the tug of the line behind you and then start the forward cast immediately, stopping it between one and two o'clock. The weight of the line will carry the lure forward toward the target.

The proper pause between upward and forward casts, of course, is the critical point in fly casting. On short casts the pause is only for a split second. On long casts it may be for a full second.

Once you can easily lay out neat casts of 30 feet, here are a few other techniques to incorporate. First, do not try to make the upward cast with slack line on the water before you. Gather it first by hand—then quickly start the upward cast. Now, hold onto that line and when making the forward cast, pull down on the line with your left hand to add power. To increase the distance of the cast, release the coils of line just as the forward cast reaches the two o'clock position. On a balanced outfit the line will then "shoot" forward. To lift the rod tip just slightly before the lure hits the water will remove slack from the line and allow the lure to "land" more delicately.

Distance is obtained by false casting—which is also an excellent drill for a beginning fly caster. This is the unbroken and rhythmic upward, forward, upward, forward, etc., casting without allowing the line actually to fall to the water. Extra distance to reach a target is obtained by allowing a little more line to "shoot" on each successive forward cast. False

casting for short periods each day on the front lawn is a splendid way to acquire the proper timing, the proper pause between upward and forward casts.

The complete bass fisherman should know two other simple casts. First is the sidearm cast, which is exactly the same as the basic cast except that it is made off to the side instead of strictly overhead. It is harder to control, but it is valuable for placing a fly or bug beneath overhanging vegetation.

The other important delivery is the roll cast, and it is the simplest of all. Try it this way. With about 25 feet of line stretched out before you, raise the rod until it reaches about eleven o'clock just behind your shoulder. Now thrust the tip forward sharply to about two o'clock and the line will "uncoil" straight ahead. This cast is used in tight situations when there is no room for the upward cast. Although the distance is limited it's especially handy for stream fishing.

In fishing with and discussing the matter with many experienced bass fishermen, virtually no two of them agree exactly on what constitutes the best or the most balanced outfit for bass. Naturally a lot depends on whether the outfit will be used for casting bugs or flies or live bait—or even all three. Casting bugs (which might weigh up to 1/16 of an ounce) requires a "softer" or "slower" action in a rod than does casting small flies and streamers. And a natural bait user would require a still "softer" action. Maybe it's best to describe the outfit I use—mostly for bugging but occasionally for streamer fishing in streams.

My rod is an 8 1/2 foot, 5 ounce Fiberglas which handles a C level line very well but which does even better with the GBG line the manufacturer recommended. Fly lines are made in so many tapers nowadays and they're so scrambled in sizes that any discussion of tapers eventually becomes a complicated affair; the best advice is simply to buy the line the rod maker recommends—or maybe even the next heavier size. Invariably this recommendation is printed on the butt end of the rod.

For all practical bass fishing, a fly line should float. That is just one good reason to avoid bargains and instead to purchase a high-grade line made by a reputable manufacturer. Since I often fish at night, I use a line with a white finish because it is easier to see. And since even the finest lines eventually become waterlogged and tend to sink in weedy waters, I always carry a spare reel full of dry line.

There are two kinds of fly reels; single action and automatic. The heavier automatics gather line by touching a lever. This is handy sometimes, but it's also a nuisance other times. Both reels do the job, but my vote goes to a sturdy and lighter single action.

Since fly lines are heavy and of large diameter it's necessary to use a leader between the line and lure. For ultrasophisticated bass or for heavily fished waters this can be a light tapered leader such as trout fishermen might use, but I have seldom had reason to change from the 8-foot section of 6-pound monofilament line which I usually use.

Doc Henshall was the first angler to use fly-fishing tackle to any great degree for bass. But even with the coarse and heavy gear of his times, he could see the great potential. At least the records and his writings show that more than half a century ago he was tying and designing flies especially for bass. Until then flies were created with only trout and salmon in mind. One of Henshall's creations, a bronze bit of

fluff fashioned from turkey feathers and named the Golden Dustman, is just as effective today as it was the first time it fooled a fat smallmouth.

Most of the first bass flies, though, were only standard trout wet flies in larger sizes—and they ran to Yellow Sallys, White Millers, Red Ibises, Parmachene Belles, and to Montreals. Of course, all of these will still take bass, but not nearly so well as the streamer flies (also first developed for trout) which came along much later. Streamers imitate minnows, and adult bass are minnow eaters more than insect eaters. Streamer fishing, then, has an important place in any bass fisherman's repertoire, especially if he frequents rivers where smallmouths live.

There are many fine bronzeback rivers throughout the eastern and northern United States. The

Perfect fly-casting form. Line is "shooting" forward. It will straighten out and deliver bug to target.

Bass bugging the weedy shoreline of Vesuvius Lake, Ohio. Bug is cast into small openings in weeds.

West Fork of the Chippewa in Wisconsin is one I think about immediately; the St. Croix on the Maine-New Brunswick border is another. But one that I know better than either of these is the Mohican in central Ohio. It isn't too far from my home, and in an average summer I'll fish there several times.

Except perhaps for live bait at times—for hellgrammites and soft crayfish—nothing produces in the Mohican like a streamer fly made to behave—or misbehave—like a native shiner minnow or a rainbow darter. I can fish either upstream or down because I cast straight across stream in any case, and as the streamer drifts with the current I shake the rod tip from side to side to give it a minnowlike, stop-and-go action. Of course, it's necessary to control line all the while to keep the streamer from sinking into crevices between rocks and becoming snagged there.

My experience is that the pattern of streamer isn't nearly so important as fishing it correctly and in the best places—as where a riffle drops off into a pool, in deep glides, in still pockets behind midstream boulders and beneath undercut banks. Still, patterns like the Hot Orange Marabou and the numerous squirrel-tail streamers are more deadly than some others, at least in the Mohican and the Kokosing, Big Darby, Whetstone, Paint, and Rattlesnake, which are creeks nearby in Ohio.

Except in large pools where largemouths may live, I've never had great success with bugs or dry flies in streams. Of the dry flies, Joe's Hopper, a grasshopper imitation first developed for Michigan brown trout, is good. So is the Muddler, a versatile trout pattern tied by Dan Bailey of Livingston, Montana.

There are almost as many bass bugs on the market

nowadays as there are bass-bug fishermen, and nearly all of them are good, both for smallmouths and largemouths. Only spotted bass seem to boycott them; spotted bass everywhere, it's well to remember, prefer a bait on the bottom, ten to one. The body materials of today's bugs run from deer hair to cork to plastic, with an increasing trend to plastic, particularly in the bugs designed to imitate crippled minnows (bullet-shaped heads) or poppers (with dished-out heads to make a popping sound on the retrieve). The plastic bodies are far more durable, and most are easier to cast than cork and much easier than deer hair. The deer-hair bugs have a slight edge in northeastern (New England) smallmouth fishing, but the difficulty of casting and waterlogging are disadvantages.

Rubber-band legs have been added to some bugs. This would seem to be gilding a lily, but actually it has made the bugs more deadly in many situations—for Andy McIntyre's fishing at Cumberland Lake, for example.

Quite a number of weedless devices have been built into some bugs, and nearly all are valuable where vegetation is thick or where other sunken obstacles are numerous. The turned-up (rather than turned-down) hook is the best of these, but it does miss good strikes occasionally. A better hooker, but heavier and therefore slightly more difficult to cast, is the bug with a weed guard of fine piano wire. It's excellent for casting among pads and bonnets or such vegetation as some of the smartweeds.

There is good bass bugging almost everywhere that bass exist, even though it may range from a brief period in springtime (as in deep, southern reservoirs) to the year around (as at Okeechobee, Florida). But the best bass bugging in America occurs in the nation's more than two million farm ponds we first mentioned in Chapter 4. Nearly all are good bugging waters because they're shallow—with enough vegetation to make them interesting to fish.

Bass bugging can become doubly absorbing because it can become a fascinating year-round pastime. On cold winter nights it's possible to spend profitable hours in basement workshops building and designing new bugs for next summer's use. Many companies sell kits or supplies for making bugs, but it isn't even necessary to buy elaborate materials. One of the best bugs I ever owned was fashioned from cork from an empty bottle of bourbon and from hackle feathers picked up from a chicken coop. Any bass fisherman who also hunts can easily save a few squirrel tails or bucktails and the skin from a pheasant or a grouse. Of course, any

Photo by Walter M. Lauftner

Bugs with deer-hair bodies or wings made specially for fishing in New Brunswick. All will take bass.

of these materials are also suitable for tying up a supply of streamer flies.

There are still other fly-fishing lures on tackle shelves today—everything from small spinners and spoons to "fly-rod size" editions of larger casting plugs. Again, nearly all of these will take bass, but too few are really suited for fly-rod fishing. At least they're not suitable when compared with the new light spinning gear which handles them better and which is also available.

I will never forget the day many years ago when I met Claire Broce. Cold thaw mists of early spring hung along the southern Ohio hillsides, and Storms Creek ran high and roily when I found him standing knee-deep in the water. Instead of fishing rod, though, he held a coal fork and a minnow bucket. With the fork he was digging into the bank below water's edge and then after scrambling around frantically, was putting something into the minnow bucket. It was a mighty strange scene.

Now I have looked into many minnow buckets in my life, but none surprised me like the contents of this one. Inside was a glistening mass of wriggling, writhing critters.

What else was there to say except: "What in the hell are those?"

"Just eels—mud eels," he answered. "I use them for bass bait."

I knew that bass will strike almost anything that's

alive and moving, but still I'd never heard of anyone using brook lampreys before—and incidentally
they *were* nonparasitic, native brook lampreys
rather than eels. I must have sounded so incredu-
lous that Broce invited me to go fishing with him the
next weekend. After what followed I bought a coal
fork of my own, because nothing is better to dig
them out of the leafy, mucky bottoms of small
streams which they inhabit over much of the eastern
half of the country. Even with a coal fork, though,
digging out lampreys is pure drudgery.

This isn't just to illustrate the value of lampreys
as excellent bass baits, which they certainly are, but
rather it's to describe a most effective use of the fly
rod which Broce pioneered, at least in his own community of Lawrence County in southern Ohio. The
same technique can be used with any of the minnows, with leeches, or even with crayfish.

Broce used a fly rod of no special size or action
because he did very little actual casting with it.
His line was the lightest level fly line he could obtain and he kept it well dressed to float for long
periods. His leader was 6 or 7 feet of 6-pound
monofilament—or maybe 8-pound test when he
traveled south to fish the sunken forests of the big
reservoirs. A thumbnail-size sliding cork was attached to the leader so that it could be moved up
and down according to the depth of the water. A
small split shot was placed about 8 inches above a
#6 or #8 hook. When he was river fishing for
smallmouths or spotted bass he omitted the shot.

The lamprey itself was hooked in the tail just behind the vent. Hooked in any other place it would
die instantly, but like this it remained lively for long
periods, sometimes long enough for its lively undu-
lations to catch several bass. Broce made some incredible catches of large bass with that combination,
even though he mostly fished in heavily fished lakes.

But a bucket of lampreys and a fly rod is no
guarantee of success. Broce was also a master of

caution and finesse. When stream or pond fishing,
he would crawl on hands and knees, if necessary,
to deliver a bait without commotion and without
alarming a bass. In a boat, he moved just as cautiously, taking care not to make unnatural noises by
banging oars or tackle kits against the gunwales.
Broce actually stalked good bass habitat in the manner of a cat creeping up on a nice, fat robin.

By holding several coils of line in his left hand,
Broce would swing to the side, rather than cast,
the lamprey toward its mark—to a stump, a ledge,
a fallen tree, or into an indentation in a weed bed.
Through practice he could "shoot" over 30 feet of
line this way. Broce would then let the lamprey
"work" in a given spot for possibly a minute. If no
strike was forthcoming he'd move a little farther
along. His was a technique which might make a
serious, dyed-in-the-wool bass bugger cringe, but
it was also a technique that's pure and unadulter-
ated murder for lunker bass. It's a good stunt for
the problem bass—the "old settler" bass which have
seen and ignored all the hardware and hackle that
has wiggled past them for many years.

The Broce method of fly-rodding with live bait
has two other applications. First is simply to eliminate the float and shot and then to drift crayfish,
say, into all likely pockets and pools of a bass
stream. The other method has to do with lakes or
ponds containing a fairly shallow and even bottom.
Call this one "chunking" for bass.

The idea here is to use a small boat and to drift
with the wind, meanwhile tossing, or swinging, a
Broce-type rig of bait and bobber ahead of the
boat. Carefully gather line as you drift, pick it up
and deliver again when you get close to it—and
always look for action. On certain summer days,
usually lazy days, it's a hard method to beat.

It's well to point out, though, that a spinning outfit in this case will do the same job at least just as
well.

Chapter 6

SPECIAL TECHNIQUES

Fishing from Shore

In our town there's a fisherman named Harry Matthews who's head and shoulders above most local anglers. Harry catches bass all through summer, and he never travels farther than a certain city water-supply reservoir. It's a spot that most other fishermen avoid.

Griggs Reservoir doesn't even look like a fishing lake. It's formed by water backing up behind a great chunk of concrete across the Scioto River. The water level fluctuates enormously in a season's time. On an average summer's afternoon the reservoir is churned to a froth by a host of speedboaters and water skiers.

It makes no difference to Harry, though. He goes fishing just the same, and it's rare when he doesn't return home with bass on his stringer. "Those hot-rodders bother fishermen more than the fish," is the way he explains it.

Matthews' method is simple. It's so simple, in fact, that some fishermen think there's something phony or mysterious about it. All he does is start early in the morning and dunk bait at carefully selected spots along the shore. These places are mostly rocky points and abrupt drop-offs, and he didn't discover them all overnight. Looking for such spots is just part of the fascinating game. The important point is that Harry has solved a situation that's typical of many waters across the nation.

The waters that offer sport for shore fishermen are practically limitless. Besides the small lakes and ponds that you think of first, don't forget to add farm ponds, which usually aren't convenient to fish in any other way than from shore. Water-supply reservoirs are generally plenty big enough for boat fishing, but—particularly in densely populated parts of the East and Midwest—boats may be prohibited or allowed only under regulations. So there's another vast category of shore-fishing waters.

In the past ten years of fishing around the country I've found out how the most successful shore fishermen catch everything from fresh-water drums to bass. Some of these fishermen are absolutely deadly at the game. For instance, I've seen them drive out from town on a Sunday afternoon, fish in a nearby pond or reservoir, and return with far more fish than if they'd spent the weekend fishing far away in the mountains.

Harry Matthews' bait-fishing technique is a good example to imitate. He casts a bait (nearly always it's a crawfish, since he's after bass) and tiny cork bobber, then lets the bait settle to the bottom. With the pickup bail on his spinning reel left open, a nibbling fish can easily run without detecting any abnormal drag such as a sinker or heavy bobber would give. (This no-drag result can be achieved with any spinning reel, open or closed-face.) It is telltale drag that causes fish to drop a bait before getting hooked.

Harry follows his fish by watching the tiny float. When it goes under for keeps he cranks the reel handle slightly to re-engage the drag on the line, then raises the rod sharply to set the hook in the fish's mouth. That's when the action starts.

If action doesn't come he moves the bait slightly. That way he covers more water. Harry gets snagged on the bottom occasionally, and his toll in hooks is high. But he also gets more than his share of bass.

An alternative rig uses a tiny sliding float or a sliding plastic bubble manufactured mostly for spinning. With these, some snagging on the bottom can be eliminated, because they can be adjusted for a certain depth beyond which the bait is held suspended off the bottom. It's a good policy to eliminate use of a sinker whenever possible.

Once you've logged some experience at bait fishing from shore, it's time to take a whirl at casting artificial lures. The average fisherman is surprised at how much this increases his catch. I feel there are fewer dull moments when I'm casting artificials, and I can't forget that the record books are full of trophies from the typical reservoirs.

There are many opportunities for tossing artificials from shore with a fly-casting outfit. Farm ponds and lakes with gradually sloping banks were made to order for bass bugging early and late in the day. But bass bugging is a slightly cumbersome technique for some shore fishing and requires more room than using spinning or bait-casting gear, but it's deadly at times when bass can't resist striking at small lures "struggling" above them. Bass bugs are seldom effective, though, in water deeper than 6 feet.

The principle of bugging can be duplicated with spinning and bait-casting tackle. All you have to do is substitute floating bass plugs (wood- or plastic-bodied lures that usually resemble small fish) for the bugs. Cast and retrieve plugs in much the same way as for bugs. The secret to using any floating bait for bass is to fish it slowly and deliberately. Take plenty of time when retrieving; let the lure rest motionless at intervals. Make it behave like a critter in trouble.

Your approach to shore fishing will depend a lot on whether you're mainly interested in relaxation or exercise. You can still-fish, walk the banks, or combine the two approaches. One technique that pays off handsomely is to walk the bank, concentrating on proved spots that you've turned up before.

When you walk the shore you're in a fine position to spot drop-offs, shoals, and sunken snags. An experienced shore walker will never pass up any of these spots for bass.

No matter what tackle or bait you use there's one trick that'll help you to cover the most water from shore. Make your first cast as nearly parallel to the shore as possible. Standing in the same spot, make the second, third—maybe even the fourth or fifth out from shore—like the spokes in a wheel. Then move forward 15 or 20 feet and repeat the spokes-of-a-wheel pattern. If one spot looks good concentrate there with several casts. Skip quickly over poor spots. For bass, a good spot is near "edge." It might be the edge of a weed bed, deadfall, drop-off, shoal, reef, channel, stump, or the edge of the lake itself.

A smart shore walker makes his casts so that he can retrieve parallel to edges rather than perpendicular to them. Casting parallel to a fallen tree is an excellent example. Then the lure will pass a fish lurking anywhere under the trunk. A cast perpendicular to the trunk might fall out of sight of the fish.

There's also a knack to casting in weed beds or other vegetation. Cast into any small openings, then retrieve as much as possible along the fringe of the vegetation. Use this method for both live bait and hardware.

When you walk the shore you inevitably have trouble with snagged lures, especially if you're casting along a rocky bank or a shore with many deadfalls. Often the difference between shore-fishing success and failure is to get the bait down close to the bottom where it is most likely to snag—but also most likely to catch fish. Particularly good in these places are the weedless spoons and the plugs which float when not in motion but dive deep when you retrieve them.

You may need several trips before you get the hang of it, but the ideal maneuver is to have the lure go almost to the bottom, then to reel it in just fast enough to maintain that same distance from the bottom throughout the retrieve. It will be a headache at first, but gradually it becomes almost automatic.

Some of the most productive sections are the hardest because they're full of brush. All but the most serious fishermen pass them by. However, the newest spinning and casting gear make it possible for you to cast where there's practically no room at all. A few hours in the back yard and you'll master the bow-and-arrow cast and the flip cast.

The bow-and-arrow cast is the simplest. You merely grasp the lure between thumb and forefinger of your free hand, and bend the rod by drawing back the lure. (If you're using a bait-casting reel you keep the line from unwinding at this point by holding the thumb of your casting hand on the reel spool. With a spinning rig you've previously released the reel's pickup mechanism, and keep the line from unwinding now by holding the line against the rod handle with the forefinger of your casting hand.) Aim the lure and let it go, and it will pull line out under gentle pressure of your thumb or forefinger. Be careful, of course, that you don't get the lure's hooks in your fingers.

For the flip cast, just poke the rod straight forward through an opening in lake-shore foliage. Allow the lure to hang 6 or 8 inches below the rod tip. Now, with elbow action only, flip the lure first

The bow-and-arrow or sling-shot cast

The flip cast

upward, then downward, and with the momentum obtained, flip it outward straight ahead. With just a little practice it's surprisingly easy. It's a good cast with crayfish and the heavier live baits.

Float and Camping Trips

No special fishing techniques, other than those already described elsewhere, are involved in camping trips or in float trips on rivers, but both have important roles in catching more bass. Let's take float tripping first.

With modern boats and outboard motors, today's fishermen have covered just about every square foot of fishing water that exists on bass lakes everywhere. Of course, some lakes are pounded harder than others, but all are fished—until now the only relatively undisturbed places remaining are on streams and rivers beyond easy walking distance from the highway bridges.

Last summer Lew Baker and I devoted about two weeks to fishing waters that were virtually virgin. What's more, we didn't travel more than fifty miles from our home, which is in Columbus, population almost one half million. Sometimes we were less than 20 miles away from Broad and High streets, right in the center of town. We enjoyed good fishing, solitude, and complete escape even though we could hear occasionally the noise of traffic on busy U.S. highways nearby or the sound of a farmer's tractor in a hayfield. We did it by making float trips on local rivers—by getting far from the bridges and popular fishing holes that other fishermen frequent. It's something that almost any angler in America can do almost any time.

Except in a few regions such as the Ozarks, float tripping is a forgotten art. It's an uncomplicated art too. It's a chance too many fishermen miss to enjoy good sport, sometimes spectacular sport, only a few hours from home. Consider a trip that Lew and I made on Big Walnut, a creek that passes al-

Float trip on West Fork of Chippewa in Wisconsin, fine smallmouth stream. It's just one of many in Wis consir

most through Columbus and which actually is heavily fished. Still we had high adventure; we caught fish and saw sections of the stream that few other sportsmen ever see.

We launched my glass canoe at a bridge just southeast of Columbus after making arrangement for a pickup the next afternoon where Big Walnut joins the Scioto. We carried plenty of tackle (that's possible when you're boating rather than wading), a small explorer tent, a cooler full of ice, trotline, and even a seine to gather bait.

It was the most leisurely sort of trip downstream. During the morning I paddled while Lew cast into pockets and eddies along the way. In one stretch of water, where the paths along the banks had completely run out, he caught a pair of fat smallmouths

and four rock bass. We ate them for lunch on a sandy bar—along with several ears of sweet corn apiece which we purchased from a farmer along the way. This is topnotch agricultural country, and it's possible to buy anything from fresh eggs and frying chickens to fresh butter or carrots while traveling downstream.

That night we camped on a peninsula formed by a long bend in the river. While I built a fire Lew unfolded the seine and collected a bucketful of crayfish and hellgrammites for bait. After dinner and after dark we stretched the trotline across the river at a point just below a shallow riffle. Then we baited up with the crayfish Lew had collected. That was good for a pair of channel cats and an 8-pound shovelhead when we "ran" the trotline first thing

in the morning. We ate the channel cats for breakfast and saved the shovelhead for bragging later on.

A river trip is an easy venture to organize. You simply get a boat, almost any sort of boat, collect the gear you need, and push off downstream. Nothing could be more simple. You can float for one day or for two weeks, depending on the time you have to spare or on the length of floatable water. First consideration, though, is the craft to use.

For two-man trips, I prefer a canoe because it's easier to handle, easier to move through dead water, and easier to carry over shallow places and deadfalls. I have an 18-foot glass canoe for larger, rocky streams and for longer trips. My 13-foot canvas canoe is perfect for short trips on slow, mud-bottomed streams. It isn't wise, though, for beginners to take canoes on turbulent or dangerous waters. It isn't comfortable either.

In those regions where float tripping is popular, or even a business, professional outfitters invariably use long, sturdy square-ended boats—johnboats, usually—because of their extreme safety and comfort. A fisherman can move around and stretch in most of them without turning the boat over. The johnboat is sluggish to handle in dead water, however, and it's completely out of the question for a fisherman who must depend on car-top delivery to and from the river. The most important requirement in *any* float boat is a shallow draft and fairly rugged construction. Until now all of them have been of wooden construction, but nowadays there are some splendid aluminum and Fiberglas models on the market.

Recently a craft has been designed that is sensational for one-man float tripping. It's an 8-foot dacron dinghy that only weighs 30 pounds. I've used it on the smallest rivers, carrying it across country around impassable sections of rivers. I simply lash the oars to the dinghy, and to these I lash a regular pack board—plus my bedroll, tackle, or anything else I carry along. I can stay out a week with only 50 pounds to carry. At night I can use the dinghy for a shelter; I've also used it as a live box for fish and bait—and even as a bathtub on occasion.

It's always wise to check the distances to be traveled before starting downstream. On an average stream in mid-America, a party can cover 10 miles per day rather easily. Figure on less if you want to

This is Lew Baker and the author on Big Walnut Creek. At this place they are only a few miles from center of downtown Columbus, Ohio.

Here is an excellent float-trip boat designed by Harry Green of Columbus, Ohio. Made of "Harborite," the boat is roomy, comfortable, almost impossible to upset, has a very shallow draft, will carry anglers with camping gear easily, is easy to cast from, can be used as a car-top carrier when traveling and as an overnight shelter when overturned and propped up.

stop frequently to fish—or more if the current is swift and the actual trip is more important than the fishing.

The best way to plan a trip is to use two cars with car-top carriers or boat trailers. Park one car at the end of the trip and drive to the starting point with the other. With two cars it's also possible to leapfrog from bridge to bridge, ending the trip whenever the mood strikes.

Float trippers can fish the back country with almost the same comforts and conveniences of an average fishing camp. Take a large tent, for example, and erect it each night on an air-conditioned gravel bar. Safari cots are handy too. Take all the cooking utensils you need to make every meal a pleasant experience. While traveling, all this gear can be completely stored away. It's no trouble at all. One float-tripping addict I know can't completely break away from civilization even for a few days—so he carries along a portable radio and a wind-up record player. But he has fun—and that's the idea.

An enterprising traveler can almost live off the country while traveling downstream. Besides the bass he catches, fresh-water crayfish are delicious (and hard to tell from shrimp) when boiled and served like shrimp. Often it's no problem to gather frogs or to catch a snapping turtle for soup. If the rivers run through limestone country there will be water cress for salad, and in springtime morel mushrooms grow along wooded banks. Look for white, button mushrooms in farm meadows during early fall. Other wild edibles a floater might find are cabbage palms, wild asparagus, any of the wild greens (dandelion, dock, lamb's quarter, mustard, horseradish, poke), walnuts, hickory nuts, pawpaws; there's no end of them.

There are some precautions that every drifter should take. For instance, do not drink or use water from the rivers for cooking. If it's absolutely necessary boil it first and dissolve halazone tablets into it. Always carry an emergency kit which contains first-aid materials, plenty of insect repellent, waterproof matches, lighter fluid (for starting a fire quickly), a flashlight, and, in the case of rubber or canvas boats, a patching kit.

On a canoe trip it starts to rain—so the author and his party pull into shore, erect a canoe shelter, and cook a meal. Here Jeep Latteral bakes a pie. The site is Basswood River near Ely, Minnesota.

I've floated many streams across the country, and there was fresh adventure in every one of them. I saw smallmouths in Ohio's Mohican which I couldn't believe. I didn't get any of the biggest fish, though, and that's excuse enough to go back.

There's another dividend to this floating too. By stopping at tiny tributaries and feeder brooks along the way I've enjoyed sport that would be hard to match anywhere. Many of the little feeders seldom ever see a lure or bait from season to season. In

just one pool hidden from the main stream last spring I caught five bass that would have averaged a pound and a half apiece. Not jumbos, of course, but it was like discovering lost gold.

By floating we've also been able to combine hunting and fishing trips—squirrel hunting especially. The pattern is simply to drift downstream, casting for bass, but keeping an eye on the trees on the bank. It's a wonderfully effective way to bag a limit of squirrels.

Floating is made to order for bass fishermen who are limited to weekend fishing. This way they can escape the heavy concentration of anglers and boating fans on most impounded waters on those busy days. It's a good family activity too, and high adventure for small boys just learning to fish. It's also a good method to stay off the highways—and to use the weekend for unwinding rather than for developing *more* tensions.

But probably the best reward of all for the float tripper, no matter where he lives, is the new and lively brand of fishing in places that less adventuresome anglers seldom see. Since many streams even in highly developed states are seldom fished in an entire summer, float tripping can be like discovering virgin bass waters—which it sometimes actually is.

Strange as it may sound, camping—either with tent or trailer—is another way to catch bass. Obviously it places an angler at water's edge at times when fish are striking; at the same time it saves a long drive from home. This is especially important for daybreak fishing. A camper can roll out of bed, brew a pot of coffee, and be casting with a minimum of effort and the maximum of sleep. In addition, camping is simply a wonderful experience that just goes hand in hand with fishing.

Thanks to the vast variety of fine camping gear that's available nowadays—everything from tents which "spring" open to effective insect repellents—it's possible to live outdoors more inexpensively than to stay at home . . . and with all the comforts of home. Several fishing friends spend almost the entire summer camping on various streams while the husband commutes from work to camp. When vacation time comes they pack and travel to Canada, where they set up camp again on a good bass lake. The number of fish they catch in a season's time sounds almost fictional.

The new camper-trailers, which are compact units while traveling but which open up into roomy living quarters, are made to order for a vagabonding fisherman. I've owned one for several years, and no other piece of equipment has been quite so handy for

Float trippers on the Buffalo River, Arkansas, one of the most beautiful and celebrated float-trip (for bass) rivers in America.

setting up a comfortable camp quickly, even in a driving rain. Quite a few models are on the market now and most of them are quite inexpensive.

Cane-Poling

Before daybreak on most warm spring mornings in the slumbering, crossroads village of Huntsville (near Indian Lake, Ohio) Walker Cline strolls the short block from his home to his barbershop (he's the town's only barber and the mayor as well). Early risers will see him turn on the light inside, not to open the shop for the day but just to pick up his cane pole and an assortment of lures to go "flipjacking." Then off for the lake in a vintage car that's not quite old enough to be back in style again.

Walker usually fishes alone because there aren't many people left who can take the rugged business of flipping. To stand all day or even for a few hours in a boat while manipulating a heavy 18-foot pole can become a chore. But Cline is built for the job. At eighty he's still erect, lean, and in splendid shape.

Years of cane-poling, and farming on occasion, have left him with thick, powerful wrists. Even on windy days, when handling the boat is quite difficult, he still refuses to use an outboard motor.

Cane-poling for bass was once a widely practiced art. In ponds and sloughs along the Eastern Seaboard it's known as skittering, and pork frogs were used for bait as often as spinners. One of the first artificial lures ever manufactured—the tandem spinner—was made for cane-polers. One model was complete with luminous blades, a forerunner of the luminous lures used today by bait casters. Other popular baits and lures elsewhere were live crayfish, strips of pickled pork, and even the large, white-rubber nipples from baby's bottles with treble hooks concealed in the open end. When chugged slowly near the surface, the latter was especially deadly on mid-western waters—so deadly, in fact, that commercial fishermen used them to catch bass when it was still legal to market them.

Still another cane-poling lure was used in shallow waters of the Deep South where alligators were abundant. Bass there have a habit of loitering in the

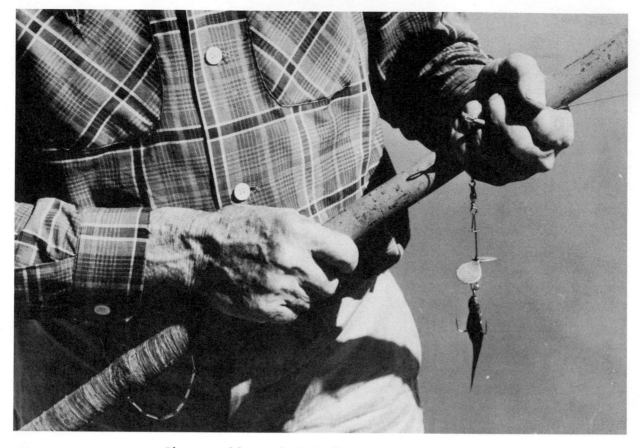

Close-up of lures which Walker uses in cane-poling.

alligator wallows, so inventive anglers cut imitation baby alligators from old black shoe leather and attached treble hooks to the feet. Years ago in Georgia's Okefenokee Swamp I saw an 8-pounder taken on such a lure.

Through the years Cline has been perfectly happy with his own lures. Occasionally he changes the color of the tails and lets it go at that. The spinners are large, about two inches from end to end, and designed to spin easily. Most of them are made from brass sheet, but Walker has used a variety of materials.

He's most particular about tails. Ground-hog hair is the best, he feels, so on certain summer afternoons he closes the shop to hunt his own. Natural bucktail is acceptable, and on occasion he will use fox-squirrel tail.

Walker has a healthy attitude for a veteran who's seen fishing pressure skyrocket in the past few years. It seems someone is casting the stumps all day long. But he is a little disturbed about the way Indian Lake has changed.

Now a 5800-acre impoundment, Indian Lake was formed from a dank wilderness swamp back in 1852. For many years thereafter the lake was full of dead trees, but eventually these decayed at the water line and toppled over. Now time is destroying these too, and only old-timers like Cline know how to find them, although younger fishermen have marked a few with iron pegs.

These stump areas were made to order for cane-poling, and Cline works them like this: reaching out as far as possible with his pole, he swings the lure and drops it gently beyond the target and then slowly draws it past—usually just fast enough to turn the spinner. If the target is a stump, he may completely circle it with his lure, and this is *really* an explosive trick if you can manage it.

Besides stump areas, Cline uses his spinners around the fringes of weed beds too. At Indian Lake, where large areas are completely choked with bonnets, he poles right into the midst of them and then drops his spinner into tiny openings that may be only a foot or less in diameter. Then he just moves the lure up and down. When a bass strikes, and this happens often enough to make the hard work worth-while, Cline immediately strong-arms it upward and swings it into the boat. He's so practiced that he can hook a bass and boat it in a space of three seconds or less.

There is still another use for the cane pole in bass fishing, and although it's used widely now in southern reservoirs in late winter or early spring, it was probably first developed at Dix Dam in Kentucky right after that impoundment first filled with murky water. The tackle here is the same as in flipjacking, but the bait is a big gob of lively night crawlers. Locally the technique is called jigging, but it isn't to be confused with jigging as we've described it elsewhere.

In this case the fisherman travels slowly parallel to a steep and rocky shore line, and at intervals he just dunks the gob of worms into the water—right up against shore or near sunken logs and tree trunks. The worm is jigged up and down a few times in each spot and then moved to another place. It does work effectively and it does catch big bass.

Trolling

Trolling is far from a traditional method of catching bass, and until recent years very little of it was ever done. But a combination of deep-living bass in southern reservoirs and dependable outboard motors with slow trolling speeds has developed trolling into quite an art. In Dale Hollow Lake, Kentucky, for example, a good portion of those jumbo smallmouths are taken by trolling.

Since bass seldom stay in extremely deep water, as in the manner of lake trout, regular casting tackle is suitable enough. A good medium to heavy spinning outfit with a 10-pound or 12-pound test line is fine.

Any lure can be trolled, but some are better than others. Many spinners tend to twist line badly, and it's necessary to use keel a foot or two in front of them. Jigs are good because they're the easiest lures of all to get down deep enough. But for some reason those fishermen who spend the most time trolling and who have learned many tricks of the game prefer to troll with plugs. And many of the most popular trolling plugs are those which float when motionless because these become snagged less often; and when

they are snagged, just to give slack line will sometimes allow them to float upward.

The secret, of course, is to troll any lure right down on the bottom—actually to thump the bottom occasionally—and this isn't a knack that is easily learned. It's absolutely necessary, though. It's a matter of "reading" the water, of practicing contours of the bottom by watching the contours on the surrounding shore and then of trying to travel parallel to a contour rather than "against the grain." The latter results in snagged lures and usually nothing more.

There are a few more important bits of advice for prospective trollers. Once you've caught bass trolling deep, keep coming back to that same spot. And second, carry a workable lure retriever in your tackle kit. And finally, troll as slowly as you can, using lure that "performs" at these very slow speeds.

In a few northern waters fishermen troll shallow, running lures or streamer flies (sometimes several of them in tandem) at night along shore and across shallow underwater bars. There are times when it works marvelously.

Lead-Line Fishing

Several line companies have been manufacturing an interesting and versatile new line which has a lead core and which is quite flexible. It's suitable both to trolling and drifting. The idea of the lead core is to sink a lure more easily and more quickly.

I first used a lead-core line when trolling for landlocked salmon in New Brunswick several years ago. The line was used with a fly rod and with a large capacity fly reel. It worked well, and later I used the same technique when trolling—and eventually when just drifting with the wind—for walleyes. In the process I kept picking up many smallmouth bass.

Since I haven't given this any lengthy trial on bass alone, and since I don't even know anyone who has, it isn't possible to go into much detail. It's very obvious, though, that here is a line and a drifting technique with great potential for any bass in medium to fairly deep water. The lead line makes it possible to feel your way better at any depth because it can be done on a much shorter line. In any case, here is room for pioneering, with better than average chances for success.

Chapter 7

WHERE TO CATCH THE BIGGEST BASS

It was in early spring of 1955 that Bill Blythe and his son returned to the camp at Dale Hollow Lake, Tennessee, after a slightly sensational day of fishing. Their stringer contained ten smallmouth bass that weighed 58 pounds. Three of these weighed 8 pounds each. The rest averaged 5 pounds each. More than likely it is the finest string of bronzebacks ever caught.

Some luck was involved in making this extraordinary catch, as there is in any catch, but the truth is that Blythe had better odds going for him than any other angler fishing that day. First, he's a pretty hot fisherman. Second, he was out fishing when smallmouths are most likely to be taken—in early spring. Finally, he was fishing in a lake which, for one reason or another, simply contains bigger smallmouths than any others. Some waters are like that.

No game fish in North America is more widely distributed than the black bass. That includes all three members of the clan: largemouth, smallmouth, and spotted, as we've pointed out. At least one of these is naturalized now in every state, in every Canadian border province, in Mexico, and on most of the Caribbean islands that contain fresh water. Catching them is no problem anywhere, but catching a lunker—a barroom-betting fish—is a different matter. It's a case of parlaying the right time and technique with the right place to go.

Bass actually do get bigger and heavier in some waters than in others. These places change sometimes from year to year, but generally certain lakes are always big-bass lakes and others are not. It's true that artificial reservoirs, no matter where they are, usually produce the biggest bass around their tenth year, but even among these a few produce bigger bass every year without fail.

A good boat which can reach remote places is helpful in finding bass.

In this day when reservoirs are built thick and fast I know several fishermen who simply concentrate on lakes as soon as they are a decade old. Next season they try a new one, and it surely pays off. It may be a matter of growing season, of nutrition in the soil, fishing pressure, or a combination of all these—not even the biologists know for sure—but there are still these premium waters. It's actually possible to predict with a certain amount of accuracy where the best fish will be taken every season!

Latitude is one definite factor in pinpointing big-bass country. They generally grow bigger the farther south they live. An angler's chances are about fifty times better of hooking a 10-pounder south of the Mason-Dixon line than north of it. They're about 250 to 1 for a 12-pounder, and the odds lengthen or narrow according to how far south or north you're fishing. The biggest bass and the most of them are in Florida.

Trophy bass live in almost every Florida lake, but some lakes are in the news more regularly than the rest with 12-pounders or better. Lake Marion (west of Melbourne), Lochloosa (near Gainesville), Griffin (near Leesburg), and Tsala Apopka (near Inverness) would probably run one, two, three, four. Others with good potential would include a favorite of mine. Blue Cypress (or Wilmington) which is west of Vero Beach, Kissimmee, Panasoffkee, Istokpoga, Tohopekaliga, and Harris.

Florida is also the only state where river largemouths often reach the same proportions as lake fish. The St. Johns River is best-known, but the Withlacoochee in the central part of the state annually produces bigmouths in the 15-pound class. I saw one of these—a big female—a year ago. It was caught just after it had spawned. The day before it might have weighed 17 pounds, but the fisherman, a local farmer, wasn't disturbed. He said he knew where there was another just like it. Maybe it hadn't spawned.

There is unlimited opportunity in Florida for the would-be record buster with a pioneering spirit. State fish technicians have frequently seined and returned to the water of some smaller, almost undisturbed lakes bass that exceeded 16 or 17 pounds. In one pond recently they weighed a bass over 20 pounds. All of these are the lakes that can be fished only by boat, but have no launching sites and so are seldom fished in a season's time. There are thousands of lakes and ponds in this category.

I was drifting on one of these ponds just west of Palm Beach one evening in midsummer. Except for several canoeloads of Boy Scouts paddling around the opposite end of the pond, it had been completely dead for the past hour. I'd just changed from plugs to live shiners when my bobber slowly disappeared. I allowed plenty of time, struck—battled—and eventually boated a bass of better than 7 pounds. I rebaited and tossed the shiner back into the same pocket in the vegetation. The bobber barely had time to settle before it slowly sank again.

I played out line until it stopped and then waited for another run. When it moved again, I struck into something I couldn't turn my way. The fish simply stayed down and cruised slowly around the boat until all the Scouts had time to come around for a

closer look. They formed a noisy cheering section as I regained about half my line, and the bass slowly came to the surface where I had a good look at it— but that was about all. It began to wallow right on the top, managed to dig into a finger of vegetation, and somehow the hook pulled out. It was at least twice as big as the first largemouth, and probably was the largest bass I've ever hooked. I felt sick. Though I cast hopefully in the area for two more hours, there was no more action that evening.

It's worth-while to note that while the biggest percentage of trophy bass are taken on artificials elsewhere in America, many of the Florida lunkers fall for large, live, shiner minnows.

The world-record largemouth, a 22 1/4-pounder which has been the record since 1932, came from Montgomery Lake, a picturesque black-water pond near Valdosta, Georgia. Of all the states today, it is the hardest one in which to pinpoint the best waters for big bass. The pattern somehow isn't clear. Just the same, some real jumbos have turned up recently in Lake Decatur near Donaldsonville and Blackshear Lake near Cordele. Heard's Lake is only a small pond near Thomasville, but still it's a big-bass special. I found jumbo bass in the Okefenokee Swamp when it was a hot spot a few years ago, but a succession of dry years has almost eliminated the fishing. Perhaps it will bounce back.

One of the finest bass ever landed at Okefenokee never reached the scales. The Atlanta fisherman who caught it figured 13 or 14 pounds, but he'll never know for sure. He netted the fish late one evening and then left it on a stringer, tied to his boat while he and his guide camped there overnight. In the morning it was gone. Alligators—or turtles—had eaten all the fish on the stringer.

Three lakes in South Carolina are worth investigating by the prospector for king-size bass. They are Lake Marion near Orangeburg, Lake Murray near Columbia, and Santee-Cooper Reservoir.

North Carolina has provided fishermen with more than a share of good bass, and of these more than a normal portion of them came from Chatuge Lake, near Haysville. Several of these fish ran from 12 to 15 pounds. That's Florida size in a latitude far north of Florida. Recently large bass have begun to show up in Fontana Lake on the edge of the Great Smoky Mountains National Park. That's also the case at smaller Santeetlah Lake, just south of Fontana.

Wheeler Dam consistently turns up the finest bass in Alabama, both largemouths and smallmouths, but doubly so with the latter. Perhaps a dozen 8-pounders have been taken here, and for several years the world record was a 10 1/2-pound Wheeler

Very few 16-pounders are caught, but this one was taken in Florida by George Smith, Sr.

bronzeback. An 8-pound smallmouth, incidentally, rates a place in any trophy room. Next to Wheeler, Wilson Lake is Alabama's best bet for trophy hunting.

Dale Hollow, a 50,000-acre reservoir on the Tennessee-Kentucky border, is certainly one of the most unpredictable lakes in America. I've had extraordinary fishing there—and I've been skunked. There are long dead periods when nothing stirs, not even the pan fish, but still it's a spot that trophy seekers can't afford to pass up. No lake has dominated the big fish of one species as Dale Hollow has with smallmouths.

The smallmouth to top them all, an 11-pound 15-ounce fish boated by D. H. Hayes of Leitchfield, Kentucky, was a Dale Hollow fish. In 1951, nine of the ten largest bronzebacks, and in 1955 the four largest bronzebacks, came from there. At least half of the best smallmouths taken nationwide in the past ten years came from this one lake, and it's possible that it hasn't reached a peak.

Just north and east of Dale Hollow is Cumberland Lake, another sprawling reservoir which biologists believe has even more potential for big bass.

Frankly, this little, old, 100-mile-long fishing hole is my favorite. It's relatively new, but already the smallmouths are running to 8 pounds and the largemouths to 10. Several 5-pound spotted bass have been taken in the Beaver Lodge area, and, speaking of trophies, it's hard to beat a 5-pound spotted bass. They're the smallest of the clan.

Eastern Tennessee nowadays is almost more water than land, because federal bureaus have dammed virtually every creek that flows the year round. As a result some fertile bass water has been created, but none of it quite as consistent through the years as the oldest of the impoundments—Norris Lake, just north of Knoxville. It's good for both smallmouths and largemouths. Watts Bar Lake west of Knoxville and Cherokee Lake just to the east are always worth a try to a wandering bass specialist. I've had better than ordinary luck at Cherokee, which is more off the beaten track than the rest.

A most remarkable example of how some lakes are simply big-bass lakes is Bedford, south of Nashville, Tennessee. It's hardly a puddle (a mere 175 acres) compared to the TVA reservoirs (average:

30,000 acres) elsewhere in the state, but for several years it hasn't failed to place largemouths, usually several of them, among the largest landed anywhere. As many as a dozen have exceeded 12 pounds and several have reached 14. That's extraordinary size, considering how close Bedford is located to Yankee country.

Spilling over into Tennessee is part of Pickwick Lake, Mississippi. Last spring, within an hour of leaving the boat dock, a fisherman caught three big-mouths which weighed 26 pounds. Two of them were 9-pounders. That same day I talked to another angler just back at the dock with a fourth 9-pounder. He'd taken it on a black pork strip. Those aren't the biggest fish ever seen in Mississippi, but bass of those dimensions are seen more often at Pickwick than anywhere else in the state. Grenada Lake is also worth a try.

Any angler is automatically stacking the odds in favor of hooking a king-size fish when he fishes any of the Arkansas reservoirs, for this is a region that spawns big bass. As elsewhere, though, several of the lakes are outstanding. The region around Hot Springs is especially good because that resort town is situated in the center of a trio of picturesque lakes —Hamilton, Catherine, and Ouachita. The first two are old reservoirs, and Catherine especially is worth quite a few old socker largemouths every season. Ouachita is the newest of the lakes, and it's also one of those for which biologists are predicting big

things. Considering the present bass populations and growth rates of fish there, it can hardly miss. It was at Ouachita last spring that Johnny Dieckman, a Costa Mesa, California, tournament caster, won the Hot Springs Professional Fishing Derby and $1000 as well. He made limit catches of big bass for all three days of the event, the largest being a 7-pound 1-ounce largemouth.

Probably the best bet for a trophy bass in Arkansas is Norfork Lake, a giant reservoir in the Ozarks near the Missouri line. This lake has been producing largemouths in the 10- and 11-pound class ever since it reached maturity, and recently jumbo small-mouths have begun to make an appearance.

Norfork is an especially good night-fishing lake all through midsummer. I've seen Bob Ketchum of nearby Mountain Home taking bigmouths right through August dog days. His formula is to fish the hour or so before dawn with an oversize spinner and pork frog. The fact that he's a consistent winner in the St. Louis *Post-Dispatch* fishing contests is evidence that it works.

Bull Shoals Lake, partially in Missouri, and Narrows Lake in southern Arkansas are also worth investigation. A word to the wise angler planning a visit to this razorback country: black salt-water jigs are all the rage for bass hereabouts. Three in every four of the best fish are hooked on these lures.

Twelve-year-old Texoma Lake on the Texas-Oklahoma line is right now reaching a peak, and it takes an 8- or 9-pound largemouth to raise eyebrows. Several years ago Medina Lake near San Antonio was the hottest place in the state for a plug caster, but the years of drought had considerable effect. It should come back now.

About 75 miles southwest of Dallas is Lake Whitney, the largest completely inside Texas. It's only five years old, but still anglers have taken many 7- and 8-pounders. That growth is so unusual that it's a lake to watch.

Lowe Fawks of Graford, Texas, has organized a not-so-exclusive club on Possum Kingdom Lake, an impoundment on the Brazos River. Catch a 7-pounder or better and you're eligible. Even though the club is only two years old Fawks already has more members than he can count. It's a good testimonial to a good lake for trophy bass.

Tenkiller, Lake of the Cherokees, Fort Gibson, and Eucha (or Upper Spavinaw) are possibilities in Oklahoma.

A 9½-pounder by the author on a fly rod in Cumberland Lake, Kentucky.

Not too many years ago there wasn't a bass to be found in the Southwest, but as in Texas, that's all changed. For many years Lake Mead near Las Vegas and Boulder City received national attention because big bass were taken there wholesale. I fished there in those days, and it's hard to recall any more lively action or bulkier bass. The truth is that this is still going on, especially in early spring, but a bass in the 10-pound bracket just seems more commonplace now. Mojave Lake, just downstream from Mead on the Colorado River, is also beginning to yield oversize bass.

Professional wildlifers in Arizona consider Roosevelt Lake just east of Phoenix potentially the best bass lake in the country.

It's significant that another, comparatively small lake, Pleasant, just north of Phoenix, has produced more than a normal share of better than 10-pounders.

Elephant Butte Reservoir, New Mexico, is one of the oldest reservoirs in the Southwest. Although fishing isn't what it used to be it's still the likeliest spot to land a largemouth of bragging size in a vast area of desert real estate.

Unless you live there it's hard to think of California as a bass state, probably because it's best known for salt-water fishing, for high Sierra trout lakes, and for some of America's finest steelhead streams. Still, Lake Henshaw, which is due east of Oceanside and Escondido, has provided unusually fine sport for bass for a long time. Several years, a decade or so ago, the top largemouths in the nation came from there. Annually the average size of Henshaw bass stacks up well with the average almost anywhere else in the South.

San Vincente Reservoir, northeast of San Diego, has been a consistent big-bass lake. More recently Round Valley and Irvine lakes fit into that category. Several 11-pounders came from Irvine during the last two years.

The truth is that there are trophy bass almost wherever there is enough water to cover them—often in extremely unlikely places. Regular inventories made by state game and fish departments rarely fail to prove it. Still the best advice is to parlay the right time and technique with a trip to those waters where the most big bass are caught—year in and year out.

Chapter 8
BASS FISHING AT NIGHT

Fishing after dark on an Ohio farm pond. Note miner's cap, a very useful item at night.

This chapter is about bass fishing's last frontier—the darkness of night. There are no new bass waters left to discover, no new wildernesses to explore for bass. Here is how I described this last frontier, and a most lively sport, in *Outdoor Life*.

For late May it was an unusually calm and quiet evening on Lake Erie. Except for the beacon that clickered atop the International Peace Monument at Put-in-Bay and the foghorn of the Catawba Ferry, we might have been in another world instead of on a rocky island just a few miles from the Ohio mainland.

We'd started in the morning by casting the shallow west shore of South Bass Island. When that didn't produce we cut across the open lake and swung into the channel between Middle Bass and the lonely Sugar Island. At this time of year that spot is almost always red-hot, but today there was nothing doing. Len Gray and I had one smallmouth apiece—and they were small fish at that. Now we were back at South Bass again, practically skunked.

The smallmouths have two big sprees in western Lake Erie—in spring and fall. All the signs were right for the spring run to be reaching a peak. We knew they moved onto the shoals and inshore shallows, because commercial fishermen had found them there in nets. And the water temperature was exactly right—57 degrees. In forty years at the Put-in-Bay fish hatchery, superintendent Ernie Miller has taken the water temperature every day. He's found that when it passes 55 the smallmouths invariably gather on the shallows to spawn. It's the only thing that's predictable about the species in Lake Erie.

We finished a fine pickerel dinner at Cooper's Island Winery with a party of weekend yachting fans from Cleveland and walked out into the balmy spring night. I was ready to turn in, but Len had another idea. "Let's try it once more," he said. Ten minutes later we were fumbling to set up casting outfits in the dark. I selected a shallow running plug.

Our boat was tied up in a gravelly bay on the west shore off the islands. As soon as Len pushed off from the dock I made a short cast that was only good for a backlash, and I needed a few seconds to untangle it and start the retrieve. That done, I made several turns of the reel handle and immediately there was a heavy roll on the surface of the lake. My rod whipped downward against gunwale, and for a second I lost control of the reel handles. I skinned a couple of knuckles before I could catch them again, while thirty feet away a good bass was jumping on his way out to the open lake. I thumbed the reel spool hard, and the fish jumped again out in the black. A few minutes later I slipped the net under a wild and fat 3-pound smallmouth.

That was only the beginning. Before my bass was on the stringer Len had hooked another, and before he lost that one on the second jump, I was in business again. It was an evening I'll never forget. We simply allowed the boat to drift across the shallow bay, and we cast at random all around us. On every third or fourth toss a big old bronzeback would boil up to the top and we'd have a time for ourselves out there in the darkness.

These were big bass for that country, too, 2- to 3-pounders with a few that would reach four. We finally stopped fishing around midnight because we were arm-weary and not because we ran out of fish. There's no creel limit on them in these waters, but we only strung a half dozen anyway. The rest of them were released to return to those same shallows next spring.

That session at South Bass was a lesson I've always remembered. It's this: if bass aren't stirring during the day, go out again after dark. The truth is that both largemouths and smallmouths are largely nocturnal anyway, probably more so than any other fresh-water fish except brown trout and catfish. And besides increasing the odds in your favor, night fishing is a sport full of suspense and uncertainty that's hard to match anywhere. It's not something to try if you have a bad heart, but for pure excitement there's nothing else exactly like it.

I had been fishing farm ponds in the Midwest for many years, and as I've pointed out before, I rate them among the best fishing holes in the region. But it was on a frog-hunting expedition several years ago that I discovered another effective way of all to fish them at night.

Johnny Adams and I were hunting slowly up a small creek in Ohio's Champaign County. The burlap sacks tied to our belts contained almost a full limit of big bullfrogs—so we stopped for a smoke. It was a quiet evening, and quickly we became aware of frogs—many frogs—"roaring" far over to our left. That was unusual, because we knew that the creek meandered away in exactly the opposite direction.

"There's water over there somewhere," John whispered. "Let's go and find it."

We climbed up the creek bank and started across country, stopping every hundred feet or so to listen. We had to cross a stubble field, a plowed cornfield, and two barbed-wire fences, but eventually we wound up on the edge of a large farm pond.

Walking in opposite directions around the pond, we made a wonderful discovery. Besides the bullfrogs, it was full of bass. At intervals all around the pond's perimeter largemouths would flush from the cattails in the beam of my light. Some of them were real jumbos; big enough, anyway, that we returned the next afternoon to ask the farmer for permission to fish. He said it was O.K. to fish any time but that we'd catch few bass. "They just won't strike," he added. But that was a story I'd heard before.

Johnny and I fished that pond thoroughly during the afternoon, and the farmer's prediction proved true enough. We couldn't raise a single bass, but we did manage to catch a good string of bluegills. I couldn't forget the bass we saw the night before, though, and, driving home, I said to John, "Remember how those bass were practically out on the banks last night?"

"Like tonight?" he answered.

"Like tonight!"

It was well after dark when we pulled into the barnyard to park and to set up our tackle in the headlights of the car. My outfit was built around my 8 1/2-foot bass-bugging fly rod. Johnny had a spinning outfit and a vestful of surface plugs. At the pond we separated again to walk or wade the bank in opposite directions. Hardly two minutes passed before there was a splash on the surface and John hollered, "Got him!"

A second or so later there was another splash and John said, "Lost him."

I made a few false casts parallel to the shore to gain line and then placed the bug a few feet from the edge of a strip of cattails. I left it motionless for a moment, twitched the bug, and left it motionless again. Nothing doing—so I walked forward

Photo by Paul A. Moore

Bass fishing at dawn in Crooked Creek, a Kentucky lake.

several steps and placed the bug farther along the cattails. I didn't even twitch that one before a bass rolled up and out and I had both hands full.

There's nothing sluggish about these farm-pond busters. They live an abundant life on the frogs, crickets, grasshoppers, and dragonflies that fall into the water. I caught a bass once which had swallowed a full-grown red-winged blackbird. When they catch something with a hook they go crazy. This one cartwheeled out toward deeper water, changed his mind, and tried to escape into the cattails. Operating mostly by "feel," I turned the bass away in time, and after another jump I had him by the lower jaw. I released him. Two casts later I had action again.

This next bass walloped my bug close by—just as I was about to pick it up for another cast. Next

it started tail-walking until it got into the weeds. Then it was just a matter of my wading to the spot and digging out my fish by hand. That was pretty much the pattern of fishing until an hour or so later when we quit. We caught enough bass to feed a platoon of hungry Boy Scouts but kept only a few fish that were hooked especially deep.

Through the seasons several of the most addicted night fishermen I know have developed a special outfit for night fishing. It consists mostly of light khaki shirt and trousers, tennis shoes, a light vest with many pockets, a head lamp, and plenty of insect repellent. This outfit is good either for wading or boat fishing. Since nearly all of this night fishing occurs in midsummer or when waters are warm, waders or hip boots are of little value. It's easier and more comfortable just to "wade wet."

A fisherman should always be familiar with the water he plans to wade at night, though. It's absolutely essential to make a reconnaissance in daylight—to check for sudden drop-offs or deep places. Even when a fisherman knows the water well, it's still wise to move slowly and cautiously. To travel slowly is a safety precaution, but it will also spook fewer bass. In unfamiliar waters it's a good idea to use a wading staff, maybe just a big willow stick, to frequently test the depth ahead.

Most night fishermen use casting rods, but on this I disagree. Nowadays I use a fly rod and bass bugs exclusively—with just one exception. That exception is when using the new, plastic worm and eel imitations that have been great killers at night as well as in daylight and which must be delivered on a casting rod.

Anyway, here's my case for the fly rod. Even experts have occasional snarls and backlashes at night, and sometimes these are a headache to unravel. It's even worse for beginners, who often find bait casting a pure headache after dark. Many of them give it up and thereby miss a world of lively sport just because casting is so complicated. With a fly rod most of this is eliminated. I use heavy (10-pound test) leaders and make short casts. I pull line from the reel only as I need it—and do not leave excess coils hanging free, especially when I'm wading. Troubles and tangles just don't exist when using this system. But more than anything else, I like bugging because it hooks more bass most of the time than casting with larger plugs.

After-dark anglers are far more in agreement on techniques than on tackle. Wading wherever it's possible is far better than boating, because a fisherman in the water is much less likely to alarm a bass (a largemouth especially) than a boat above. No noises like the rasp of an oarlock, of a paddle scraping the gunwale, or a thumping tackle box accompany a man wading.

The best technique is just about the simplest too. It's a case of using surface (or sometimes in the case of plug casters, plugs that run very shallow when retrieved) lures just about as slowly as the angler's patience permits. It just isn't necessary to hurry a retrieve in this type of fishing. Tom McNally, outdoors editor of the Chicago *Tribune* and a terrific bass fisherman, believes that underwater plugs are most effective at night.

Nearly any bass bug will work after dark. The frog imitations are deadly, and so are the spent-wing hair bugs. All the hair bugs are a little harder to cast accurately, though, and in areas of heavy vegetation this can be troublesome. They also tend to sink quickly. Recently bugs with turned-up (rather than turned-down) hooks have appeared on tackle shelves everywhere. Perhaps they actually were made for night bugging; in any case they're perfect for weedy waters or for ponds full of pads and bonnets.

In night bass bugging it's doubly necessary to have a floating fly line. Nearly all modern lines float well, but after extended use in ponds thick with algae even the best begin to sink. So in this instance the extra reel and line I always carry is most valuable. I change as soon as the first line begins to sink.

For several years straight running the winner of all bass-fishing contests at Ohio's fine Burr Oak Lake was Dwight Hartley, a store owner in nearby Glouster. His business is such that except on Sundays he doesn't have much opportunity to fish in daylight. It doesn't matter, though, because Hartley believes that once summer arrives, night is the *only* time to fish for bass. He catches enough 6-pounders, which are bragging size hereabouts, to prove it, and his method is precisely described before. He fishes floating lures ever so slowly along the fringes of shallow water.

To fish at night is certainly an angler's best weapon after dog days arrive. It gives relief from the heat as well as a chance to catch some fillets for the home freezer. A few years ago Charlie McClellan and I fished regularly—almost daily—at Vesuvius Lake in southern Ohio. But all through July and August we'd seldom wet a line until nightfall when all of the picnickers, pleasure boaters, and swimmers would leave. Then we would travel slowly up the lake, stopping to cast in places that had been churned to a froth all day long.

One of our favorite places was the bathing beach which in daylight was always alive with people. The outer, safe edge of the beach was marked with a series of posts or pilings connected with a heavy rope. We would cast around these pilings and make truly remarkable catches on popping bugs. One night Charlie and I caught 16 bass up to 5 pounds around a dozen pilings!

Boat docks and stump areas are also good places to try at night. Sometimes in such spots it's possible to locate bass by the sounds of their surface feeding. To present a surface lure to a bass chasing minnows or hunting for frogs will almost surely produce a strike.

A night fisherman needs a calm and quiet night for the best results. If there is any breeze at all it's best to stay home, because it's harder to control both the boat and the casting in a wind. Eventually an angler learns to "fish by ear" after dark, and even this is impossible except on quiet, velvety nights. Some fishermen closely watch the stage of the moon, but I believe it's far better to watch the weather vane.

One year we planned a trip to New Brunswick—to Palfrey Lake near the Maine border at Vanceboro—to catch the smallmouth fishing at its peak in early June. The idea was a week of bugging for them, but it just didn't work that way. They wouldn't strike in daylight at all; action didn't begin until sundown. But that wasn't all; almost every morning a fresh wind would develop, and then last all day and well into the night. Bass bugging was eliminated even after sundown. Fortunately we were kept pretty busy trolling for landlocked salmon and on a couple of occasions had all the action any sportsman could handle. Then I made a discovery.

I woke up before daylight one morning and found the lake was glassy calm. Alone I slipped out of the cabin and paddled slowly along a rocky shore. When I reached a shallow point where I'd found a few bass several evenings before, I made a cast and a heavy fish rolled under my bug but didn't take it. It was a temptation to pick up the bug and cast again, but instead I just twitched it gently and left it motionless again. That did it. The bass rolled up a second time and inhaled the bug. It was out of the water, shaking, almost before I could raise my rod and set the hook. Somehow the hook held, though, and I had a fish for my stringer.

For about an hour that morning I had the sort of action that every bass fisherman dreams about. It should happen to every one of them. The fish were lying in tight against the shore and just to place a bug in close was to coax a strike.

In the first faint light of daybreak I noticed the movement of a bass between two rocks just offshore and barely a foot apart. My bug fell on one of the rocks, and easily I pulled it off into the water. The

It's dusk and the author and Don Ray are casting toward the shoreline at Sepdnic Lake, N. B.

bass swirled beneath it but didn't strike. It swirled again when I gave the bug the long-pause-and-twitch retrieve . . . and still didn't strike. Then when the bug was a full yard from the rocks the pressure was too much. The fish surged up and was hooked.

We had a fast and furious contest going there for several minutes. That smallmouth took much more line than most bass; six times it catapulted clear of the surface, and once more it rolled up but couldn't jump clear. That's when I regained my line and led him alongside the boat. The fish weighed 4 1/2 pounds if it weighed an ounce

I caught one more bass after that before the wind rose again. Then I paddled back to camp and to the hot coffee which was then abrewing.

Night fishermen are always developing something —a new gadget to eliminate some of the discomforts of the sport or, more often, a new lure. One winter recently, the late Carl Abell of Glendale, who was one of California's best bass fishermen, sent me several "parachute" flies. They're large-size imitations of dragonflies tied with deerhair wings and tails. The design is such that they fall slowly on the cast and alight softly on the water. Carl reported they were murder on certain California ranch ponds where dragonflies are numerous—and maybe I would find them useful too.

Well, dragonflies are also numerous here in the Midwest, and I tried them in several places, including one "problem" farm pond where the bass are shy about striking even at night. So far it has been a great producer here; it just might be great anywhere.

Another good bet to try at night is the Muddler, a large grasshopperlike imitation originated by fly tier Don Gapen for large eastern brook trout in Ontario. More recently it has been popular on western trout streams (particularly in Montana). After dark several Columbus, Ohio, anglers have found it extremely effective on pond largemouths and on the smallmouths in small meadow rivers. I've had a lively evening or two using it myself.

The truth is that black bass are usually easier to fool, and sometimes more fun to fool, after night has fallen.

Chapter 9

BASS
IN THE PAN

The bass is known as the fish with the "muddy taste." Nothing could be more absurd if a bass fisherman keeps one important item in mind; preparation for the table must begin the minute the fish is caught.

There are two ways to handle bass as they are caught—either alive on a stringer or in a portable refrigerator. In the latter the fish should be placed so that they do not slosh around in melting ice water. Lacking both a stringer and a cooler, soak a burlap bag and then wring it out as much as possible. Wrap the bass inside and place the bag in a shady place. Of course, this isn't so effective as the other methods.

When fishing is finished the bass should be cleaned immediately. From small fish remove the scales, gills, fins, head, and entrails. Wipe the body cavity clean and dry. Fillet the larger bass, say from 1 1/2 pounds and upward. Avoid using water as much as possible in the cleaning, and, instead, sprinkle either the whole fish or the fillets with lemon juice. Water makes the flesh mushy, while lemon tends to "firm" it. If water is used, wipe the fish dry with a cloth before cooking or refrigerating.

If a "muddy" taste actually exists at all in the bass, simply skin them.

Largemouths are "lean" or nonoily fish, and general cooking instructions are pretty much the same as for other such fish. Most important is not to overcook them, no matter what the method. Overcooking always leaves bass very dry, flaky, and tasteless. No matter whether it's frying, baking, or broiling, the best idea is first to briefly subject the bass to high heat to seal in flavors. After that reduce

The complete bass fisherman cooks his bass fresh out of the water.

the heat, except in frying, where a bare six or seven minutes will take care of small pieces of fish.

Just as largemouths are unsophisticated fish, so should cooking them be uncomplicated. The flavor of bass is pleasant, and there is no reason unduly to disguise it.

Fried Bass

Frying bass is as simple as heating a skillet of butter, bacon drippings, or other cooking fat and then dropping salted and peppered pieces of bass into it. Three minutes or so on each side will do it. That's the most convenient and least complicated of methods for cooking on the trail or in a light camp. Otherwise, roll the fish in a mixture of flour, yellow corn meal, and salt and pepper before frying. Still another alternative is to make a batter of pancake flour, egg, and milk to cover the fish before

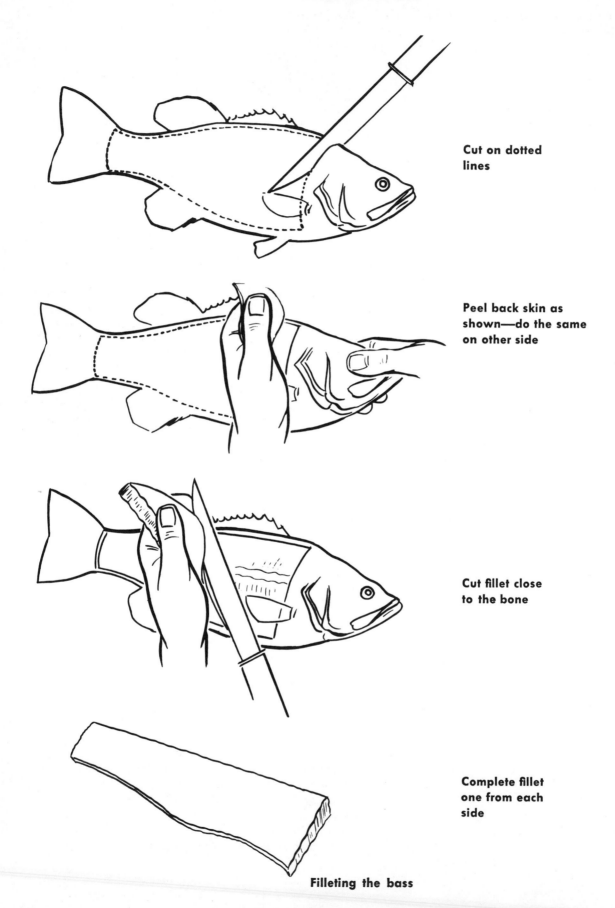

Cut on dotted
lines

Peel back skin as
shown—do the same
on other side

Cut fillet close
to the bone

Complete fillet
one from each
side

Filleting the bass

cooking. Never allow fried fish to remain in the fat after cooking is finished.

Grilled Bass

Clean a medium- to large-size bass but leave it whole. Split it and place the flesh side down on a grill from 10 to 12 inches above a bed of hot hardwood coals. After 10 minutes (for a 2-pounder) turn over and sprinkle with a half teaspoon of monosodium glutamate, salt, and pepper on the flesh side. The bass will have a robust, somewhat smoky flavor. It should be served with potatoes baked in the coals.

Bass can be "grilled" at streamside just by spitting the pieces or whole fish on green willow sticks and holding them over the coals.

Planked Bass

Tack large fillets or split whole bass to a strip of clean, bleached driftwood with skin side to the wood. Prop the wood near the fire and brush the fish frequently with hot strips of bacon or bacon drippings as they broil. Baste also with lemon if it's available. Season with salt and pepper. This is a leisurely method of cooking that was designed for a warm midday on a wilderness pond.

Baked Bass

Take a whole 3- or 4-pounder (or the fillets from several fish) and rub all surfaces with olive oil. Lay in a well-buttered casserole, add a finely chopped onion and a half cup tomato juice—and bake for thirty minutes in a 350° oven, basting frequently. Remove the fish, cover it with a creole sauce and buttered bread crumbs. Put it back in the oven and brown it under the broiler. Serve it with rice and a green salad.

Boiled Bass

Place either fillets or whole fish in a clean cheesecloth bag. Place the bag in two quarts of boiling water in which three tablespoons of salt and six tablespoons of vinegar have been dissolved. Poach for about ten or twelve minutes and remove the bag gently. With a spatula lift fish from the bag and transfer them to a serving plate. Cover them with a hot fish sauce.

Hundreds of delicious fish sauces have been prepared. Some are simple to make. Some are even available on grocery shelves. The easiest thing to do is to select one from a cookbook. It's adventuresome eating—just as it's adventuresome business fishing for bass—anywhere.

Chapter 10

LIVE BAITS FOR BASS

Speak of live bait and minnows or crayfish immediately come to mind. Or maybe night crawlers. These are effective sure enough, but a bass will tackle anything that moves, native to the water or not, and it's a wise bait fisherman who considers all the possibilities. The truth is that some of the lesser-known baits are the most effective. Here are some statistics on most of them.

Alewife: also called killifish, the alewife is sometimes found landlocked in lakes, although it is a salt-water species. They may migrate into fresh-water coastal streams to spawn. Caught, kept, and hooked in the same manner as minnows, they make excellent bait.

American brook lamprey: found in the mud bottoms of streams, brook lampreys are harmless members of the family to which the parasitic sea lamprey belongs. In areas where they occur they can be dug from the muck in fairly shallow water, a common digging implement being the hay fork. They are tough and long-lasting baits. They can be hooked in various ways: through the tail so that the lamprey continues to swim freely; through one of the gill openings; or strung on the hook like a worm. They are especially favored for bass, but they also make good baits for walleyes, catfish, northern pike, and pickerel.

Australian cricket: wingless cricket accidentally introduced into U.S. Good bait. Has been grown commercially.

Baltimore minnow: name for goldfish.

Bee: adult bees can be used for catching bass. More frequently, the grubs of bees, hornets, and wasps are used as bait.

Beetle larva: beetle larvae, called grubs, make excellent bait for bass, bluegills. One of the most popular of the grubs is the meal worm. Other grubs can be dug from rotting logs and stumps, from beneath tree bark, grass roots, or manure piles.

Blackfin shiner: one of the many shiners used as bait. See Golden shiner.

Blackhead minnow: see Fathead minnow.

Black-nosed dace: a small minnow common in cold waters, preferring fast-moving waters to slow. It is dark above and white below, with a dark stripe down the side; sometimes the dark line will appear to be yellow or tan, and the sides are often blotched. Maximum size, about three inches.

Blacknose shiner: one of the many shiners used as bait. See Golden shiner.

Bloodsucker: see Leech.

Blowfly maggot: these maggots, along with those of the housefly, the stable fly, and others, make excellent bait. They can be obtained by hanging out a piece of meat or dead animal and collecting the full-grown and fattened maggots that accumulate within about a week. If the meat or dead animal is hung up and a container placed beneath it the maggots will drop into it automatically. Frequently, such a container is filled with corn meal to dry and to cleanse the maggots.

Bluntnose minnow: one of most popular for pond propagation. Prominent spot at end of lateral line, just in front of caudal fin. Head is broad, blunt. Maximum size, about 3 inches.

Brandling: name for English redworm.

Brassy minnow: a common bait minnow in the Midwest; found in creeks and ponds. It gets its name from the brassy color of the large scales along its sides.

Bream: a name sometimes used in referring to one of the various shiners used for bait.

Brindled mad tom: mad toms are the smallest members of the catfishes; distinguished by continuation of adipose fin into caudal fin. Generally 5 inches or less in length. They prefer swift waters, are frequently found under rocks. They have poison glands at the base of each spine. Can inflict painful injuries. Good bait for variety of fish, especially black bass. Durable on hook. Clip their spines for safety.

Bullfrog: frogs, because they are lively and will attract a fish's attention, often catch fish where other baits fail. The leopard frog, pickerel frog, and the green frog are favorites, although small bullfrogs also make good baits; tadpoles, too, can take fish.

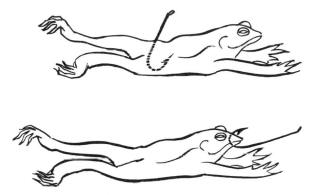

For still fishing, hook the bullfrog through the back. For casting, the bullfrog should be hooked through the lips.

You can catch the frogs by hand or scoop net; at night, blind them with a flashlight. They can be kept in a large wooden cage partly submerged in the water if you have provided them with rocks or pieces of wood for resting places. When you go fishing take them in a small container filled with damp grass and leaves.

Bullhead: bullheads make good bait for bass and other game fish when they are 5 inches or less in length. Larger ones are sometimes used for trotlines, set lines, etc. The horns on the pectoral and dorsal fins are generally clipped so that the bait is more attractive and less dangerous. Young bullheads can be seined from ponds and quiet backwaters and can be kept for long periods of time in bait buckets. They also live for a long time on the hook.

Butterfly: see Caterpillar.

Caddis creeper: see Caddis worm.

Caddis fly: see Caddis worm.

Caddis worm: caddis worms, the larvae of small, winged insects which belong to the same order as the dobson fly (adult hellgrammite), live in the water and are generally encased in a portable protective sack made of sticks, leaves, stones, and other material which they cement together with a secretion from their mouths. The exact construction of these cases is so exact as to material and method that the species can be identified from the character of the case. Caddis worms can be caught by hand as they crawl about on the bottom. Removed from the case and strung on a hook, they are excellent bait for bass. Sometimes more than one can be used on a hook.

Carp: carp are the largest members of the minnow family and were introduced to this country in the 1800s as a food and forage fish. Their closest relative, also an introduced species, is the goldfish. Both are good baits, but both are considered undesirable when placed in waters still free of them. State laws frequently ban the use of either goldfish or carp as bait.

Caseworm: see Caddis worm.

Catalpa worm: the catalpa worm is the caterpillar or larval stage of the sphinx moth. It sometimes reaches a length of 3 inches and can be found only on the catalpa tree, its only source of food. They can be harvested by shaking the tree and picking up the worms that fall to the ground. You can keep them alive in a cage, feeding them catalpa leaves; or you can save them in corn meal in the refrigerator. They can be housed in ordinary coffee cans, provided they have leaves to eat. No holes need to be punched in the cans, as the empty space provides plenty of oxygen. They can be strung on the hook like a fishing worm, or the heads can be cut off and the soft body inside shucked from the skin, to make a possibly more appealing bait.

Catawba: see Catalpa worm.

Caterpillar: caterpillars are the larvae of butterflies and moths, and most of them can be used for bait. Smooth-skinned ones are better than those that are hairy or horned. Some of the hairy or spiny ones can sting.

Catfish: see Bullhead.

Chub: chubs are stocky minnows with big heads and large scales. Generally caught in gravel-bottomed areas of creeks and large streams, they often reach a length of 8 inches or more. They are sometimes caught on hook and line for sport. Small ones are good baits for bass. They are hardy.

Chub sucker: see Sucker.

Cicada: cicada (seventeen-year locust) makes good

bait for bass during years of abundance. Found in all years, but particularly at seventeen-year intervals.

Clam: clams and mussels live in mud, sand, or graveled bottoms of creeks, rivers, or lakes. There are many species. You can get them by wading and feeling for them with your feet, then digging them out by hand or by raking the bottom. There are regulations in some states specifying the size, number, and the season for taking clams. They can be kept in water-filled containers for long periods of time on a fishing trip. Soured clams (the soft insides placed in a jar with sour milk for several days) are used for catfish, but fresh clams work well too. The clams are removed from the shell by inserting a knife blade and cutting the hinge muscle.

Clipper: see Hellgrammite.

Cockroach: there are four common species of cockroaches: German, Oriental, American, wood. The first three can be raised easily for bait or can be trapped by baiting them with raw or cooked vegetables. The containers in which they are kept should be tightly covered to prevent their escape, perhaps oiled near the top so that they cannot climb out. Make certain that the container holds an adequate supply of water. The entire roach is placed on the hook and is an excellent bait.

Common chub: see Chub.

Common eastern mad tom: see Brindled mad tom.

Common killifish: see Alewife.

Common shiner: see Golden shiner.

Common white sucker: see Sucker.

Conniption bug: see Hellgrammite.

Corn earworm: see European corn borer.

Crab: another name for Crayfish.

Crane fly: also called gallinipper, crane flies are long-legged, extremely fragile flies whose water-dwelling larva, called leatherjacket and waterworm, make excellent bait for a variety of fish. The maggotlike larva, found under debris in streams, ponds, and lakes, has a tough skin and a small, hard head. Hook one or two through the head.

Craw: see Crayfish.

Crawdad: see Crayfish.

Crawfish: see Crayfish.

Crawler: see Hellgrammite.

Crayfish: also called craw, crab, crawdad, crawfish. The crayfish, which looks like a miniature lobster, is another good bait which many fresh-water fish can't resist. A number of different species are found in the swamps, brooks, streams, rivers, and lakes. They come out of hiding mostly at night, but during the day they can be caught by hand or with a small net by lifting up stones or searching in weed beds. Minnow traps baited with dead fish or meat scraps will often catch them if the funnel openings are wide enough for them to enter. For a day's fishing you can keep them in damp weeds or moss in almost any container. The best crayfish for bait are those which have shed their hard shells and are soft and helpless. Tie these to a hook with fine thread and fish them for trout, black bass, walleyes, catfish, carp, and large pan fish. To use hard-shells, break off the large claws and hook them through the tail or back. The tail alone often makes a good bait. Frogs and crayfish require plenty of water and space, and it's not practical to try and raise them in small numbers. You can catch more than you need for yourself in most lakes or rivers.

Creek chub: see Chub.

Cricket: catch crickets from under leaves and stones by hand or with a small net. Keep them in a box of grass on trips. For fishing, fine wire hooks are best. Run point under collar carefully so it doesn't kill the cricket. Good bait for bass. Two common species: gray and black. Easily grown.

Croton bug: another name for German cockroach. See Cockroach.

Dace: see Black-nosed dace.

Damsel fly: see Nymph.

Dark meal worm: see Meal worm.

Darter: also called Ohio log perch, sand pike, and zebra fish. Smallest members of perch family. Named because of habit of rapidly moving from place to place, then pausing. Found principally in and below currents. Catch on hook and line, or seine. Good bait.

Dewworm: see Night crawler.

Dobson fly: the adult stage of a hellgrammite.

Dragon: another name for Hellgrammite.

Dragonfly: dragonfly nymphs, often called perch bugs, ugly bugs, bass bugs; live in ponds, lakes, and quieter stream sections. They hide in mud, vegetation, and debris, where they can be caught in seines or dip nets. Bringing debris from bottom with rakes and examining for nymphs is also productive. Good bait for black bass.

Dung worm: also called the stink worm or fecal earthworm, a manure worm is a rather uncommon bait because of its scarcity and its habitat. It lives in manure and sewage and other such undesirable places. When cut or hooked it gives off a yellowish liquid with a disagreeable odor. It is

Photo by Karl H. Maslowski

The dragonfly, familiar around all bass waters, is also a good bait for fly rodders.

thinner than a regular earthworm, although it sometimes reaches a length of 4 or 5 inches. It is also more lively.

Earthworm: earthworms are one of the best all-round live baits used in fresh-water fishing. Whether they are common earthworms, night crawlers, or dung worms, they should be taken along on most fishing trips. You can dig them with a garden fork, grab the night crawlers when they emerge at night, or buy your worms from bait dealers. If you obtain your own look for them in rich, moist soil. Worms can be kept for long periods in almost any large can or box filled with earth. For shorter periods or on the fishing grounds you can keep the worms in any small container filled with earth. But keep the worms

The best method of hooking the earthworm is the one which keeps the worm on the hook securely, yet allows it to wiggle freely.

out of the sun and rain. If kept for more than a week or two the worms can be fed corn meal, bread crumbs, chicken mash, or other animal or vegetable matter mixed into the soil. When hooking the worms the best method is the one which keeps the worm on the hook securely, yet allows it to wiggle freely and to live the longest time. For trout, hook the worm under the sexual band or anywhere else near the center. In heavy weeds or when fishing on the bottom, the point and barb can be covered. When drifting the worm in fast, running water, the point and barb should be exposed. For bass from one to a half-dozen or so large worms can be used on a hook. Earthworms can be kept or raised almost anywhere, indoors or outdoors, and take up little space. If an angler just wants enough worms for himself and perhaps a friend or two, he can usually dig the worms in the spring of the year and keep them in boxes or cans throughout the fishing season. Just keep the soil moist by sprinkling some water into the containers ever so often and feed the worms bread crumbs, chicken mash, ground oats, or almost any other vegetable or animal matter, small amounts of which can be mixed into the soil. You can also obtain special, prolific worms from tackle stores, bait dealers, or worm farms if you want to raise large quantities of them. From 100 to 300 of these worms can be used to start a colony in a large watertight box or metal container filled with rich soil. This container can be kept indoors in a cool spot, and after the worms are added the only attention it needs is occasional food and water to keep the soil moist. About 1 pound of corn meal to 1/2 pound of vegetable shortening or lard can be mixed into the soil every two weeks or so. The larger the container, the more food should be added. The worms will breed, and you can remove the adult ones for bait at regular intervals. Outdoor pits can also be dug or constructed in a shady spot and filled with rich soil and manure or compost. Breeder worms can be added to this, and for best results the worm bed should be fenced with boards or concrete extending well below the surface to keep the worms inside. If organic materials are used for worm compost, wet thoroughly and turn daily until all heat is gone before stocking the worms. Best bed material is cottonseed meal, flue bran, or cotton waste from gins. Add cottonseed meal if bed material is low in protein.

Eastern banded killifish: see Alewife.

Eastern mad tom: see Brindled mad tom.

Eel: see American brook lamprey and eel.

English redworm: also called brandling. Excellent for earthworm-bait production.

European corn borer: also called corn earworm, is found on the leaves, husks, and tassels of corn during the summer months. During the fall and winter they can be taken from dry stalks. They make excellent bait both in summer and winter. To keep them alive on the hook, it's best to hook them through the tough head or to tie them onto the hook with thread.

Eye: fisheyes are often used as bait for other fish.

Fairy shrimp: a transparent, fresh-water crustacean growing to 1 1/2 inches; found in streams, ponds, potholes in grass, weed beds, and edges. They can be caught with "drag" bucket of closely woven wire mesh, or seined. Excellent bait.

Fathead minnow: also called blackhead minnow; are among the most popular and the most easily raised minnows in ponds. They rarely exceed 3 inches in length and can be caught in many streams, ponds, and lakes.

Fecal earthworm: see Dung worm.

Fidding: method of harvesting earthworms by driving wooden stake into firm but moist ground and then rubbing board or metal strip across stake top to develop a vibration in the ground. Within a few moments worms will be found lying on the ground surface.

Field cricket: see Cricket.

Field mice: see Mouse.

Fish (as bait): Strips of fish, particularly belly meat, with the skins attached are trolled for bass occasionally.

Fish fly: the larva of an insect resembling the hellgrammite, used in the same manner. Found in quiet water.

Fishworm: see Earthworm.

Flip-flap: another name for Hellgrammite.

Freckled mad tom: see Brindled mad tom.

Friar: see Golden shiner.

Frog: see Bullfrog.

Gallinipper: see Crane fly.

Gall worm: gall worms are the larvae of flies, moths, and wasps which cause the swellings called galls on the stems of plants. Gall worms are good wintertime bait and can be cut from the gall when other baits are not available.

Garden hackle: another name for Earthworm.

Garden worm: another name for Earthworm.

Garter snake: see Snake.

German cockroach: see Cockroach.

Gizzard shad: like the alewife, the gizzard shad is a member of the herring family. It is also used for bait and is an important food fish.

Golden shiner: the golden shiner is one of the several species of shiners which make excellent bait. Their bodies are compressed to form a sharp lid on the belly just behind the pelvic fin. Shiners are generally in the shallower parts of lakes, ponds, and in slow-moving streams. They can be raised successfully in ponds for bait.

Goldfish: species of minnow. It is not a carp. It is a successful minnow for bait production in ponds. Very prolific and hardy.

Grasshopper: like crickets, grasshoppers can be caught in fields and gardens and can be kept for long periods of time in containers before actually using them on a fishing trip. They're hooked in much the same manner as a cricket, which see.

Photo by Maslowski & Goodpaster

Live grasshoppers are especially good when fishing small streams and farm ponds. A fly rod is required.

Grub: see Beetle.

Grubworm: usually a whitish, thick-bodied larva of May beetle or June bug dug from soil. Fair catfish and trout bait. See Beetle larva.

Harvest fly: another name for Cicada.

Hawk moth: a large, narrow-winged moth, the larvae of which live on tomato plants, tobacco plants, cotton plants, and other crops. The larva, like the catalpa worm, is an excellent bait.

Helldiver: another name for Hellgrammite.

Hellgrammite: this popular water insect bait, also known by other names—such as alligator, water grampus, conniption bug, snipper, flip-flap, and helldiver, to name a few—is the larval form of the big, winged insect known as the dobson fly. It is black or dark brown with two sharp pincers, six legs, and numerous "appendages" on both sides of its long body. Hellgrammites live under rocks in the riffles of streams and rivers. They can be caught by turning over the rocks and holding a wire screen or net below the rocks. Keep them in damp leaves or grass in a cool spot. They make a tough bait and can be hooked under the collar, in the tail, or turned inside out after cutting the head off. It's a great bait for smallmouth black bass, especially in rivers, but it will often take largemouth bass, trout, sunfish, yellow perch, and walleyes.

Hog sucker: see Sucker.

Horned chub: see Chub.

Horned dace: see Black-nosed dace.

Horned pout: see Bullhead.

Hornet: see Bee.

Hornyhead chub: see Chub.

Housefly maggot: see Blowfly maggot.

House mouse: see Mice.

Indiana minnow: another name for Goldfish.

Japanese beetle: see Beetle.

Jerker: another name for the hornyheaded chub, see Chub.

June bug: see Beetle, Grubworm.

Katydid: like grasshopper. Fish in same manner as cricket.

Killifish: see Alewife.

Lake emerald shiner: see Golden shiner.

Lamprey eels: see American brook lamprey.

Lamprey: see American brook lamprey.

Larva: name used for the soft-bodied stage of various insects, such as the grubs of beetles; maggots of flies; caterpillars of moths.

Leather back: another name for Northern pearl dace. See Black-nosed dace.

Leatherjacket: another name for the larva of the Crane fly.

Leech: there are many species of leeches (also called bloodsuckers), varying in size from less than an inch to several inches in length when stretched out. They belong to the same group as the earthworm, but most of them have a sucking disk at each end of the body and live by sucking blood from various animals. They can be caught in traps baited with blood or meat. Sometimes fishermen rub liver or bloody meat across their waders and then wade through a mucky pool where leeches can be found. The leeches will attach themselves to the waders. They can live a long time without food, so can be easily kept in aquaria. They are very durable baits for bass.

Leopard frog: see Bullfrog.

Locust: see Cicada.

Long-jawed goby: another name for Mudsucker.

Maggot: see Blowfly maggot.

Manure worm: see Dung worm.

May fly: also called Willow fly. Adult and immature May flies are important fish food. The immature or nymphal stage of May fly is often used as bait. Adults and nymphs are often copied in fly patterns and used by trout anglers. Nymphs are captured by scooping up muck and mud from bottom of streams and pools, then draining mud away from the insects. They can be kept in aquaria where water is well aerated and the bottom covered with debris similar to that from which they were taken.

Meal worm: large numbers of meal worms are easily raised in a large washtub or box filled with alternate layers of burlap and layers of chicken mash or other grain meals. This should be stocked initially with a few hundred meal worms. This container will need a sprinkling of water every day or so; you can add some raw carrots or potatoes to provide the necessary moisture. Keep the container covered with wire screen to prevent the meal worms and the adult beetles from escaping. See Beetle larva.

Mice: see Mouse.

Mouse: both field mice and house mice can be used as bait for big bass. They are frequently tied onto the hook with wire or thread.

Miller's-thumb: another name for the Sculpin or Muddler.

Minnow: most fresh-water fish like minnows, and so they are a popular bait with anglers. There are many kinds, such as the bluntnose, fathead, and the various chubs, dace, and shiners. These small bait fish can be caught in most fresh-water streams, lakes, and rivers with seines, drop nets, minnow traps, and tiny hooks baited with bread, dough, or bits of worm. They can also be bought from bait dealers. In minnow buckets which keep the water cool and fresh, minnows will live for days if not too crowded. For longer periods keep them in "live boxes" submerged or floated in clean, cool water. Minnows from 1 1/2 to 10 inches long are usually used for bait, depending on the size of fish sought. They can be hooked through both lips or the back for still-fishing and "sewed" on the hook for casting and trolling. Minnows can

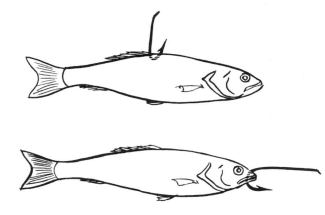

Hook the minnow through the back for still fishing—and through the lips for casting.

also be raised, but if you need only a small number during the fishing season it is cheaper and less trouble to buy them or seine them from a pond or stream. To raise them in large quantities to supply several anglers or to raise them for sale, you need one or more ponds or tanks. Since there are many kinds of minnows which can be raised and different parts of the country call for somewhat different methods, it is best to consult your state conservation or fish and game department for information on raising minnows in your area. They can supply the necessary literature on construction or selection of ponds, species, proper breeding, feeding, control of diseases, and handling.

Mountain mad tom: see Brindled mad tom.

Mud minnow: a small, hardy bait fish; lives a long time on a hook.

Muddler: see Sculpin.

Mudsucker: also called the long-jawed goby. It is a small salt-water fish found along the Pacific Coast, often used as bait for bass.

Mummichog: another name for the killifish. See Alewife.

Mussel: see Clam.

Newt: newts and salamanders are amphibians which are sometimes found near rocks and logs and damp places near the water. They must be grabbed by their heads or midsections because their tails break easily. They are cared for in the same manner as frogs and can be hooked through the tail or through one of the feet and used as bait.

Night crawler: night crawlers are the largest of the worms used for fishing, many reaching the length of ten inches. On warm, moist nights they come

out and stretch across the surface of the ground, where, with the aid of a flashlight and a bit of dexterity, they can be caught. See Earthworm.

Nightwalker: see Night crawler.

Northern blacknose shiner: one of the many shiners used as bait. See Golden shiner.

Northern common shiner: one of the many shiners used as bait. See Golden shiner.

Northern creek chub: one of the chubs used for bait. See Chub.

Northern log perch: one of the most popular perches used for bait. See Darter.

Northern muddler: see Sculpin.

Northern pearl dace: one of the common daces used as bait. See Black-nosed dace.

Northern redfin shiner: one of the common shiners used for bait. See Golden shiner.

Nymph: a name used for the immature stage of certain water insects. In these insects there are three stages of development—egg, nymph, and adult.

Ohio log perch: one of the common darters used for bait. See Darter.

Oriental cockroach: see Cockroach.

Peeler: name of crayfish which can be peeled when hard shell loosens. See Crayfish.

Perch bug: name commonly used to refer to dragonfly nymphs. See Dragonfly.

Perch: see Yellow perch.

Pickerel frog: see Bullfrog.

Pork rind: although pork rind is used mostly with artificial lures, it is considered to be a natural bait. The rind can usually be purchased in a butcher shop which sells salt pork. All the fat should be scraped off the skin, and then a very sharp knife or razor blade is used to cut the rind into the desired shapes. After being cut the strips should be put in a strong brine solution for two or three days. Then they can be removed and bleached by soaking in a dilute hydrochloric or acetic acid solution until they turn white. After this the strips can be packed in airtight jars containing a solution of 10 to 20 per cent formalin and a little glycerin. Another preservative is a solution of 1 per cent sodium benzoate in water. Or you can use ordinary rubbing alcohol or a heavy brine to preserve the rind until used. Pork rind can also be bought already made up in almost any tackle store.

Prawn: small salt-water shrimp sometimes seined and used in fresh-water fishing for bass.

Pupa: pupa is the third stage in the development of insects which pass through the egg, larva, pupa, and adult stages of development. This is the resting stage and is frequently the stage at which the insect is used for wintertime fishing.

Rainworm: another name for Night crawler.

Redbelly dace: one of the dace commonly used for bait. See Black-nosed dace.

Redfin: bait minnow. Popular in the Southeast.

Redside dace: see Black-nosed dace.

Red horse: one of the members of the sucker family caught on hook and line when full-grown and used as bait while young.

Redworm: see Earthworm, English redworm.

Reedamite: a name sometimes used to refer to the Caddis worm.

River chub: see Chub.

River shiner: one of the shiners commonly used as bait. See Golden shiner.

Roach: a common name sometimes used for the Western golden shiner.

Round shiner: popular bait minnow in midwestern and southern waters.

Salamander: the salamander is an amphibian like the newt.

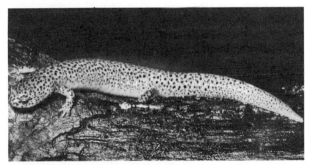

This red salamander is one of more than 100 salamanders found in North America that make good bass baits. Some call them spring lizards.

Salmon eggs: the eggs from a female salmon or steelhead trout are used to catch fish in the states where this bait is legal. These eggs can often be obtained from a freshly killed salmon or steelhead trout, but most anglers buy them already packed in small jars at tackle stores. The eggs can be used singly on a small hook or in clusters of many eggs. They can be tied to the hook with thread or enclosed in small bags of cheesecloth or mosquito netting around a treble hook. Salmon eggs are used mostly for trout.

Sand pike: a common name sometimes used to refer to darters. See Darter.

Sculpin: sculpin, or muddler, is a small bottom-dweller which has a rather large black head and permanently protruding pectoral fins. They re-

semble in general appearance small catfish and make good and hardy baits for bass. They can be taken from streams by turning over rocks and catching them as they wash down into a net.

Sea horse: name used for the nymph of a May fly.

Sea lamprey: a parasitic member of the lamprey family. See American brook lamprey.

Seventeen-year locust: see Cicada.

Sewn bait: a term applied to bait fish attached to spoons or spinners. Such rig is usually used in trolling.

Shiner: see Golden shiner.

Short-horned grasshopper: a common grasshopper, often used as bait. See Grasshopper.

Shrimp: a salt-water shrimp, like prawns, it is often used as bait for fresh-water bass and trout. See Fairy shrimp.

Silver chub: a common chub used for bait, also known as the Storer's chub.

Silver lamprey: one of the parasitic lampreys. See American brook lamprey.

Silverside: a long, thin minnow sometimes used for bait. The name is also used when referring to a shiner minnow which is also called friar. See Golden shiner.

Slug: the slug is a large, shell-less land snail which can be found under stones, logs, and in other damp places. They are especially prevalent in gardens and can be used as bait for bass.

Smelt: smelt are small fish found in the lakes. They are frequently used as bait for smallmouth bass.

Snail: the snail is sometimes used as bait after removal of its shell. See Slug.

Snake: many of the smaller snakes such as garter snakes, green snakes, and small water snakes can be used as bait for larger carnivorous fish such as bass.

Snipper: another name for the Hellgrammite.

Soldier fly: a fly larva that feeds on organic matter. Larvae are usually those squirming masses of maggots found in outdoor privies. They can be grown in clean materials. About an inch in length, they are hardy and make excellent bait.

Sphinx moth: the adult stage of the Catalpa worm.

Spotfin shiner: common shiner used as bait. See Golden shiner.

Spottail shiner: common shiner used as bait. See Golden shiner.

Spring lizard: see Newt.

Stickbait: a name used to refer to the Caddis worm.

Stickworm: a name used to refer to the Caddis worm.

Stinkworm: this is another name for the Dung worm.

Stone cat: see Brindled mad tom.

Stone fly: the stone-fly nymph resembles the nymph of the May fly. They are found under rocks in swift water rather than in the mud and muck of stagnant water. Nymphs are used as bait for trout and are frequently copied in fly-pattern design. Wire hooks are used in hooking them, either threading them on like a worm or hooking them on underneath the collar.

Stone pike: one of the common names for Darter.

Stone roller: minnow found in streams. Hardy on hook.

Storer's chub: see Silver chub.

Striped dace: a dace often used for bait. See Black-nosed dace.

Sucker: the sucker is a bottom-feeding fish which has thick, protrusible lips. There are several species, all of which may be used as bait when they are small for bass.

Sunfish: small sunfish, particularly with their spiny dorsal fins trimmed, are sometimes used for bass.

Tadpole: the tadpole is the immature, water-dwelling stage of the frog, sometimes good as bait. See Bullfrog.

Tadpole mad tom: a species of mad tom used as bait. See Brindled mad tom.

Toad: small toads, like frogs, are good bait on occasion. They are especially abundant near water during the dry season.

Tuffy: name for Fathead minnow.

Ugly bug: name for Dragonfly nymph.

Wasp: the larvae of wasps are good bait. See Bee.

Water grampus: another name for Hellgrammite.

Water snake: see Snake.

Waterworm: another name for the larva of the Crane fly.

Western golden shiner: see Roach.

White sucker: member of the sucker family. See Sucker.

Willow fly: see May fly.

Wood cockroach: see Cockroach.

Wood sawyer: also called wood borers. Beetle larva that burrows into decaying or cut wood. Rasping of sawyers beneath bark of pine logs can be heard long distances. Good bluegill bait.

Worm: see Earthworm.

Wriggler: another name used for the May-fly nymph.

Yellow meal worm: one of the meal worms used as bait. See Beetle larva.

Yellow perch: a small perch sometimes used as bait for larger fish, with the spiny dorsal fin often cut away to make the bait more attractive. Strips of perch belly with the fins attached are also used for trolling and skittering.

Zebra fish: another name for Darter.

How to Use Live Bait

There are so many potential and proven live baits that describing how to use all of them would require an entire library of information. There are some general points, however, which apply to nearly every type of live-bait dunking.

Since the only reason for live bait in the first place, as versus artificials, is because of an appeal and an "action" which is impossible to duplicate, live bait should be used in the most free and unhampered manner possible. That means an absolute minimum of sinkers and bobbers, if not eliminating them altogether.

Probably the ideal live-bait tackle is a light or medium spinning outfit; with it a crayfish (just for the sake of an example) can be hooked in the tail and without sinker or float be cast to a productive spot exactly like a plug. The crayfish then swims to the bottom and acts like a crayfish would naturally act until a bass comes along and nails him. Now, the minute this happens the fisherman flips open the bail on his spinning reel and allows the bass to run with bait with virtually no suspicious drag at all because the light line is pulling easily off the end of the spool. When the bass pauses to swallow the crayfish the angler closes the bail, gently gathers slack line, and then strikes. Another bass for the stringer.

This live bait-spinning combination is equally good in lakes and running water. Critters like leeches, hellgrammites and large grasshoppers as well as crayfish can be allowed to drift with the current in a completely genuine manner. Actually this is a deadly technique, particularly on a rising water level or when a stream is somewhat roily from recent rains.

Of course, there are times when it just isn't possible to do without a sinker or a float—either to get a bait closer to the bottom or to keep it from burrowing *into* the bottom. In that case, use the smallest and lightest sinker possible. Often a single split shot will do the job. Or when using a float, a small sliding, thumb-sized cork with a matchstick to fit in the core is enough. With this simple kind of float, it's easy to adjust lure depth. In any event, remember that the larger and more buoyant a float, the more "drag" is evident to a fish taking the bait.

It isn't necessary to use large hooks in live-bait fishing, either. Only rarely is it necessary to use something larger than #8, and usually #10 is good enough. You can get much more mileage out of the bait, too, with a small fine-wire hook.

Too many bass fishermen cast a live bait and then allow it to soak for much too long in one small place.

It's much better to move it often, to test, to thump it along the bottom, and to toss it into likely "edge" in the same manner of a plug caster. And always try to keep a *fresh* bait on the hook. Nowadays it isn't difficult to carry a large supply of bait on any trip and to keep it lively for a long time, thanks to the many new containers and devices that are available. Several of these are illustrated elsewhere in this book.

Live bait is most important for winter fishing— and essential in fishing through the ice. This may surprise some fishermen, but bass *can* be taken through the ice with some regularity. Strangely enough, ice-caught bass are usually big ones, and Ohio's record largemouth is a 9-pounder taken in 1956 in Pine Lake near Youngstown. Nor is it unusual to make good catches at Indian and Buckeye lakes, both also in Ohio.

This is a good place to say something about pork baits—the pork strips, frogs, chunks, etc. Actually these have been in use almost as long as Americans have been bass fishing. Fred Harlow, who lives in Newark, Ohio, and who has seen almost eighty-five summers come and go, once caught bass commercially for a living. For many years he would catch up to 100 fish a day, daily, and nearly all on some sort of pork bait he prepared himself on Sundays, his only days off.

Pork rind or skin has an undulating action in the water which has been hard to match until these last few years when the soft plastics came on the scene. Chamois skin has a similar quality when soaked. Still, pork-rind and pork-fat baits that have been

Pork rind cured in brine is a productive bait.

properly "cured" in brine have an important place today. Probably bass fishermen will always depend on them. Although they're most often fished in combination with other lures, maybe with a weedless spoon or behind a June-bug spinner, pork strips and pork frogs are deadly when fished alone.

Try this someday when action is slow. Put a pork frog on a weedless hook and cast it into "islands" of lily pads. Then retrieve it erratically, stop and go, half over the pads and half between them. Stop altogether for several seconds, then jerk the bait hard. Pause again. It's explosive.

Here's another possibility. Put a 3-inch strip of pork on a bare hook and with a fly-casting outfit drift it into small pools and pockets. Let it sink to the bottom, then raise it and let it sink again. Raise and sink repeatedly. Sometimes you can catch bass, catfish, and pan fish this way—and all without moving from the same spot. Try this method especially below low dams or along the "shelves" of limestone streams.

Any way you look at it, pork is an excellent bait in the hands of a fisherman who likes to experiment —to give his bait an action few bass ever saw before.

Chapter 11

LURES

Pal-O-Mine

Such a vast number of bass-fishing lures exist on tackle shelves that it's virtually impossible to catalogue them. And every year hundreds of new lures are introduced. Some survive because they attract fish; others survive because they attract fishermen. But those which attract both fish and fishermen survive the longest and sell the fastest.

The plug—the wood or hard-plastic imitation of a swimming minnow—was developed initially for bass fishing, and until recent years it was the most popular type of lure for bass. But recently a new trend is noticeable, a trend toward the soft-plastic imitations of natural bait creatures. More manufacturers are entering this field, and it's no wonder. The new plastic earthworm counterfeits, for example, are the hottest bass lures in any tackle boxes right now.

A wise bass fisherman will have a good selection of lures in his kit. Besides a number of plastic worms or eels, he should have several good surface plugs, probably of both the noisy and silent-when-retrieved types. He should also have a number of different sinking plugs, the difference being that they run at different depths when retrieved. Let's say he should have a shallow-, a medium-, and a deep-running model. For weedy situations a fisherman should always carry a number of weedless spoons, plus a supply of pork strips. A few jigs are valuable to have on hand too.

The kit of a fly caster will mostly contain floating bass bugs of various designs, a few streamer flies, and perhaps some tiny plastic worms or crickets. Occasionally strips of pork rind are deadly too.

Any of the following lures listed here will catch bass, but of course a few are much better day in and day out than all the rest. In any case, much of the fascination of the game comes from testing new lures and new ways to fish them until . . . you find the one which works best for you.

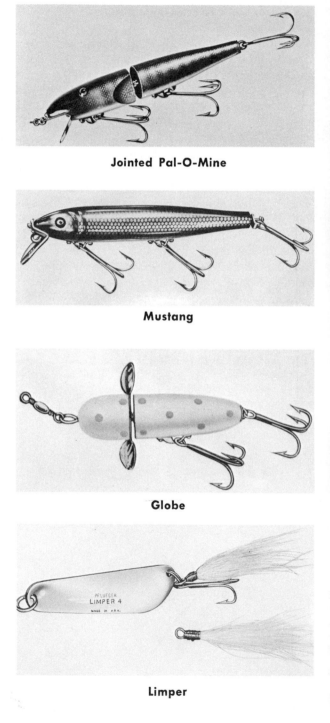

Jointed Pal-O-Mine

Mustang

Globe

Limper

Chum Spoon

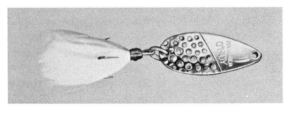

Yahuddi

Cyclone Asst.

O'Boy

Niftee Asst.

Patrol

Surety

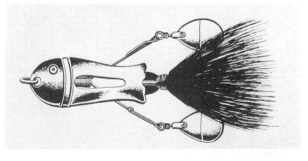

Zam

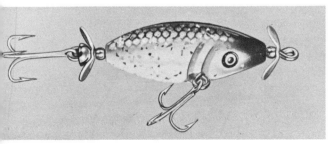

Baby Scoop

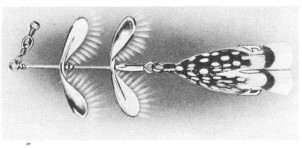

Luminous Tandem Spinner

Pal-O-Mine, shallow-running minnow imitation, 2 sizes (7/16 and 9/16 ounce), 11 colors, golden shiner is deadly for Florida bass. By Pfleuger.

Jointed Pal-O-Mine, shallow-running minnow imitation, two sizes (5/8 and 3/4 ounce), 8 colors including golden shiner. By Pfleuger.

Mustang, floating or near-surface wiggling-minnow imitation, good hooker, 5/8 ounce, 8 finishes, 4 1/4 inches long. By Pfleuger.

Globe, propeller-headed, noisy surface plug which has accounted for some extra-large bass. Two sizes (5/8 and 3/4 ounce), 3 finishes, also fine for pike, muskies. By Pfleuger.

Limper, versatile spoon with bucktail and double hooks, spinning sizes, chrome and gold finish. By Pfleuger.

Chum Spoons, among most effective and most popular bass lures ever built. Weedless, rides with hooks upright, has wiggling, snaky action. With or without feather hooks, pork strip can be attached, in 3 bass sizes (1/4, 6/16, and 5/8 ounce), chrome and gold. By Pfleuger.

Cyclone Asst., swept-back spinner, 1/4 ounce. By Pfleuger.

Niftee Asst., deep-running, luminous spinner, interchangeable feathered treble hooks, 1/4 ounce. By Pfleuger.

Surety, a weighted streamer fly, fairly weedless, 6 patterns, 1/4 ounce. By Pfleuger.

Baby Scoop, excellent injured-minnow type of surface lure with counter-rotating propellers, 2 inches long, for spinning. By Pfleuger.

Pippin, an old favorite spoon that is also good for pan fish, white bass, trout. By Pfleuger.

Yahuddi, spinner with weighted body which casts well, 1/4 ounce, 4 body colors and feathered hooks. By Pfleuger.

O'Boy, hammered wabbler that casts well, 1/4 ounce chrome with bare or feathered treble hook. By Pfleuger.

Patrol, spoon with chrome on one side and zigzag paint pattern on other. Catches bass but better for pike, walleyes, trout (1/4 ounce). By Pfleuger.

Zam, a weedless spoon and spinner combination that works very well around pads and bulrushes. Chrome with 4 bucktail colors, 1/2 or 5/8 ounce. By Pfleuger.

Luminous Tandem Spinner, one of the greatest old-time bass lures still being manufactured—is as good today as when developed almost a century ago. Weighted or unweighted, 5 sizes from 1/8 to 9/16 ounce, good for casting, trolling, or skittering with a cane pole. By Pfleuger.

Spin-Nik, wiggly plug with plastic skirt that is unusually weedless. Three finishes, 1/4 ounce. By Pat's Fishing Tackle.

Little Suzie, a deep-running and lively spinner plug of unique design. By Pat's Fishing Tackle.

Min-O-Eel, an unusually effective, black and white plastic eel. Completely weedless with hooks hidden during retrieves, it has bait oil blended into plastic. Excellent for casting or trolling or "bottom bouncing." Also can be fished like live bait. Has taken countless extra-big bass. By Hutt's Tackle House.

Mirrolure, minnow imitation with unusual flashy finish, angler must apply action, versatile, in 12 finishes, 5 sizes (1/16, 1/6, 1/4, 3/8, 3/4 ounce) by L. & S. Bait Co.

Mirrolure, a medium-depth minnow imitation in 12 finishes, in 3 sizes from 1/4 to 5/8 ounce, by L. & S. Bait Co.

Mirrolure, a very deep-running minnow imitation in 12 finishes, in 1/8- and 1/4-ounce sizes, by L. & S. Bait Co.

Bass-Master, medium-running, effective minnow imitation. In 12 finishes, 3 inches long, weight 1/2 ounce, sinks quickly when motionless, by L. & S. Bait Co.

Panfish Master, very good sinking minnow imitation in 12 finishes. Weight 1/4 ounce, 2 1/2 inches long, by L. & S. Bait Co.

Baby Cat, sinking imitation of small catfish with lifelike "fisheyes." In 4 finishes, weight 9/16 ounce, 3 1/4 inches long, by L. & S. Bait Co.

Mouse, a top-water or very shallow plug which has been most effective for many years. Has fine action. In 3 sizes (1/4, 3/8, 1/2 ounce) and in 5 finishes. Gray and glo-pearl are especially good. By Creek Chub.

Darter, one of the best of all surface plugs for bass, in use many years. In 7 finishes and from 1/4 to 5/8 ounce. Silver flash finish is very good. Hot bait during early season. By Creek Chub.

Plunker, a plunking or popping type surface lure in use many years. Weights from 1/4 to 5/8 ounce and in 7 finishes. By Creek Chub.

Pikie Minnow, an old and well-known shallow-running minnow imitation. Weights from 1/4 to 3/4 ounce and in 12 finishes. Floats when motionless but runs medium on retrieve. By Creek Chub.

Jointed Pikie Minnow, same as Pikie Minnow except jointed. By Creek Chub.

Nikie, a minnow imitation that floats when at rest and runs fairly deep on fast retrieve. Six colors, 1/2 ounce, 3 1/4 inches long. By Creek Chub.

Injured Minnow, top-water plug that floats on its side, in use many years, in 10 finishes, from 1/4 to 5/8 ounce. By Creek Chub.

Snarkie, a minnow imitation that runs to medium depth, 3/8 ounce in 6 finishes, 3 inches long. By Creek Chub. Similar lures: Snark and Snark-Eel.

La Rue 92, an effective-hooking, weedless lure that is great in shallow water. In 3 (chrome, frog, orange and black) finishes and 2 (1/4, 1/2 ounce) sizes; pork strip, rubber skirt, or streamer fly can be attached. By La Rue Mfg. Co., 3000 Sheridan Rd., Chicago 14, Ill.

Wounded Spook, crippled minnow action on surface, 5/8 ounce, 3 3/4 inches long, in 6 finishes. By Heddon.

Vamp Spook, shallow-running minnow imitation which floats at rest. In 5 finishes, 3/4 ounce, 4 1/4 inches long. By Heddon.

Chugger Spook, surface lure with built-in bubbling noise. In 6 colors and 2 sizes, 3/8 and 1/2 ounce. By Heddon.

Punkinseed Spook, lifelike imitation of small pan fishes with 7 natural finishes. Sinks. Weight 5/8 ounce. By Heddon. Also 1/3-ounce size.

Tadpolly Spook, a diving lure that floats at rest. Good action on slow retrieve, 3/8 ounce, 6 finishes, 3 inches long. By Heddon.

River Runt Spook, a wonderfully effective and versatile plug—and probably the best-selling lure of all times. Many millions have been sold and used. Sinks slowly, has good action, in 8 finishes; 1/5-, 1/4-, 3/8-, and 1/2-ounce sizes. By Heddon.

Midgit Digit, a small version of the River Runt Spook with transparent body. In 8 finishes, weight 3/8 ounce. By Heddon.

Go-Deeper River Runt Spook, the deepest running of the Runts. Probably best for walleyes, but will catch bass. In 4 finishes, 1/2- and 5/8-ounce sizes. By Heddon.

Sonic, a plug said to send out high frequency vibrations and to attract fish. In 3/8-ounce size (Super Sonic in 1/2 ounce), sinks, runs fairly deep, in 8 finishes. By Heddon.

Firetail Sonic, same as Sonic, plus added tail which glows and is designed for sure hooking. Sinks, in 6 finishes, 3/8 ounce, 3 1/2 inches long. By Heddon.

Sonar, a unique metal lure which makes fishing deep quite easy. Has "fast" action. Good for trolling too. In 8 finishes and 3 sizes (1/4, 1/2, 1 ounce). By Heddon.

Dowagiac Spook, a deep-sinking minnow with flashing spoons added. Designed for hot-weather fishing. Four colors, 3/4 ounce. By Heddon.

Dying Quiver Spook, a surface lure to be used very slowly. Light twitch gives it quiver of injured fish. Deadly lure at times, 4 colors, 3/8 ounce. By Heddon.

Dying Flutter Spook, a floater similar to Quiver, designed for slow, erratic use over weed beds, around shore. Has mirror insert, in 4 colors, 3/8 ounce. By Heddon.

Zara Spook, modern version of an old, tested plug. Floats at rest but either dives or jumps up when twitched. Good in salt water too. In 6 colors, 3/4 ounce, 4 1/4 inches long. By Heddon. Baby Zara is 3/8 ounce.

Lucky 13, a chugging surface bait that has good action under water when retrieved quickly. In 8 colors, 5/8 ounce (Baby Lucky 13 at 3/8 ounce). By Heddon. Also Tiny Lucky 13 at 1/5 ounce.

Tiny Tad, small plug with good action that catches pan fish too. In 7 finishes, 1/5 ounce. By Heddon.

Crazy Crawler, a noisy and sometimes deadly surface lure that has accounted for big bass. In 6 colors, and 2 sizes, 1/3 and 5/8 ounce. By Heddon.

Meadow Mouse Spook, a fur-covered mouse imitation that floats at rest and dives when retrieved. Four finishes, 1/2 ounce, 2 3/4 inches long. By Heddon.

Tiny Torpedo, a surface, crippled-minnow type of plug. Will twist line. In 8 finishes, 1/5 ounce, 2 1/8 inches long. By Heddon.

Spinfin, a very fine deep lure for bottom-bumping or jigging, especially in large reservoirs of the South and West. Has taken jumbo largemouths. In 4 finishes, 3 sizes (1/8, 1/4, 1/2 ounce), pork strip can be added. By Heddon.

Hep, a silver or gold spinner, with or without feathered hooks. In 1/8- and 1/4-ounce sizes. By Heddon.

Jitterbug, a surface plug with a gurgling noise. A night-fishing favorite for many years, but it has some daytime use, too, especially on windy days. In 11 colors, 1/4 and 5/8 ounce. By Fred Arbogast.

Hula Popper, a versatile top-water plug that can be popped, plunked, or twitched to make a variety of noises. In 10 finishes, 1/4- and 5/8-ounce sizes. By Fred Arbogast.

No. 1 Hawaiian Wiggler, a deep-running, very weedless, rubber-skirted spinner that has taken many bass since its development years ago. Several varieties with trailer hooks, weed-guard spinners, and double spinners. Six colors, 1/4 and 5/8 ounce. By Fred Arbogast.

No. 1 1/2 Hawaiian Wiggler, medium- to deep-running spinner, 1/4 and 5/8 ounce. By Arbogast.

No. 2 Hawaiian Wiggler, medium-running spinner with interchangeable rubber skirts, 1/4 and 5/8 ounce. By Fred Arbogast.

No. 3 Hawaiian Wiggler, shallow-running, next-to-impossible-to-snag lure that wiggles through toughest places. Fine in southern waters. In 3 body colors, 1/4 and 5/8 ounce. By Fred Arbogast.

Spin Liz, wabbling spoon, 1/4 ounce. By Fred Arbogast.

Hula Dancer, a good casting plug in weedless, snagless waters, in 1/4- and 5/8-ounce sizes, in 8 finishes. Perch finish is especially good. By Fred Arbogast.

Arbo-Gaster, similar to Hula Dancer, but much deeper running, is surprisingly snagless on rocky bottoms. In 12 finishes, in 1/8-, 1/4-, 5/8-ounce sizes. By Fred Arbogast.

Skinny Minny, designed for salt-water surface fishing but works with bass too. At rest, floats with nose out of water. Five finishes, 1/4 and 5/8 ounce. By Fred Arbogast.

Scooter, another salt-water surface lure that's adaptable to bass. Darts off to sides when twitched. Five finishes, 5/8 ounce. By Fred Arbogast.

Rib-Lip, a slow-sinking, medium-running minnow imitation that works in open water. In 8 colors, 1/4 ounce, 3 inches long. By Fred Arbogast.

Sputterbug, a noisy surface lure with a paddling sound. Must be fished slowly for most effect. In 11 finishes, 1/4 and 5/8 ounce. By Fred Arbogast.

Busy Body, an excellent deep lure for bottom thumping in big waters. Running depth can be measured by sinking time. Easy to cast and control. In 5 colors and 3 sizes (1/4, 3/8, and 1/2 ounce). By Fred Arbogast.

Cisco Kid, a most effective, fairly deep-running minnow imitation. In 12 finishes, 3 sizes (1/4, 3/8, and 5/8 ounce). By Wallsten Tackle Co.

Cisco Kid Topper, a good surface plug that's best on glassy calm water. In 12 finishes, 1/3 ounce, 2 1/2 inches long. By Wallsten.

Jointed Cisco Kid, a mid-depth lure that can be cast or trolled. It's best in open water. In 12 colors, 1/4- and 3/8-ounce sizes. By Wallsten.

Injured Cisco Kid, a crippled-minnow type of surface lure. Must be used slowly. In 12 finishes, 1/2 ounce. By Wallsten.

Spin Injured Cisco, a crippled-minnow pattern in 12 colors, weight 3/16 ounce, 1 3/4 inches long. By Wallsten.

Salty Cisco, was designed for salt-water casting, but it takes bass too. In surface (1/4 ounce) and weighted (1/2 ounce) models, 12 finishes. By Wallsten.

Cisco Kid Diver, a minnow imitation that casts well enough and runs deep enough to make fishing for bass possible in 30 feet of water with normal retrieves. In 12 finishes, 7/16 ounce, 2 1/4 inches long. By Wallsten.

Nightcrawler (plastic) on harness with tandem spinner is one of effective new baits. Weed guards on this one. Bait is deadly in ponds. Weight 3/8 ounce. By Sportsman's Products. In many colors.

Plastic Nightcrawler with single spinner. Excellent pond bait, weight 3/8 ounce. By Sportsman's Products. In many colors.

Floating Eel with lead jig head. Excellent lure for slow, deep fishing in large reservoirs, black, jig weight 1/4 ounce. By Sportsman's Products.

ABU Reflex, a widely selling and versatile spinner that has taken bass in every sort of situation. Best bass sizes are 1/8, 1/3, 1/4 ounce. Orange with zebra blade is good pattern. By Garcia.

Can-Can, a good spinner with counter-rotating blades which will not twist line. Good on trout too. In 4 finishes and 1/8- and 1/4-ounce sizes. By Garcia.

Eelet, probably the first in the long line of eel imitations that have been so effective on bass. This one is hard plastic, dark green, in 3 sizes (3/16, 3/8, 9/16 ounce). By Garcia.

Little Tilly, a fish-shaped, scale-finished spoon in 3 finishes and weighing 1/4 ounce. Good also for pike, trout, walleyes. By Garcia.

Pecos Dace, an exact imitation of a stream dace. Has lively wiggling action, 3/16 ounce. By Garcia.

Spoonplug, a lure which caused a sensation recently in Southeast. Designed for deep casting and trolling. Must be used slowly. By Buck's Baits.

Bayou Boogie, a slow-sinking lure which is very versatile. Will work near surface or quite deep. In 18 finishes from 1/3 to 1/2 ounce. Also a 1/4-ounce Fly Boogie and a Bayou Boogie Topper. By A. D. Mfg. Co.

Stinger, a jig and crawler rig that is great for deep fishing the big reservoirs. In 1/4 or 1/2 ounce in 3 colors. With 1 or 2 hooks (second in tail), of vinyl plastic, worm portion can be replaced. By Whopper Stopper.

Hellbender, a deep-running bait that can be cast or trolled effectively. Reel fast to get right depth, then erratically. In 18 finishes, 1/4- and 5/8-ounce sizes. By Whopper Stopper.

Silver Minnow, one of great, all-time spoon baits. Has excellent action and is very weedless and snag-proof. Five sizes from 1/24 to 3/4 ounce. In 9 finishes; among best for bass are silver, black nickel, and hot pearl. By Louis Johnson.

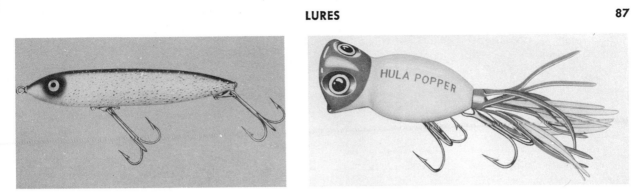

Zara Spook   **Hula Popper**

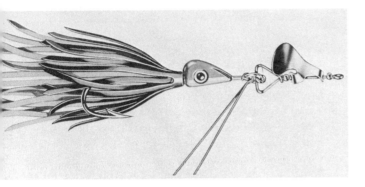
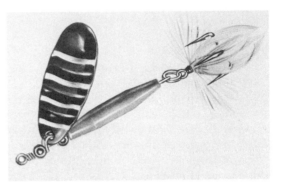

No. 1 Hawaiian Wiggler   **ABU Reflex**

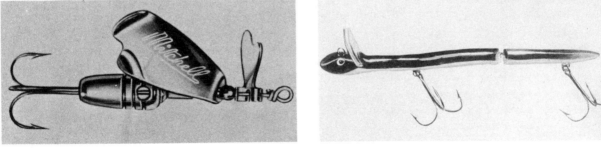

Can-Can   **Eelet**

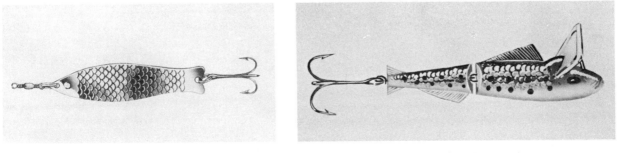

Little Tilly   **Pecos Dace**

Barnstormer, a potentially fine jig with rubber whiskers and streamer tail. Should be great for deep fishing. In 1/4 and 1/2 ounce. Would be O.K. for trolling. Six colors. By Louis Johnson.

Mr. Whiskers, a deep-running spinner which has great possibilities for bass in midsummer. In 1/4 and 1/2 ounce. By Louis Johnson.

Jig Head Crawler, a deadly deep bait. Plastic crawler floats and when jig head rests on bottom, crawler wiggles upward. Slow, erratic retrieve gives lure a weird action. With 1 or 2 hooks, in natural and red colors, size 1/0 hook. By Weber.

Rattle Spoon, a take-off on a common type of spoon. Although better for pike and walleyes, will catch bass. In 4 colors; 1/4, 3/8, 9/16 ounce. By Marathon.

Spin-O-Hawk, a spinner that's especially effective in early season fishing. Three colors; 1/16-, 1/8-, and 1/5-ounce sizes. By Marathon.

Joe's Deep Runner, a lively, deep-running minnow with a glitter finish. Can be trolled, weight 1/4 ounce, designed for cloudy days. By Marathon.

Valse, an imported spinner with squirrel-tail treble hooks. In nickel, gold, copper; from 1/12 to 2/3 ounce. By Marathon.

Valse Spinner, with plastic tail and unusual glitter in water. By Marathon.

Large Crawfish, a completely authentic imitation of a live crayfish with weedless hook, in natural color, 1/3 ounce, 3 inches long. By Creme Lures.

Small Crawfish, authentic imitation of small crayfish. By Creme.

Lizard, a completely accurate imitation of a mud puppy. Has excellent potential for big bass. In 6 colors and from 3 1/2 to 5 1/2 inches long. By Creme.

Redworm Rig, a plastic night crawler rigged up with 2 hooks and single spinner. A fine bass lure in shallow waters, available with other model spinners. By Creme.

Nightcrawler Rig, a reddish-brown crawler rig with single spinner and 3 hooks. Also a deadly bass getter. Crawler 6 inches long. By Creme.

Spotted Crawler Rig, a plastic night-crawler imitation with single spinner. In numerous color combinations. By Creme.

Wiggle Jig Rig, a deep-running night-crawler imitation with curved jig head and two hooks. This is a deadly bass catcher when used slowly and erratically along the bottom. Best in big lakes, reservoirs; has good potential in river fishing. By Creme.

Wiggle Worm, amazing lifelike imitation of night crawlers and dewworms. Feel, look, and act alive in the water. Sold without hooks or other attachments. To be rigged at home by individual angler. By Creme.

Godart, a deep-running spinner with weedless single hook. For light spinning. By Airex. Can be used with pork strip or cut bait.

Brown Godart, deep-running spinner with treble hooks, 1/4 ounce, for light spinning. By Airex.

Big Name, a weighted head with marabou tail designed for deep fishing; 1/6, 1/4, 3/8 ounce, 6 patterns. By Weber.

Rani, a spinner lure with bird-wing blades, assorted finishes, 1/8 ounce, for light spinning. By Airex.

Frenchi, a spinner in nickel or brass which is effective in open water, 1/4 ounce, treble hooks. By Weber.

Whirl-Atom, a spinner with "ripple" or striped blade, best for early season fishing, 1/4 ounce, 6 colors. By Weber.

Gold Digger, an effective spinner for early spring and for weedless waters. Gold finish with hackled hooks, 1/8 ounce, for light spinning. By Airex.

Merry Widow, a gold-finished spinner with hackle and streamered treble hooks, 1/3 ounce. By Airex.

Preska Perche, very effective rubber-bodied spinner with brass blade. Should be used with swivel and antitwist keel, 1/5 ounce. By Airex.

Popit, a plastic-bodied surface popper with a perch finish and palmer flies attached, 1/3 ounce. By Airex.

Plucky, a rubber-bodied, weedless minnow imitation. By Airex.

Hoppie, a 3/8-ounce lure which runs deeper the slower it is retrieved, with 2 treble hooks. By Airex.

Preska Toff, rubber-bodied spinner with brass, scaled blades striped in red. Requires use with swivel and antitwist keel, 3/16 ounce. By Airex.

Babalu, a 1/4-ounce streamer designed for light spinning in six colors. By Airex.

Pet Spoon, a fine wabbling spoon with or without weed guard, can be used with or without pork strip, in many sizes from 1/24 to 3/4 ounce. By Tony Accetta.

Bug Spoonet, a tiny spinner-spoon combination that's weedless and snagless, 1/6 ounce in chrome and gold. By Tony Accetta.

Hollo Head, a plug with a hole in the head and a wounded-minnow action. Sinks slowly but runs deep, in 6 finishes, 1/6 ounce. By Tony Accetta.

Jigaroo, a versatile jig with spinner underneath. Fairly snagless even when bumped over uneven bottom. Can be used with pork strip or eel, from 1/8 to 3/4 ounce, in 4 colors. By Tony Accetta.

Snubnose, a fairly weedless and snagless jig designed for bottom bumping. In 4 colors, 1/4 ounce, 2 inches long. By Tony Accetta.

Mystic, an effective spinning plug with unusual, ribbed Tenite body. Sinks quickly, 1/4 ounce, 3 finishes. By Weber.

Name, a jig-streamer combination that is most effective for bottom bouncing and is versatile enough to catch many species. From fly-rod size to 3/8 ounce, in several finishes, with Marabou streamer. By Weber.

Tri-Trix, a metal darting spoon that can be adjusted for fishing 3 separate depths. Effective when allowed to settle to bottom after raising rod tip quickly; this should be repeated. Gold and nickel finish, 1/6 and 1/3 ounce. By Weber.

Hi-Gloss Jig, a fairly weedless jig with larger than usual body, with bucktail streamer, in 4 colors, 1/8 to 1/2 ounce. By Weber.

Ball Fly Jig, good deep lure with ball-shaped head and either deerhair, marabou, nylon, or unusual plastic tails. In 4 colors, from 1/32 to 1/2 ounce. By Weber.

Crawler or Worm, a very soft, pliable imitation worm or night crawler, to be rigged by individual fishermen, in natural and exotic colors, from 2 1/4 to 5 1/2 inches long. By Weber.

Shyster, a successful spinner in many situations where waters are fairly open. In 17 finishes, including pearl (which is extra-good) and fluorescent, in 4 sizes from 1/8 to 1/2 ounce. By Evans.

Super Shyster, a weighted spinner with hackle streamer fly tail. Good in open, clear waters. In 11 finishes, from 1/8 to 1/2 ounce. By Evans.

Cherry Buoyant, a fluorescent, fire-red lure with cork-float body and hammered spinner blade. It's an excellent lure for river fishing; cork body allows lure to drift with current at mid-depth while spinner "kicks" back and forth instead of revolving. In several sizes. By Evans.

Skirt Twerp, a plastic surface popper with natural scale finish and plastic streamer skirts. By Evans.

Undertaker, a spinner with rubber "feelers" which casts well and could be a good bass catcher. In 3 colors, 1/4 ounce. By Evans.

Thunderbird, a spinner with a rubber skirt which has great potential in relatively weedless waters. In 10 colors, 1/8 and 1/4 ounce. By Evans.

Herb's Dilly, a spinner-spoon that will work under water but which also can be given a noisy, churning retrieve on the surface. On rare occasions, especially at lakes like Okeechobee, the latter is a deadly technique. In 7 finishes, 1/4 and 3/8 ounce. By Evans.

Maribou Jig Fly, a quick-sinking jig for bottom fishing, in 6 colors, from 1/32 to 1/2 ounce. By Evans.

Hair Jig Fly, a quick-sinking jig for fishing deep, in 6 colors, from 1/32 to 1/2 ounce. By Evans.

Weedler, an effective weedless, snagless spoon for shallow fishing, in mirror and wrinkle finishes; in gold, silver, and half-and-half colors; in 1/4 and 5/8 ounce. By Williams.

Wabler, a spoon which will take bass but is at its best for pike. In gold and silver, wrinkle or mirror finish, from 1/8 to 3/4 ounce. By Williams.

Weighted Bass Fly, a somewhat weedless bass fly with weighted body, for spinning, in 6 patterns, 1/0 to 5/0 hooks. By Marathon.

Weedless Spinning Popper, a high-riding spinning popper which is good in shallow waters; good lure in small Michigan lakes, in 6 patterns, 1/12 ounce. By Marathon.

Spin-o-jack, a fairly snagless, jig-type lure with spinner tail that's good for probing around in sunken brush piles and in submerged vegetation. In 6 patterns, 1/5 ounce. By Marathon.

Snooper, a novel spinning lure with weighted body and matched wings. In 6 patterns. By Marathon.

Rock and Roll Junior, a shallow-running minnow imitation with good action. Three finishes, 1/4 ounce. By Marathon.

Porkrine Hook, a weedless device for casting pork strips or frogs. Casts well and is almost snagless. A very handy item for bass fishermen. In 5 colors, 1/2 ounce. By Marathon.

Fresh Water Jig, an unusual metal jig for bottom fishing, in 4 colors, 3/32 ounce. By Marathon.

Bushwhacker, an excellent, deep-running bottom lure for large-reservoir fishing with 1 or 2 spinners, feather or rubber tails, in 18 patterns, 1/4 and 1/2 ounce. By Bomber.

Bomber, a deep-running plug in 33 finishes. Plug bores almost straight down on retrieve, is excellent for trolling as well as casting. In 5 sizes from 1/4 to 3/4 ounce, from 2 1/2 to 4 1/4 inches long. By Bomber.

Water Dog, an extra-deep running plug with a fast vibrating action, in 21 finishes. Is surprisingly snag-proof. Three sizes from 1/4 to 5/8 ounce. By Bomber.

Bomberette, a medium-depth plug which can be cast or trolled. Has good action, in 19 finishes, 3 sizes from 1/4 to 1/2 ounce. By Bomber.

Gimmick, a weighted spinner fly that casts well. Spinner turns on very slow retrieve. Good in open water. In 14 patterns, 1/2- and 1/4-ounce sizes. By Bomber.

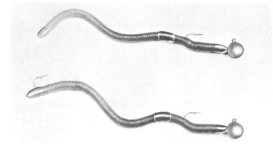

Jig Head Crawler

Tri-Trix

Lizard

Redworm Rig

Ball Fly Jig

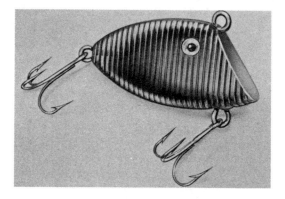

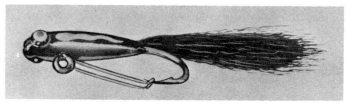

Hi-Gloss Jig

Mystic

Crawler or Worm

Big Name

Herb's Dilly

Top Bomber, a surface lure in 19 colors with propeller tail. Rests with tail down and nose pointed out of water. Good hooker, 3/8 and 1/2 ounce. By Bomber.

Jerk, a floater at rest and originally designed for salt water, it takes bass when given a jerky retrieve. In 12 colors, 1/4 and 5/8 ounce. By Bomber.

Stick and Spinstick, top-water lures with counter-rotating spinners, float in vertical position, slight twitch causes lures to dance and bob. Good action all around. In 14 finishes, 1/4 and 3/8 ounce. By Bomber.

Bomber Jig, a standard jig in 12 colors with nylon tail, of durable construction, 1/4-, 1/2-, and 3/4-ounce sizes. By Bomber.

Possum, a weighted spinner with feathers or plastic teaser on hooks. Three colors, 1/4 ounce. By Ce-Bet.

Spinning Poppers, top-water lures in 4 finishes with novel nylon hitchhiker loop to attach smaller popper or fly as trailer. Idea worth trying to pick up bonus pan fish, even bass. In 3/16 ounce. By Ce-Bet.

CP Swing, ultralight spinner for spinning. Best for smallmouths in water clear of vegetation, 1/12 to 1/4 ounce. By Rockland.

CP Deluxe, a weighted spinner fly, 1/12 to 1/4 ounce, for light spinning. By Rockland.

CP Fly, a tiny spinner fly for the lightest spinning tackle and for clear waters minus vegetation. From 1/12 to 1/4 ounce. By Rockland.

Cybele, a weighted spinner which casts very well. Blade turns on slowest retrieves; silver, gold, or black; 4 sizes from 1/8 to 1/4 ounce. By Rockland.

EGB Blinker, erratic wabbling spoon with novel "tab" tail. Finish designed to imitate natural color reflections of bait fish. Five sizes from 1/10 to 1/2 ounce. By Rockland.

Li'l Spike, a light, compact spoon with a fluttering action, for ultralight spinning, 6 finishes in 1/10 ounce. By Rockland.

Panther Martin, a weighted spinner with curiously different design. Blade will revolve even on upstream casts. Somewhat snagless. Three finishes, 6 sizes from 1/16 to 1/4 ounce, for ultralight spinning. By Rockland.

Rocky, a jointed plug with minnowlike action, in 6 colors, 1/16 and 1/8 ounce, for ultralight spinning. By Rockland.

Paul Bunyan 66, a weighted spinner-fly combination which has been effective for many years. Versatile, deep-running, with hair or hackle streamer tails. Five models from 1/25 to 1 ounce. By Paul Bunyan.

Flash Eye Weedless Spoon, a glittering spoon that retrieves well over most snags and through vegetation. In spinning sizes. By Paul Bunyan.

Flash Eye Spoon, a wabbling spoon in nickel or gold finishes, #2 treble hook, 1/4 ounce. By Paul Bunyan.

Bill Upperman's Bucktail, a typical jig in 4 colors and 8 sizes from 1/13 to 2 ounces. Perhaps these were the first jigs to be used on fresh-water bass, and they are just as successful today. By Bill Upperman's Bucktails, Atlantic City, N.J.

Black Widow Eel, a lamprey imitation made from pork rind with cuts in the "fat" part to give it an alive action. Perforated for trimming. Can be used alone, with spinner or with jig. Two sizes: 5 inches and 1/8 ounce; 9 inches and 1/4 ounce. By Uncle Josh.

Pork Frog, a famous old bass catcher cut from salt pork. Can be used with weedless hook (light spinning), with jig or weedless spoon. Three sizes: 1/40, 1/10, and 1/4 ounce. By Uncle Josh.

Pork Chunk, an egg-shaped chunk of pork usually used with June-bug spinner or weedless spoon, 1/4 ounce. By Uncle Josh.

Pork Strip, plain strip of pork in 4 colors. Can be used with hook alone, on jig, spinner, or spoon. In many sizes. By Uncle Josh.

Pork Strip with Hook, a pork strip with imbedded trailer hook. Usually used with other spoon or spinner lures, in 4 colors. By Uncle Josh.

Pollywoggler, an imitation pollywog with side whiskers and tail. Use alone or with other lures. White, 1/8 ounce, 2 3/4 inches long. By Uncle Josh.

Shammy Strip, a frog-shaped piece of chamois skin that's pliable and ready for reuse without storage in water or brine. Works with single hook alone, with jig, spinner, or spoon. Three sizes from 2 to 4 1/2 inches long. By Nature Faker.

Ewelure, a curious, jointed plug in which the tail wiggles when sinking, even though angler gives it no action. Speed of retrieve regulates depth. In 9 finishes, 3/8 ounce. By Parker.

Daredevle, a very versatile spoon and one of the oldest and best-known of all artificial, fresh-water fishing lures. In many finishes, but for bass, red and white stripe remains a favorite. Also in many sizes, from 1/32 ounce for fly rod to 3/4 ounce, which is about the largest practical for bass. By Daredevle.

Spinnie and Midget, very weedless spoons fine for casting in vegetation. In many finishes; 1/4 and 3/16 ounce. By Daredevle.

Mousiedevle, a 2 1/2-ounce spoon with good wiggling action. By Daredevle.

Osprey Bass Fly, a weighted spinner-bass fly that's fairly weedless, in 8 patterns, 1/4 ounce. By Daredevle.

Deep-r-doodle, a deep-running minnow imitation which can be cast or trolled. Dipsy Doodle and Spot-Tail Minnow are similar but medium-running. In several finishes, from 1/6 to 1/4 ounce. By Horrocks-Ibbotson.

Freakfish, a lively plug that is a good hooker. In 19 finishes, 3 inches long, 1/2 ounce. By Horrocks-Ibbotson.

Rangley Minnow, a light spinning lure with a spinner-leaf tail. In several finishes, 1/8 ounce, 1 7/8 inches long. By Horrocks-Ibbotson.

Fur Mouse, a field-mouse imitation that leaves a rippling wake on the surface when retrieved slowly. Finish resembles wet fur, 3/8 ounce, 2 1/2 inches long. By Horrocks-Ibbotson.

Miracle Minnow, a good minnow imitation in jointed and one-piece models. In 19 finishes, for casting or trolling, in 1/8-, 1/4-, 3/8-ounce sizes. By Wright-McGill.

Dixie-Dandy, a standard type of surface lure with propeller tail and weighing 1/4 ounce. In 12 finishes. By Wright-McGill.

Right-Fish, a wriggling, fish-shaped spoon, in 6 finishes, 1/4 ounce. By Wright-McGill.

Weighted Spin Popper, a weighted top-water bug with or without rubber legs, with hackle or hair tail. In 6 finishes; 1/8 or 1/4 ounce. By Evans.

Ideal Bass Fly, a fly with weighted body and hook that rides upward during retrieve. Can add pork strip. In 5 standard patterns. Sizes 1/6 and 1/4 ounce. By Pfleuger.

Crippled Killer, an effective floater that's effective for dawn and dusk fishing, 1/2 ounce, in 20 finishes. By Phillips.

Midget Killer, a tiny underwater plug which sinks slowly and has counter revolving spinner blades. In 20 finishes. By Phillips.

Weedless Popper, a surface bug that works well among pads and bonnets. Has wire weed guard and hackle tail. In 15 finishes, 3/16 ounce. By Phillips.

Spin Devil, a fairly snagless spinner-jig combination that retrieves well over almost any kind of bottom. Good bait for smallmouths, spotted bass. Fine for fast water too. In 7 finishes, 1/4 ounce. By Phillips.

Flash-o-mino, a good shallow pond, minnow imitation with oversize spinner in front. In 9 finishes, 1/4 ounce. By Phillips.

Spin Popper, a very deadly surface lure with spread wings, resembles a small bird fallen to the water, 3/16 ounce. By Phillips.

Big Boy, a surface popper. Best to leave at rest 30 seconds, then start slow, erratic retrieve. Size 3/8 ounce. By Phillips.

Old Joe, a surface popper that should be raced across surface in short and fast jerks after resting for 30 seconds or so. 3/8 ounce. By Phillips.

Jigging Worm, excellent combination for deep bottom fishing, with 1 or 2 hooks, with or without weed guards. Worm portion floats. 3/8 ounce, 7 inches long. By DeLong.

Jigging Eel, fine combination for deep fishing, to imitate three kinds of lampreys, plastic part floats, with or without weed guards, 7 inches long, 3/8 ounce. By DeLong.

Silver Flash Minnow, a clear plastic minnow imitation with a metal reflector strip inside. In several sizes from ⚡8 hook to 3/8 ounce. By DeLong.

Weedless Witch, a good, weedless, 8-inch-long bottom lure which depends on stop-and-go action of the angler. Has taken many extra-large bass. In black and orange, 3/4 ounce. By DeLong.

Heavy Duty Eel, a 7-inch eel of soft plastic with two hooks molded into the eel. Depends on action of rod tip. In clear, fluorescent red or black, 5/8 ounce. By DeLong.

Tiny Eel, greenish-black, 2-inch-long lamprey imitation with two hooks molded into plastic body. For very light spinning. By DeLong.

Silver Ghost, a lamprey imitation with opalescent body and strip of silver through center. Two hooks, 6 1/4 inches long, 1/5 ounce. By DeLong.

Lucky Harnessed Silver Ghost, opalescent lamprey imitation with silver reflector and swivel-spinner ahead. Two hooks, body 6 1/4 inches long, 1/4 ounce. By DeLong.

Weedless Jigging Worm, with 2 1/4 inch flexible floating tail and single weedless hook, 3/8 ounce. By DeLong.

Weedless Lucky Harness Dew Worm (also a WLH Crawler), natural earthworm imitation with 2 weedless hooks and spinner ahead. Worm is 5 1/2 inches long. Weighs 1/6 ounce. By DeLong.

Rigged Crawler, a natural night-crawler imitation with two hooks, either bare or weedless, 5 1/2 inches long, 1/7 ounce. By DeLong.

June Bug Crawler, plastic night-crawler imitation with double June-bug spinner ahead. Single hook, hook sizes from 2 to 6/0, 1/2 ounce. By DeLong.

Slim Tapered Worm, with two ⚡8 hooks in red, black, or yellow. For lightest spinning. By De-Long.

Shrimp, good imitation of shrimp, translucent with fluorescent red eyes. Might prove killer in some situations. Hook sizes 1/0 and 3/0. By DeLong.

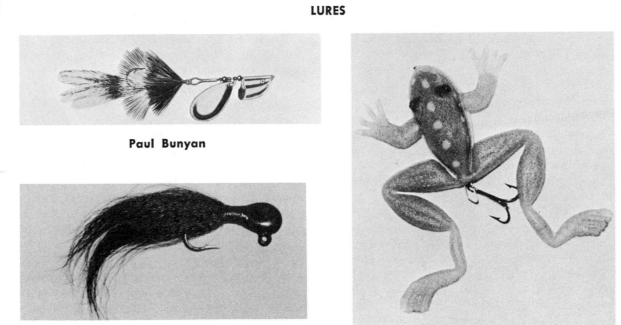

Paul Bunyan

Bill Upperman's Bucktail

Floating Frog

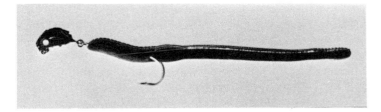

Jigging Worm

Spinning Mouse

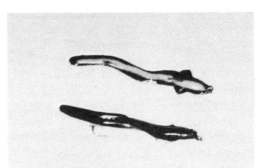

Tiny Eel

Jigging Eel

Little Sam

Floating Frog, the most realistic frog imitation, and perhaps with the greatest potential of any frog-type lure this writer has ever seen. Back legs are completely "alive" and work beautifully when rod tip is twitched. Whole body even feels like frog. Size 6 treble hook, about 1/4 ounce. By DeLong.

Black Jack, shiny black arrowhead-shaped jig with black nylon tail. Designed for bottom bouncing, with 3/0 hook. Weighs 3/8 ounce. By DeLong.

Tadpole, exact imitation of tadpole, 3 1/2 inches long, with double hooks, with or without spinner ahead, in several colors. By DeLong.

Eel, a soft and wiggly eel imitation that even feels slimy in the water, is 4 3/4 inches long, 1/6 ounce. By DeLong.

Spring Lizard, a soft plastic imitation of a salamander, 4 inches long, with 2 hooks, 1/6 ounce. By DeLong.

Bass Bomb Popper, a surface plug with cupped face, hackle tail, and weed guard (which is optional). Size-3/0 hook is molded into Dylite plastic body. Very sturdy construction. In 7 patterns, 1/4-ounce size is great for spinning. By Weber.

Spinning Frog, a fine frog floater with Dylite plastic body and hook molded in, with weed guard and forked bucktail legs, easy to cast, in 3 colors. The 1/4-ounce weight is great for spinning. Size 3/0 hook. By Weber.

Spinning Mouse, a floating mouse with a natural "hairy" body, weedless hook molded into a Dylite plastic body. Has glass eyes, whiskers, ears, and a tail. In 3 patterns, 1/4 ounce, 3/0 hook. By Weber.

Little Sam, an injured-minnow type of lure with arched body and wobbling action on surface when retrieved. Propellers both ends, 1/4 ounce in 9 patterns, Tenite plastic body, has been great producer in Ontario early in season. By Weber.

Lifelike Eel, a black 5 3/4-inch eel imitation which is available either plain, with or without weedless or bare hooks. The eel "floats" upward when not in motion, with or without spinner. Very effective lure. In black only. By Weber.

Jig-Head Eel, same as Lifelike Eel except that head is a ball jig for bottom fishing. Eel body floats upward when at rest. Good lure. Hook size 1/0, 5 3/4 inches long, in black. By Weber.

Weedless Crawler, a 5 1/2-inch imitation night crawler, rigged with 2 or 3 weedless hooks, and with or without spinner. One model has ball-jig head instead of spinner. Good lure for bass everywhere. In 6 colors, including fluorescent. By Weber.

Jig Head Floating Crawler, a natural imitation crawler with jig head for deep fishing. Worm is 5 1/2 inches long. 1/0 hook, in 2 colors. By Weber.

Flies, Baits, Bugs for Fly-Rodding

Hula Spinner, a rubber-skirted spinner that's effective in shallow water but a little too heavy (1/16 ounce) for best casting. Six colors. By Arbogast.

Hula Popper, rubber-skirted popping bug that is most effective, but also a little too heavy at 1/16 ounce for best casting. Six finishes. By Arbogast. Also 1/32 ounce.

Tin Liz, a good fly-rod spoon for many years. Takes pan fish too, 1/64 and 1/32 ounce. By Arbogast.

Helgramite, a very lifelike imitation of a hellgrammite in brown and black, about 1/20 ounce. By Creme.

Water Cricket, a brownish-green imitation of a cricket which should be great for farm-pond fishing. About 1/32 ounce. By Creme.

Roach Floater, a faithful counterfeit of a live roach, has been effective at Reelfoot Lake, Tenn., about 1/32 ounce. By Creme.

Fly Boogie, a slow-sinking minnow imitation with good swimming action. Six colors, 1/14 ounce, 1 1/4 inches long. By A. D. Mfg. Co.

Dot Pop, a rubber-legged bass bug that's very effective. Plastic body, several colors and in #4, #8, and #10 hook sizes. By Pfleuger.

Woole Worm, a deadly spinner-fly combination in #8 and #2 hook sizes, spinner turns easily on slow retrieve. By Pfleuger.

Wizard, an effective plug with good action, but too heavy at 1/20 ounce for the best fly casting. Several colors, 1 1/2 inches long. By Pfleuger.

Chum, a small spoon with good action in nickel, gold, and red-white. Size-2 hook. By Pfleuger.

Pilot Fly, an excellent fly-and-spinner combination with a sensitive nickel blade, in 6 patterns. In 10, 8, 4, 1/0 hook sizes. By Pfleuger.

Choicy Streamer Fly, a standard #8 streamer in 12 old patterns from Cahill to Coachman. By Pfleuger.

Flilite Popping Bug, standard plastic-bodied popper in several colors, sizes 4 and 10. By Pfleuger.

Hoptoit, plastic-bodied, hackle-tailed popper in sizes 10 and 12. By Pfleuger.

Divided Wing Fly, a standard upright trout dry fly, really, in 12 standard trout patterns, but an occasional possibility for bass. Sizes 10 to 12. By Pfleuger.

Splittail, a sponge-bodied bug with rubber-band legs. Floats but has unique action just under surface when retrieved. Sizes 8, 10, 12. By Nature Faker.

Skippet, concave-faced, standard popping bugs with hackle tails and rubber-band legs. In sizes 8, 4, 1/0. By Ce-Bet.

Spinofly, a good fly-spinner combination that probably is best in stream fishing. In 18 old favorite patterns. Sizes 8, 4, 2, 1/0. By Marathon.

Streamwing Hair Fly, standard streamer with hair wings in 6 favorite patterns. Sizes 2, 4, 6, 8. By Marathon.

Salmon Egg Jig, a novel jig-type lure with streamer tail. In 4 colors with 1/0 hook. By Marathon.

Salmon Egg Streamer, made of salmon-egg imitation beads and streamer tail in 4 colors. Size 1/32 ounce. By Marathon.

Bass Houn, a spentwing bug with deerhair body which is tricky to cast but which is deadly fished on still-water ponds. Slight side-to-side twitching of rod tip gives this a terrific action. In 12 patterns and 1/0 or 2/0 hooks. By Marathon.

Hot Pop Popping Minnow, a standard surface bug with streamer tail in 15 colors. Sizes 1, 4, 6, 8, or 1/0. By Marathon.

Crazy Legs, a standard-type popping bug with rubber-band legs. In 15 colors. Sizes 1, 4, 6, 8, 10, 12. By Marathon.

Popping Minnow, a standard, fast-selling popper in many sizes from 14 to 2/0. In many colors of enamel finish. Sturdy in construction. Also a similar Popping Frog. By Marathon.

Wiggle Popper, typical surface bug with rubber legs and with wiggling action on top when retrieved slowly. Sizes 12 to 1. By Marathon.

Hair Frog, surface bug with deerhair body and long hair legs. Very effective bait. Sizes 1 to 8. By Marathon.

Bucktail Crab, a crayfish imitation made with natural deerhair. In sizes 1 to 8. By Marathon.

Peerless Bass Fly, the old standard upright bass fly in 24 old standard patterns. Well tied. Size 1 or 1/0. By Marathon.

Namakagon Streamer Fly, good minnow imitation in 12 old trout patterns. Sizes 6, 8, 10. By Marathon.

Weighted Streamer Fly, with weighted ball head and thin squirrel-tail wings. Good smallmouth stream possibility. Sizes 8, 1/32 ounce. By Marathon.

Streamer Hair Fly, bushy deerhair-winger fly which should take smallmouths. Sizes 1, 1/0, 2/0. Four original patterns. By Marathon.

Williams Nymph, a tiny spoon in gold or silver which runs hook upward. In 1/80 and 1/40 ounce. Good for stream fishing. By Williams.

Explorer, standard type of popper with hackle tail and large popeyes. In 6 colors. Sizes 1, 4, 6, 8. By Evans.

Band-it, a popper with striped body and extra-long rubber-band legs. Cork body is long, slim. In 6 colors. Sizes 4, 6, 8, 10. By Evans.

Prankster, popper with acorn-shaped body and weed guard. It's 1/10-ounce weight makes it better for spinning than fly casting. Six patterns, 1/0 hook. By Evans.

Double Feature, a novel, rubber-legged popper with a trailer hook attached to hook short strikers. In 4 colors, sizes 1/0 and 4. By Evans.

Playboy Popper, standard popper design with Dylite body. In 6 colors. Sizes 1, 4, 8. By Evans.

Giddy Popper, standard popper with tapered body and streamer tail. In 6 finishes; sizes 1, 4, 8. By Evans.

Firefly Popper, standard popping bug in fluorescent lacquer. Six colors. Sizes 1, 4, 6, 10. By Evans.

Bingo Bug, heavily hackled and probably a moth imitation. Also has fan-shaped wings of Saran material. In six colors, size 8 only. By Evans.

Pan Handler, a popper of the usual design and rubber-band legs. In 6 patterns. By Evans.

Long Tom, a popper with elongated body to imitate crippled minnow. In 6 patterns. Sizes 4, 6, 8, 10. By Evans.

Seducer, a spinner fly best in stream fishing. In 8 standard patterns. Size 8. By Evans.

Bull's Eye Popper, surface bug with unique round head and large eyes. In 6 colors. Sizes 2, 4, 6, 8, 10. By Evans.

Closed Wing Bass Fly, a large upright bass fly in the old style and in old patterns. Sizes 2/0, 1/0, 1, 2. By Evans.

Weighted Sinker Fly, a curious lure with rubber-band legs and marabou tail and a weighted round head. It's recommended for ice fishing, but it could be a great stream bait. Size 10 only. By Evans.

Wickam's Fancy, Black Wooly Worm, Blonde Wulff, Muddler, Joe's Hopper, Dan Bailey Salmon Fly, and *Robert Page Lincoln.* These patterns are tied by Dan Bailey of Livingston, Mont. All are tied primarily for western trout, but all of these are also quite effective stream flies for bass. Other good bass possibilities include Dan Bailey's BiFly, White Muddler, Sawtooth Popeye, and McGinty tied in large sizes.

Multi-Winged Streamer, a long hackle streamer with plastic head that could be fine for small-mouths. In many colors, size 1/o. By Phillips.

Weedless Wiggle Popper, a multi-rubber-legged popping bug with weed guards which give it a good appearance in shallow water. Best around pads, weed beds. In 8 colors, 3/64 ounce. By Phillips.

Fly Rod Popper, a surface bug with unusually good hooking properties because hook is placed at low angle beneath body. Good, sturdy bass catcher in 10 colors, 3/64 and 1/32 ounce. By Phillips.

Shiner, a most unique, tiny minnow imitation with transparent plastic body and gray floss tail. Could be a killer for stream fisherman who likes to experiment with new lures. By DeLong.

Black Roach, a good plastic imitation of a roach which does well with pan fish as well as small bass. Size 8. By DeLong.

Slim-Bug, a floating bug with long, thin body, rubber legs, and hackle tail. This bug is an extremely good bass producer. It has worked especially well in sandy, glacial lakes of Michigan's Upper Peninsula. In 4 sizes (10 to 4) and 6 patterns. By Weber.

Crazy-Pop, a disc-headed popping bug with rubber-band legs and hackle tail. In 3 sizes (4 to 10) and 6 patterns. By Weber.

Nitwit, a popping bug with hackle tail and an unusually shaped head. A Creepy Nitwit also has rubber-band legs. In 2 sizes and 12 colors. By Weber.

Scaly Popperakle, a sturdily built Dylite plastic popper with a forged, hump-shank hook molded in the body. Has big popeyes. This bug can be given hard use for a long time, and it will stand much abuse. The writer has even used it on salt-water fish. In 3 sizes from 2 to 8, in 4 patterns. By Weber.

Scaly Creepy Popperakle, is same as Scaly Popperakle, except also has rubber-band legs. By Weber.

Poppin' Frog, an imitation frog bug with hook molded inside Dylite popper-type head and with forked bucktail legs. In green-frog pattern only, 3 sizes. By Weber.

Dylite Super Duper, a popping-bug type floater with bucktail "whisker" wings. Very effective on southern bass. In 3 sizes and 6 colors. By Weber.

Dylite Frog, an excellent surface-swimming frog with upturned hook—which makes it possible to pull over or across pads, bonnets, and other obstacles. In frog finish, has popeyes, cupped face, bucktail hair legs. Size 1/o. By Weber.

Dot Pop

Woole Worm

Pilot Fly

Hoptoit

Choicy Streamer Fly

Dylite Frog

Divided Wing Fly

Scaly Creepy Popperakle

Scaly Popperakle

Dylite Super Duper

Bass Houn   **Double Feature**   **Black Roach**

TOP ROW: Wickam's Fancy, Black Wooly Worm, Blonde Wulff. **MIDDLE ROW:** Muddler, Joe's Hopper. **BOTTOM ROW:** Dan Bailey Salmon Fly, Robert Page Lincoln.

Bass Streamer Flies

Here follows a list of streamer flies and their dressing which a fly-tying bass fisherman can make at home. For most, only a few inexpensive materials are required. Others are a little more elaborate, but all are very effective. Fly-tying materials for any of these can be obtained from Herters, Inc., Waseca, Minn.

Golden Dustman, originated by, and one of the favorites of, Dr. James Henshall. He considered it best on dark days. Body: peacock herl. Hackle: golden yellow. Wings: bronze (from wild turkey if possible, but domestic turkey suitable). Tail: fibers from a golden-pheasant crest.

Irish Iron Blue Dun, a real antique among trout flies, but good for bass when tied as streamer on long-shanked hook. Tail: fibers of red feather from the breast of a golden pheasant. Body: fur from the belly of a muskrat ribbed with about 5 turns of silver tinsel. Hackle: dark gray. Wings: gray squirrel tail.

Shenandoah, originated by smallmouth fishermen in the Blue Ridge Mountain region. Could be good elsewhere too. Wings: black bucktail or tail of black phase of gray squirrel. Tail: same. Body: black chenille tied fat. Head: black with a small wiggling disc attached. Tie on ⌗4 or ⌗6 long-shanked hook.

Black Dazzler, same as Shenandoah except that the chenille body is not used. Instead cut some blue and clear cellophane strips about 1/16 inch wide. Tie these alternately along the full length of the body as you wind it with black silk. Strips should be crinkled and trimmed so that the projecting bits are about 3/8 inch long, forming a body that looks "bushy."

Hot Orange Marabou, a great pattern for roily water and midsummer stream fishing. Use ⚞4 or ⚞6 streamer hooks. Wings: bright orange-dyed marabou feathers topped with several strands of peacock herl. Body: a clear strip of cellophane wound until it's about 3 times the size of the hook shank. Shoulder: jungle cock.

Yellow Marabou, same as Hot Orange except substitute yellow marabou.

Beltrami ⚞13, a strange creation developed by George Herter and named after Beltrami County, Minn. It was meant for big brook trout, but it works well on brown trout and bass too. Body: oval silver tinsel. Hackle: about 8 lengths of white rubber band tied on as a throat. Wing: barred orange topped off with black-bear hair. Head: coated with waterproof cement and covered with finely chopped-up black hair. Shoulder: flat plastic yellow and black eyes—or jungle cock.

Bumblepuppy, an old trout streamer designed by legendary Theodore Gordon almost 50 years ago. Said to be a fine clear-water streamer. Tag: silver and red silk. Tail: Scarlet ibis, 2 mated feathers back to back. Butt: red or yellow chenille. Body: full with white silk chenille and ribbed with flat silver tinsel. Hackle: badger, large, long and lots of it. Wings: strips of white swan or goose over white deer- or goat hair. Sides: jungle cock. Head: black.

Smelt Marabou, a good one for New England and New Brunswick smallmouths. Wings: pale green marabou topped with 2 strands of peacock herl. Body: black and thin-ribbed with silver tinsel. Eye: jungle cock.

Mickey Finn, a well-known streamer developed by John Alden Knight. Head: black. Body: medium thick made of flat silver tinsel and ribbed with oval silver tinsel. Wing: a small bunch of yellow bucktail; then a medium bunch of red bucktail on top; then a medium bunch of yellow bucktail on top of all. Shoulder: jungle cock.

Warden's Worry. Head: black; red eye with white painted center. Tail: a small section of red goose-wing feather. Body: rear half flat silver tinsel; front half yellow seal fur-ribbed with gold tinsel. Wing: natural brown bucktail with several yellow polar-bear hairs tied on top. Shoulder: jungle cock. Hackle: yellow.

Chief Needabeh. Body: medium thick made of flat silver tinsel. Wing: 4 yellow neck hackles. Shoulder: jungle cock. Hackle: red.

Moose River. Body: thin of flat silver tinsel. Head: black. Wing: small bunch of white bucktail with peacock-eyed tail fibers tied above as a topping. Cheek: golden pheasant tippet.

Parmachene Belle, an old, old pattern. Head: black. Body: yellow chenille ribbed with flat silver tinsel. At rear of body put a ruff of peacock-eyed tail fibers. Wing: 2 white neck hackles tied between 2 red ones. Shoulder: jungle cock. Hackle: one red and one white one tied together.

Red Angel, developed for fishing West Virginia streams. Wing: angel hair dyed crimson tied long and sparse. Body: flat silver tinsel. Tail: black bear or squirrel hair. Head: black with black wiggling disc. Tie on ⚞6 long-shanked hook.

Burlap Fly, a western pattern originated for steelheads by Wayne Buszek, but with splendid potential for bass. Tail: stiff bristle of deerhair tied to flair. Body: piece of burlap tied full. Hackle: soft grizzly. Wing: none.

Zebray, a surface bass bug rather a streamer, designed by Art Kade of Sheboygan, Wisc., easy to tie. Tail: yellow Asiatic goat hair. Body: alternate black and white bars of bucktail deerhair, shaped wide at the rear or bend of the hook and tapered toward the front; the front end shaped deepest below the wings with a lift line to provide easy lifting from the water; body shallow above the hook to provide sufficient clearance for hooking fish. Wings: divided, spent wings of bright orange. Asiatic goat hair. Head: black silk waterproofed. Hook: hollow point ⚞4 Sproat with turned-down eye.

Golden Pheasant, an old English wet pattern which somehow, and with some revision into a streamer, will catch smallmouths in small rivers. Body: orange chenille with gold tinsel ribs tied medium fat. Tail: strands of black feather. Wing: 2 golden pheasant feathers. Hackle: red.

Oriole, a streamer version of one of Dr. Henshall's favorite old patterns. Body: black chenille tied thin with gold tinsel ribbing. Tail: sliver of black feather above a thinner sliver of white feather. Hackle: black. Wings: 2 long white hackle feathers dyed bright orange; long golden pheasant feathers could be substituted. Use ⚞6 long-shanked hook.

Chapter 12

TACKLE

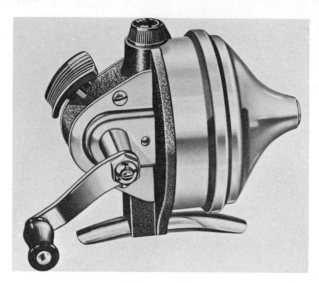

Pfleuger 88

No group of anglers have had as much serviceable, foolproof and easy-to-use tackle designed for them as have bass fishermen today. And although other costs have constantly increased, volume and production of fishing tackle and new technological developments in their manufacture have kept the prices within reach of anyone.

Modern bait-casting reels are light, with very lightweight spools, and much less formidable to use than those of twenty years ago because of effective, new antibacklash devices. A plug caster can buy any of the reels listed herewith—and do so with complete confidence.

The light spinning reels which are most suitable for bass fishing have also been developed to a maximum of simplicity and ease of handling. Any improvements in this type of reel would have to be made, it seems, in an entirely new direction. It is possible, just possible, that the enclosed spin-bait casting reels are in the process of making the open-faced type of spinning reels obsolete.

There was a day not too long ago when the most serious bass fishermen looked on the first spin-bait casting reels with horror. Here was a device that upset the status quo—but which also made accurate, pinpoint casting much easier for more sportsmen. And it is true that the first models released had many bugs in them. But the current models are entirely practical, and what's more, nearly all of them are good bargains; you get plenty of pleasant fishing for a low price.

It's a rare bass fisherman nowadays who doesn't use Fiberglas rods, no matter what type of fishing he prefers. And except for sentimental reasons there simply isn't any excuse to use anything but glass right now. Modern tubular stocks have been designed with actions impossible to match. And besides, they're far more durable than bamboo or anything else.

New developments and improvements in fishing lines have come so fast and so frequently that it's impossible to follow them. It's a wise bass fisherman, though, who figures what test casting line he needs—and then selects the line with the finest diameter for the test. A spin caster has one other consideration to keep in mind; "softness" or pliability of the line. It's far more pleasant to use a line which coils well on the reel spool. One important test of any fly line is in its buoyancy.

Spin-Bait Casting or Closed-Face Reels

Pfleuger 88, features immediate line control, carboloy line pickup, silent antireverse, easy to use, extra line spools. Medium price range. Enterprise Mfg. Co.

Pfleuger Saturn, features instant line control, smooth drag, silent antireverse, extra spools, 3 to 1 gear ratio. Approximately 100 yards of 6# monofilament with reel. Medium price. Enterprise Mfg. Co.

Johnson Century, a versatile, light reel with interchangeable right- or left-hand retrieve. Selecto-dial gives positive and visual control. About 100 yards of 6# mono line. Medium price. Denison-Johnson.

Johnson Princess, same as Century, but finished in pink color for distaff anglers. Denison-Johnson.

Johnson Citation, big brother of the Century, has larger line capacity (125 yards of 10# mono). Medium price. Denison-Johnson.

Johnson Century

Abu-Matic ✳40

Johnson Citation

Flash

Johnson Centennial, features rugged and dependable construction, double handle, extra spools, "duo-matic" drag which gives steady and even tension. Medium price. Denison-Johnson.

Abu-Matic ✳60, features "synchro-drag" for foolproof playing of fish, no line twist, automatic antireverse, the finest material available, star drag. Comes in leather case with oiler, etc. Fairly expensive. Garcia.

Abu-Matic ✳40, is anodized against corrosion, star drag, etc. Medium price. Garcia.

Zebco 33, features continuous antireverse, easily adjusted drag, interchangeable spools, easy to clean and change spools, feather-touch control. Medium price. Zebco Co.

Bronson Savage, features radial-type adjustable drag, positive antireverse, precision-cast alloy drive gear. Very inexpensive. Bronson Reel Co.

Bronson Classic, comes with 100 yards of 8✳ mono line, slip-type drag with click, ventilated closed face to dry out line. Inexpensive. Bronson.

Bronson Pilot, features visual drag adjusting device, smooth action spool, slip-type drag with click. Medium price. Bronson.

Bronson Dart, features an antireverse crank, weighs 7 ounces, preset drag that's adjustable, and at less than $6 retail is lowest price spin-bait cast reel on market. Bronson.

Shakespeare Cast (or *Spin Reel*), makes it possible for fly fishermen to spin with fly rod, has fly-rod seat, weighs 6.7 ounces and fits easily in a pocket. Moderately priced. Shakespeare.

Shakespeare Wonder Cast, push-button reel with adjustable full-circle drag and excellent workmanship all around, has extra spools, new level wind. Altogether there are 6 models which range from medium price to fairly expensive. Shakespeare.

Shakespeare Spin Wondereel, a closed-face spinning reel which fits at the bottom of the rod rather than as a true spin-bait casting reel. It's manufactured in 8 separate models with various line capacities and which range from medium to expensive. Shakespeare.

Martin 75, has eliminated line twist, has handy crank-handle tension control, a high-gear ratio and quick retrieve, automatic antireverse, is easy to take down. Moderately priced. Martin.

Langley 999, precision-made, equipped with star drag and double handles, has quick retrieve, fits any casting rod, factory-filled with 120 yards of 6# monofilament. Medium price. By Langley. Also manufacture Cast Flo 900 Deluxe spin-bait casting reels at a slightly higher price.

Impala, features micro-disc drag brakes, automatic antireverse, guarantees no pinched lines, extra spools available, weight 8 ounces, 100 yards 6# mono line prewound on reel. Low priced. By Airex.

Eldorado, has effective cross-wind on spool, automatic feathering, extra spools available and gathering face is removed easily, no pinched lines. Medium price. By Airex.

Flash, has larger-than-usual diameter spool, a smooth and powerful drag, fits any casting rod, supplied with 8# test monofilament. Medium price. Horrocks-Ibbotson.

Stream & Lake 88, guarantees trouble-free casting, can handle from 4 to 20# test line, smooth and adjustable drag. Medium price. Wright & McGill.

Stream & Lake 7L-SL, fits at bottom of spinning rod, gives finger-tip touch control, smooth drag, changeable spools. Fairly expensive. Wright & McGill.

Fre-Line All-Purpose, a versatile reel that's good for spinning, spin-bait casting, and for use on fly rods. Could also be used for trolling. In 3 models, all inexpensive. Wright & McGill.

Fre-Line 58, a spin-bait caster with adjustable drag on handle, fast-geared retrieve, changeable spools,

right- or left-handed. Medium price. Wright & McGill.

Ocean City Flipline, has handy drag-control dial, automatic antireverse, double handles, comes with 6# mono line. In two models. True Temper.

Lawrence 405, spin-bait casting reel with top-mounted drag control, automatic antireverse, sensitive drag. Medium price. Lawrence Tackle.

Bait-Casting Reels

Supreme, a fine old bait caster that's almost legendary in performance and dependability. Rugged in construction, gears, and bearings of phosphor-bronze, gears spiral-cut and hand-lapped for precision and smooth running. Lightweight aluminum spool. Level-wind mechanism can be removed for cleaning without taking reel apart. Comes with accessories. Expensive. By Pfleuger.

Summit, a handsome and dependable caster with brass gears, bronze bearings, and aluminum spool. Level wind can be removed easily. Comes with spare pawl. Line capacity: 175 yards. 15# test. Moderately priced. Pfleuger.

Nobby, an especially lightweight casting reel, well suited to longer, lighter action rods. Precision-machined gears and bearings. Aluminum spool. Medium price. Pfleuger.

Skilkast, casting reel with mechanical thumber, installed to prevent nuisance backlashes when night fishing. Good point is that antibacklash device works only when line is going out and not on retrieve. Medium price. Pfleuger.

Akron, one of best-selling of all bait-casting reels. Has brass gears, bronze bearings, removable level wind. Low price, by Pfleuger.

Trump, has brass and nylon gears with brass bearings. Made of plated solid brass, is dependable. Inexpensive. By Pfleuger.

Trusty, lightweight reel with adjustable antibacklash and sliding click. Very inexpensive. By Pfleuger.

Ambassadeur 5000, an outstanding bait-casting reel which combines a free spool with a level wind and centrifugal brake. Backlash is virtually impossible. Also has mechanical brake to adjust for casting various weights, a soundless retrieve, corrosion-proof, red finish, easy to lubricate, comes in handsome leather case with tools. Very expensive. By Garcia.

Ambassadeur 6000, is very similar to 5000 but is meant mostly for salt water with a wider spool and single handle. Would make fine bass-trolling reel. Very expensive. By Garcia.

Abu 2100, a fine narrow-spool tournament reel with free spool, automatic centrifugal brake and no level-wind mechanism. Weighs only 7 3/4 ounces, has checkered thumb rest, great for light lure fishing. Expensive. By Garcia.

Abu 2300, a tournament reel with free spool and centrifugal brake, no level-wind mechanism. Lightweight spool stops easily. Dependable, fine for light lure casting. Fairly expensive. By Garcia.

Streamlite, an excellent caster with dependable level wind, an anti-inertia spool, corrosion-resistant finish, weighs only 5 ounces, difficult to backlash. Medium price. By Langley.

Speedcast, lightweight reel in green "Alumalite" finish, with level-wind, anti-inertia spool. Is dependable, smooth-running, and quiet. Very moderately priced. By Langley.

Lurecast, a fine caster with narrow spool and level wind, lightweight, for serious plug fishermen who use light lines and lures. Maroon Alumalite finish. Pleasant reel to use. Medium price. By Langley.

Reelcast, a lightweight reel with level-wind and anti-inertia spool. Inexpensive. By Langley.

Shorty, a narrow spool, level-wind casting reel designed for use with light gear. Has anti-inertia spool. Inexpensive. By Langley.

Coronet, an excellent reel with automatic spool, is precision-machined, has 10-second take-down without tools. Phosphor-bronze gears and bearings, adjustable drag, comes in leather case. Also a narrow spool, tournament-casting model, weight 4 1/2 ounces. Expensive. By Bronson.

Symbol, a direct-drive, level-wind reel with nylon gears and antibacklash device. Inexpensive. By Bronson.

Topflight, a dependable reel with nonbacklash control, smooth spiral gears, lightweight spool, stainless steel pawl. Is chrome-polished with plastic arbor. Weighs 8 3/8 ounces. Inexpensive. By Horrocks-Ibbotson.

President, a splendid direct-drive, 2-nylon gear reel of stainless steel (and one model in aluminum) with carboloy bushings. Handsome, has oiler-type spool caps, stainless-steel bearings, chromed level wind, automatic thumb spool-cap drag. Capacity: 100 yards of 15# line. Weight 9.3 ounces. Very expensive. By Shakespeare.

Direct Drive. There are 6 separate models of this dependable reel, in various weights (from a very light 5.5 ounces to 8.5 ounces) and ranging from inexpensive to medium price ranges. All have direct drive, quiet nylon gears, and sturdy over-all construction. One model has star drag. Shakespeare.

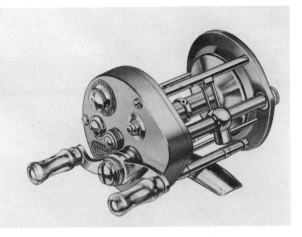

Supreme

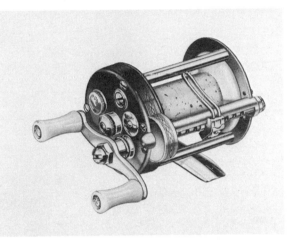

Nobby

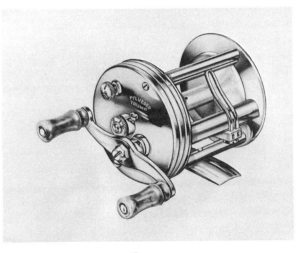

Trump

Speedcast

No. 1921D

Wondereel

Glaskyd, a 2-gear direct drive with end plates and spool of glaskyd. Capacity 200 yards of 10⁂ monofilament. In 3 models from 8.3 to 8.5 ounces. One model has star drag, good for casting or trolling. Medium price. By Shakespeare.

Wondereel. There are 3 models of well-known Wondereels which vary mostly in price from inexpensive to medium. All are extremely serviceable, and if antibacklash mechanism is adjusted correctly no thumbing is really necessary in casting. Good values. By Shakespeare.

Marhoff, another very well-known bait-casting reel for many years. Is light and handsome. Weight 7.6 ounces; capacity 50 yards. 15⁂ test, has stainless-steel spool. Moderately priced. By Shakespeare.

Triumph, an inexpensive reel that has such features as a dependable level wind and hard brass, spiral-cut gears. Weight 7.3 ounces. By Shakespeare.

True Blue, a rugged bait caster made of chrome-plated brass with knurled head cap. Has stainless-steel bearings, dependable level wind. Inexpensive. By Shakespeare.

Leader, very rugged reel weighing 7.2 ounces, dependable. Inexpensive. By Shakespeare.

Star, a dependable reel in same class as Leader. By Shakespeare.

Deuce, similar to Star and Leader. Inexpensive. By Shakespeare.

Intrinsic, similar to Deuce, except somewhat lighter, is sturdy. By Shakespeare.

Thrifty, similar to Deuce, Intrinsic. Very inexpensive. By Shakespeare.

Service, rugged double-grip reels that were built for heavy fishing but which would work well for bass, especially when deep trolling. Level wind and star drag. In 4 models from medium to fairly expensive. By Shakespeare.

Spinning Reels

Pelican, a reliable reel with die-cast aluminum frame, a drag that's easy to adjust while playing a fish, and a bail that snaps into position on only 1/6 turn of the reel handle. Lays on line in smooth basket weave. In right- and left-hand models, extra spools. Moderately priced. By Pfleuger.

Freespeed, a lightweight reel with effective drag that has extra-good quality for the price. Durable, of die-cast aluminum frame, holds 175 yards of 6-pound line. Inexpensive. By Pfleuger.

Mitchell 300, a well-known and popular reel that is extremely rugged and which has given outstanding service. Left- and right-hand models. Also a fast-retrieve (⁂350) model. Has smooth, dependable drag. Extra spools available. Fairly expensive. By Garcia.

Mitchell 302, actually designed for salt water but would do well for fresh-water deep trolling. Expensive. By Garcia.

Mitchell 314, a light and serviceable reel with push-button spool release, "planamatic" gears, anti-reverse control, extra spools. Moderately priced. By Garcia.

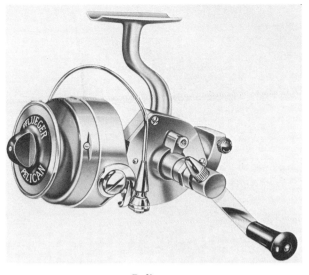

Pelican

Mitchell

Mitchell 306, a sturdy, durable reel in the Mitchell tradition that would serve for deep trolling for bass. Expensive. By Mitchell.

Mitchell 304, lightest and most compact of the Mitchells. Sturdy and very serviceable reel. Medium price. By Mitchell.

ABU, a sturdy reel with handy antireverse control, full bail pickup, bottom-mounted drag, extra spools, right- and left-hand models, holds 350 yds. of 6-pound line. Fairly expensive. By Garcia.

Mignon 33, world's tiniest spinning reel, excellent for ultralight tackle fishing with thread lines. Weighs only 5 3/4 ounces, has reliable drag, double ball-bearing construction, in left- and right-hand models. Expensive. By Rockland.

Majestic 44, dependable and versatile reel with built-in drag, lever-type antireverse button, weighs 11 ounces. Fairly expensive. By Rockland.

Mariner 55, heavy duty, rugged reel with ball-bearing mountings. For right-handers only. Expensive. By Rockland.

Magnum 66, an extremely durable, heavy-duty reel designed primarily for salt water. Could be used for bass trolling. Very expensive. By Rockland.

Fin-Nor, probably the ultimate in fine spinning reels. Of exquisite design and precision craftsmanship, but too heavy for most bass fishing. Great for deep trolling, though. Very expensive. By Tycoon/Fin-Nor.

Larchmont, a rugged reel with antireverse button at finger tip, "quadrant" brake, 3.44- to 1-gear ratio, extra spools, positive line pickup. Expensive. By Airex.

Spinster, has nylon expansion-type drag brake, finger-tip antireverse control, extra spools. Weight 9.6 ounces. Medium-priced. By Airex.

Astra, quite similar to Spinster, except with larger line capacity, other refinements. Left or right hand. Moderately priced. By Airex.

Martin 27, has double-post, trigger guard grip. Also has aluminum housing, precision helical gears, dependable drag, and full bail pickup. Holds 200 yards 6# line. Medium-priced. By Martin.

Spinlite DeLuxe, a small, compact, high-quality reel. Has beveled, machine-cut brass main gears, dependable antireverse and self-centering bail, very smooth retrieve because of two-point shaft suspension. Extra spools, holds 100 yards of 6# monofilament. Expensive. By Langley.

Spinlite Special, virtually the same as Spinlite DeLuxe except not quite as elaborate in construction. Weighs only 6 ounces, is grand for using very light lures, holds 100 yards of 6# monofilament. Moderately expensive. By Langley.

Langley 777, a popular reel with automatic antireverse, excellent balance, and a reliable drag. Has all-aluminum spool, holds 200 yards of 6# monofilament. Medium-priced. By Langley.

Spinator 870, actually a salt-water reel, but with potential for deep trolling in fresh water. Expensive. By Langley.

Spin DeLuxe 830, a lightweight reel precision-made for long service. Has corrosion-resistant finish, weighs 8 ounces, holds 200 yards 6# monofilament, available in right- or left-hand models. Moderately priced. By Langley.

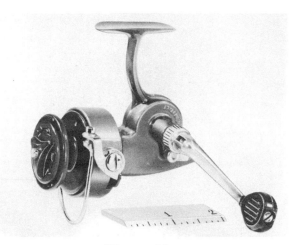

Mignon 33

Larchmont

Hi-Spin

Jet 500, a standard spinning reel durably made with full bail, effective drag, antireverse. Holds 150 yards 6⚡ monofilament. Medium-priced. By Bronson.

Buddy 800, a compact reel with full bail and which weighs only 7 ounces. Serviceable for a long time, but low-priced. By Bronson.

Hi-Spin, a very lightweight (at 6 ounces) reel of noncorrosive metal throughout. Has noiseless gears, reliable adjustable drag. Capacity: 175 yards 4⚡ monofilament or 125 yards of 6⚡. Extra spools, also a de luxe model. Inexpensive. By Horrocks-Ibbotson.

Lightning 400, has full bail, 3 1/2- to 1-gear ratio, cross-wind. Holds 150 yards 6⚡ monofilament, weighs 11 ounces. Inexpensive. By Lawrence.

Orvis 100 and 101, a popular and very dependable reel with smooth drag and sturdy construction. Weighs 10 ounces, left and right hand. Expensive. By Orvis.

Fly-Fishing Reels

Russell Intrinsic, a very light, sturdily built, single-action fly reel of noncorroding aluminum alloy. Weighs 5 ounces, holds 50 yards of D level line. Inexpensive. By Shakespeare.

Tru-arT, a silent-winding, free-stripping automatic reel, for right- or left-handed use. Weighs 9 1/4 ounces. Inexpensive. By Shakespeare.

OK Automatic, a serviceable aluminum reel with clock-spring steel spring. Friction clutch slips even when reel tightly wound. Inexpensive. By Shakespeare.

Sportscraft, an aluminum, single-action reel with generous line capacity. Has reversible click, weighs 5 ounces. Very inexpensive. By Horrocks-Ibbotson.

Royal-Matic, a fully automatic reel with bronze bearing and free-stripping. Capacity: 30 yards HCH plus 50 yards 15⚡ test backing. Weight 9 ounces. Inexpensive. By Bronson.

Royalist, strong but light single-action model with on-and-off drag. Capacity 30 yards HCH plus 50 yards 15⚡ test. Weight 4 1/8 ounces. Inexpensive. By Bronson.

Royal 360, single-action reel with click-type drag. Same capacity as Royalist. Weight 4 ounces. Very inexpensive. By Bronson.

Kalahatch, made of corrosion-proof aluminum, has durable fly-line guard, is precision-built, for right- or left-hand use, weighs 6 ounces, holds 100 feet of D level line. Very inexpensive. By Weber.

Tru-arT

Sportscraft

Landex

Royalist

Medalist

Magnetic, a handsome single-action reel which features a permanent magnetic drag. Case is stainless steel, spool is hand crafted of aluminum, exclusive line backing furnished with each spool, has lifetime guarantee. Fairly expensive. By Denison-Johnson.

Fly-Wate, an automatic reel which is the descendant of the first automatic designed and built by Herman Martin 75 years ago. It's lightweight, has audible click and silent wind, and adjustable line-release lever. Takes down quickly and easily. Inexpensive. By Martin.

Blue Chip, an extremely handsome and serviceable automatic reel with mechanical precision of a watch. Each reel has extra spool, case, and bag. Weighs 8 1/4 ounces, holds 100 feet of D level line. Fairly expensive. By Martin.

Ablette, a rugged but lightweight single-action reel. In right- and left-handed models, also in various sizes and weights from 5 1/2 to 6.7 ounces. All have reliable click drag, extra spools available, noncorrosive finish. Inexpensive. By Airex.

Beaudex, a fine single-action reel with simple lines and designed in 3 different spool diameters. Has positive drag and one-piece frame. Moderately priced. By Garcia.

Pridex, a fine single-action reel with simple lines and designed in 3 different spool diameters. Has positive drag and one-piece frame. Moderately priced. By Garcia.

Landex, a high-quality reel with adjustable drag. Also, handle remains stationary when fish pulls out line. Heavy-duty, one-piece frame, ventilated spool. Rather expensive. By Garcia.

Medalist, probably the most popular single-action fly reel ever built. Of sturdy construction, easy to take apart, with lightweight aluminum frame. In 4 spool diameters and 4 weights from 4 ounces to 8 3/4 ounces. Has positive drag. From inexpensive (in small size) to medium price. By Pfleuger.

Superex, a dependable automatic that takes apart for cleaning with the press of a button. Light in weight (9 ounces), it holds 32 yards of C level line. Retrieves 24 yards on full winding of spring. Low priced. By Pfleuger.

Gem, a 5-ounce, single-action reel with gun-metal finish and a smooth acting click. Inexpensive. By Pfleuger.

Sal-Trout, a single-action fly reel with large-capacity spool. This one could be used for trolling or drifting with lead core line. Weighs 4 1/4 ounces. Very inexpensive. By Pfleuger.

Progress, a simple, lightweight, but sturdy single-action reel. Very, very inexpensive. By Pfleuger.

Casting Rods

Actionrod 1200 Series, 5 foot, 5 1/2 foot, and 6 foot, one piece, medium price. Finished in maroon with green, black, and white wrapping. Four stainless-steel wire-frame guides (on longer lengths) and Allanite tip top. Chrome-plated chuck handle with nylon collet and screw-type reel lock. Aluminum foregrip and long 5 1/2 inch specie cork grip give this balanced rod a distinctive appearance. This 5 foot, 5 1/2 foot, and 6 foot light Actionrod has one-piece action and makes a true fisherman's companion. Good grade tube and bag. By Orchard Industries.

Companion 2201, 2202, 2214, 2215, 6 foot medium action and 6 1/2 foot light action, moderately priced. Two-piece construction with detachable handle, chromed stainless-steel or agate guides; agate tip top, black finish with offset reel seat and cork grip; keeper ring; self-aligning chuck; screw-type reel lock; protective butt cap; flannel bag, fiber carrying tube. By Garcia.

Companion 2211, 2212, 2213, same one-piece construction as 2201, but designed with "tournament" action. In 5 1/2 foot medium, 6 foot light, and 6 foot medium actions. Moderately priced. By Garcia.

Chieftain, a versatile, tubular glass, two-piece rod in 6-foot, 6-foot-4-inches, and seven-foot lengths. Has 5 chrome-plated guides, aluminum cast offset handle with aluminum collet and specie cork. Inexpensive. By Phillipson. Also available: *Scout* rod, inexpensive, 5 feet to 6 feet 4 inches.

Regal Lancer, there's fine quality in these two-piece rods—6 lengths from 5 feet to 7 feet. Have detachable handle, positive reel locking, 5 chrome-plated guides. Will handle standard casting or spin-bait casting reels. Inexpensive. By Phillipson.

Eponite DeLuxe, precision-made rods with excellent action. Two-piece models in 5 lengths from 5 feet to 7 feet. Has chrome-plated guides and tip top. Offset handle with positive reel locking. Also a handsome, high quality *Eponite Royal* model. Fairly expensive. By Phillipson.

Magnum, in 3 models: PT110—1 piece, 6 feet. Designed for use with closed-face reels, this rod is also capable of casting an extreme range of lures with conventional casting reel. The sensitive tip will cast 1/8-ounce lures while the power progression enables rod to cast 5/8-ounce lures. PT100—1 piece, 5 1/2 feet. Supplied with nine-inch all-angle handle. Casts lures from 1/4 to 3/4 ounce. Can be used both with conventional bait-casting reel and

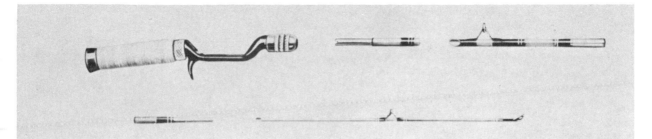

Companion

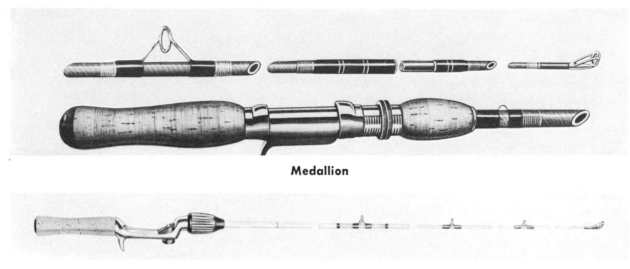

Medallion

Hedliner

closed-face reels. PT120—6 feet. Casting rod. Featuring a new revolutionary action, this rod will cast from 1/4- to 1-ounce lures. All angle handle. Very expensive. By Silaflex.

Perfexion, fine Fiberglas rods in 8 models, both one- and two-piece, from 5 1/2 feet to 6 feet 3 inches, with various actions. Beautifully made with splendid action. Expensive. By Silaflex.

Medallion, is of excellent quality, 6 feet long. This casting rod in the *Medallion Series* features the offset handle, is a three-piece rod that breaks down to only 24 inches. It becomes the third member of the Executive Sets which conveniently pack in your "two-suiter" yet possess unbelievably fine action. Very expensive. By Silaflex.

Medallion, is two-piece and 6 1/2 feet long. True precision for the caster. This rod was designed for use with light test lines and ultralight casting reels. It will handle lures from 1/8 to 1/4 ounce. The lightest casting rod (the blank weighs 1 5/8 ounces) on the market. Also another MC65-2 model with heavier action. A 1 7/8-ounce blank,

designed for use with lures 1/4 to 3/8 ounce. Other than action it is identical with the lighter *Medallion.* Expensive. By Silaflex.

Hedliner 6616, with two-piece, 6 1/2 foot, universal action. "Sunburst Yellow" tubular glass, two-piece. Wound with forest-green nylon thread, vinyl coated for toughness. Graduated spinning-type guides, durable chrome, with extra spiral group winding on butt section. Nickeled ferrule, handle is offset type, aluminum, permanently joined to butt section of rod. Select cork on full-size grip. Screw-locking reel seat that locks reels tightly. By Heddon.

Hedliner 6054, 6057, in "Sunburst Yellow" tubular glass tip, one-piece, wound with forest-green nylon thread, vinyl coated. Graduated spinning-type guides, durable chrome, with spiral trim winding on butt guide. Handle is offset type, aluminum with green chuck-type foregrip. Screw-locking reel seat holds all reels firmly. Select cork grip, full size. 6054—5 1/2 foot, universal action. 6057—6 foot, universal action.

Seven-Footer, 7 feet long with two-piece tip. For fishermen who want a "long reach" casting rod, for extra-long casts with both casting and spinning lures. Natural-tone tip has black vinyl guide winds, trimmed in orange. Extra-long handle has 8-inch rear grip. "Screw-lok" foregrip registers tip in position, locks it tightly. Sliding hood holds reel securely. Hard chrome guides, tip top. Moderately priced. By Heddon.

Mark IV, tubular glass, two-piece rods in 3 sizes from 6 to 6 1/2 feet. Tip in natural tone. All spincasting guides and tip top are carboloy for maximum wear. Aluminum offset handle in durable "Poxibond," rich gun-metal finish. "Screw-lok" foregrip registers tip in position—locks it tightly. Sliding hood holds reel securely at all times. Foregrip, slide, and butt cap are aluminum-satin anodized. Packed in handsome leatherette case, reinforced tube. Expensive. By Heddon.

Hedliner 5058, solid glass with one-piece tip, 6 feet long. Very inexpensive. By Heddon.

Hedliner 5501, 5503, solid glass, two-piece, 5 1/2 and 6 feet long. Inexpensive. By Heddon.

Hedliner 6601, 6603, tubular glass, two-piece, 5 1/2 and 6 feet long. Inexpensive. By Heddon.

Hedliner 6703, 6706, tubular glass, two-piece, 6 and 6 1/2 feet. Inexpensive. By Heddon.

Mark IV, tubular glass, one-piece tip, 5 1/2 and 6 feet. Fairly expensive. By Heddon.

Mark I, tubular glass in 3 actions, 6 and 6 1/2 feet long. Medium price. By Heddon. In one- and two-piece tips.

Mark II, tubular glass in 3 actions, 6 and 6 1/2 feet long. Medium price. By Heddon. In one- and two-piece tips.

Mark III, tubular glass in one- and two-piece tip, in 3 actions, 6 to 6 1/2 feet long. Fairly expensive. By Heddon.

Hedliner 5020, solid glass, one-piece, 4 feet long. Very inexpensive. By Heddon.

Hedliner 5052, 5055, solid glass, one-piece, 5 and 5 1/2 feet long. Inexpensive. By Heddon.

Hedliner 6105, 6108, solid glass, one-piece, 5 1/2 and 6 feet long. Inexpensive. By Heddon.

Thunderbird, solid glass, tapered, 5 and 5 1/2 feet long. Also in tubular glass. Made for long, hard use. Medium price. By Horrocks-Ibbotson.

Thunderbird, tubular glass, tapered, 6 and 6 1/2 feet long. Rod is iridescent pearl color. Medium price. By Horrocks-Ibbotson.

Wonderod, a famous name in casting rods which has meant quality and good casting for many years. In many grades, sizes, and actions from Super DeLuxe (fairly expensive) to Jim Dandy (very inexpensive). All models are handsome, beautifully finished. From 5 feet 2 inches to 6 feet long. Guides of stainless steel. By Shakespeare.

Spin 'R Cast Wonderod, tubular glass, two-piece rods with swelled butt construction. In every type of action and from 5 feet 8 inches to 6 feet 6 inches long. De luxe model is fairly expensive, but others graduate down to inexpensive. All well built for long service. By Shakespeare.

Spinning Rods

Spin Wonderods, white, two-piece, tubular glass rods of high quality and fine workmanship. In numerous grades, lengths, and in all actions from light to fairly stiff. Some have fixed reel seats, others are movable. One model, the 7-foot ⚹1288, is a combination spin-fly rod. It has seats for both spinning and fly reels. Most models are fairly expensive. By Shakespeare.

Spinning Wonderods, two-piece, tubular glass rods in 22 different models. Actions run from very light to heavy. Lengths from 6 1/2 to 7 feet. Have both fixed and adjustable reel seats. Two models (1458, 1459) are combination spin-fly rods with 2-reel seats. Workmanship is good on all models which range from inexpensive to fairly expensive. By Shakespeare.

Hi-Power, tubular glass, two-piece in 6 actions from featherlight to heavy, from 6 1/2 to 8 feet long, all with stiff butt and sensitive tips. Fairly expensive. By Horrocks-Ibbotson.

Spinlite, ultralight, one-piece, Fiberglas in two lengths, 4 1/2 and 5 feet. Smallest weighs only 1 3/4 ounces. Well built. Moderately priced. By Langley.

Airex Tubular Glass, altogether 17 models available in every action, from 6 1/2 to 7 feet, of lightweight and skillful construction, all two-piece. From inexpensive to fairly expensive. By Airex.

Mark I, tubular glass, two-piece, 6 1/2 and 7 feet long, with either fixed or movable reel seat, fixed reel seat, sturdily built, 16-inch tapered handle. Moderately priced. By Heddon.

Mark II, same as Mark I but more elaborate, 6 1/2 and 7 feet with fixed or movable reel seat. Fairly expensive. By Heddon.

Mark III, handsome, two-piece, tubular glass model in 6 1/2- and 7-foot lengths. Expensive. By Heddon.

Mark IV, custom-made quality in two-piece, tubular glass rod. Lengths of 6 1/2 and 7 feet. Beautifully constructed. Expensive. By Heddon.

Hedliner, tubular glass, two-piece, movable reel seat in 4 models, 6 1/2 and 7 feet long. Inexpensive. By Heddon.

Hedliner, solid glass, two-piece, fixed reel seat, 6 1/2 feet long. Inexpensive. By Heddon.

Medallion, splendid rod in 5 models from 5 1/2 to 7 feet long. In two- and three-piece models, several good actions from very light to heavy. Very expensive. By Silaflex.

Perfexion, 6 models of a fine tubular glass rod, all with rather light action. From 6 to 7 1/2 feet, two- and three-piece, will toss very light lures, handsomely made. Expensive. By Silaflex.

Magnum, tubular Fiberglas with new progressive taper, 6 1/2 feet long, one- and two-piece. Beautifully made, has movable reel seat, will handle wide variety of lure weights. Very expensive. By Silaflex.

Chieftain and *Scout,* tubular glass rods of golden beige stock with chrome-plated mountings, fixed on movable reel seats. Inexpensive. By Phillipson.

Regal Lancer, two-piece, tubular glass, finest construction. In many actions, from 6 feet 4 inches to 7 1/2 feet long. Medium price. By Phillipson.

Eponite Aristo, tubular glass of best construction from best materials. Chrome-plated guides and tip top. Positive reel-locking. In 6-foot-4-inch and 7-foot lengths. Moderately priced. By Phillipson.

Eponite DeLuxe, handsome rod, two-piece, fine construction throughout, movable reel seat, from 6 to 7 feet long, comes in square, aluminum case. Fairly expensive. By Phillipson.

Actionrod 1700 series, two-piece tubular glass rod with simulated bamboo finish, trimmed in azure blue, black, and white. Ferrule is brown anodized aluminum. Spiraled guides. Actionrod's fixed reel seat. Large No. 24 butt guide. Allanite tip top. Select specie cork handle with protector butt cap. De luxe bag and tube. Moderately priced. By Orchard Industries.

Mignon Mate Standard and *Mignon Mate DeLuxe,* designed for ultralight spinning, tubular glass, with featherweight ferrules and guides, select specie cork handle, packed in aluminum tube. Moderately priced. By Rockland.

Companion Ultra-Light, two-piece construction; deep-chromed stainless steel guides; genuine Agate tip top; handsome black and red windings; tapered golden sliding rings on finest specie cork handle; keeper ring; protective rubber butt cap and winding check; flannel bag; fiber carrying tube. Ideal for light-tackle bass angler. Fairly expensive. By Garcia.

Companion Multi-Purpose, two-piece construction; genuine Agate guides and tip top; handsome black and yellow windings; black anodized aluminum reel seat with golden sliding rings; finest specie cork handle; keeper ring; protective rubber butt cap and winding check; flannel bag; fiber carrying tube. Very versatile rods. The 6 1/2-foot model is excellent for all fresh-water fishing such as bass. The 7-foot model, slightly heavier in action, is also ideal for bass. Expensive. By Garcia.

Companion 2111 to 2132, two-piece construction; deep-chromed stainless steel or Agate guides; Agate tip tops; handsome windings; black and gold anodized aluminum screw-locking fixed reel seat; finest specie cork handle; keeper ring; protective rubber butt cap and winding check; flannel bag; fiber carrying tube. Expensive. By Garcia.

Companion Popping & Boat Rod, designed for Texas and Florida weakfish but also a good possibility for deep trolling for bass. Very well-made rod. Expensive. By Garcia.

Fly Rods

Companion 2403, 2404, 2405, 2406, excellent quality, two-piece construction; handsome black and yellow windings; stainless-steel snake guides and tip top; Agate stripping guide; keeper ring; black and gold anodized aluminum reel seat; half Wells grip of finest specie cork; rubber winding check; flannel bag; fiber carrying tube. Available in various lengths—7 1/2 to 9 feet and various actions. Expensive. By Garcia.

Actionrod 1600, two-piece tubular glass. Striking green, black, and white wrapping on maroon finish. Stainless-steel guides and tip top. Chromed ferrules and anodized reel seat. Keeper ring and large stripper guide. Shaped specie cork grip. Good grade bag and screw-cap fiber carrying case, 8 to 9 feet. Moderately priced. By Orchard Industries.

Actionrod 4300, an ideal bass-bugging rod in two-piece tubular glass, finished in natural tan, accentuated by brown and white spiral wrapping over rich metallic gold with matching brown anodized aluminum ferrule and reel seat. Stainless-steel guides and tip top. Large No. 14 and 10 spiraled stripper guides. This sturdy rod is also ideal for bonefish and salmon. De luxe bag and screw-cap carrying case, 8 to 9 feet. Expensive. By Orchard Industries.

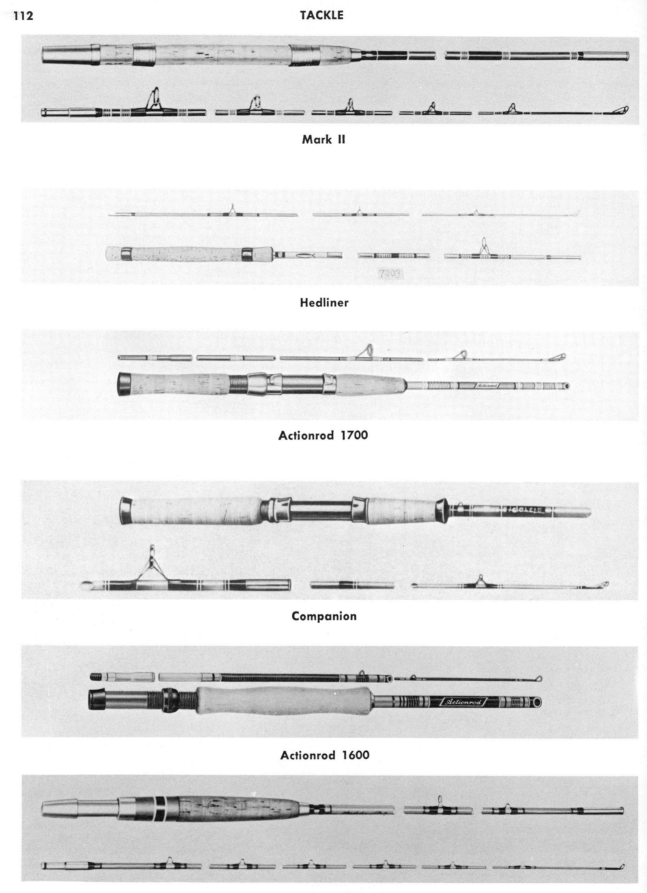

Mark II

Hedliner

Actionrod 1700

Companion

Actionrod 1600

Mark IV

Aristo, excellent value in an eponite, tubular glass rod with hard chrome-plated guides, nickel-silver ferrules, anodized reel seat, and excellent action. Three sizes: 7 1/2, 8, and 8 1/2 feet to handle HDH and HCH lines. Packed in cloth bag and aluminum case. All models two-piece. Moderately priced. By Phillipson.

Eponite DeLuxe, made of eponite tubular glass blank, with highest quality guides, ferrules, reel seat, and nylon windings. Two-piece rods in 7 1/2, 8, 8 1/2, and 9 feet. Three-piece rods in 8, 8 1/2, and 9 feet. Fine action in all models. Expensive. By Phillipson.

Perfexion, comes in 5 models from 7 1/2 to 8 1/2 feet and many different actions. All are of finest construction and have splendid action. Most interesting rod of the line is a four-piece, 7 1/2-footer which will fit into a small suitcase. Expensive. By Silaflex.

Medallion, an extraordinarily fine series of fly rods from two-piece, 5 1/2 feet (weighing only 1 1/4 ounces), to a two-piece, 9 1/2-footer. Workmanship and materials are of the best. Extremely expensive. By Silaflex.

Hedliner, tubular glass line of rods in two- and three-piece models from 7 1/2 to 9 feet and in so-called quality. Rods run from inexpensive to medium price. By Heddon.

Mark I, in 5 popular lengths from 7 1/2 to 9 feet and all with "fast tip" action. Rods are handsome, sturdily made. Medium price. By Heddon.

Mark II, beautifully finished models in 4 sizes from 7 1/2 to 9 feet. All metal parts of high quality, rods have fast tip action, specie cork grip. Moderately priced. By Heddon.

Mark III, handsome fly rod in 4 sizes from 7 1/2 to 9 feet with fast tip action. Craftsmanship and all material is high grade. Expensive. By Heddon.

Mark IV, a fine, tubular glass rod with best quality materials and craftsmanship throughout. In 4 sizes from 7 1/2 to 9 feet with fast tip action. Positive reel seat. Expensive. By Heddon.

Airex 191, 193, two-piece rods in 7-foot-4-inch and 8-foot-4-inch lengths, light and medium actions, with high-quality metal parts, tubular glass blanks, and good action. Inexpensive. By Airex.

Airex 194, 195, same as 191 except more elaborate finishing. Inexpensive. By Airex.

Hi-Power Woodsman, tubular glass rod with smooth action. In light and medium actions from 6 3/4 to 8 1/2 feet long, all two-piece, well made, and neatly finished. Expensive. By Horrocks-Ibbotson.

Fly Wonderods, a complete line of fly rods in all actions and many weights and sizes from 6 1/2

to 9 feet. They range from inexpensive to very expensive. All are beautifully made of high-quality materials. DeLuxe and Super DeLuxe models rate with best fly rods available. Available in two- and three-piece models. There's a rod in this line to fit any angling need or any budget. By Shakespeare.

Here is a list of assorted tackle and accessories that many bass fishermen have found useful.

De-Liar, a unique accessory which not only weighs the catch accurately, but measures it by means of a spring-tensioned steel tape. When not in use the De-Liar folds compactly to fit the watch pocket. Two sizes are available, both in green crackle finish. The small De-Liar (Model 208) weighs fish up to 8 pounds and 24 inches long. The large size (Model 228) weighs to 28 pounds and measures to 42 inches. By Langley.

Garcia Mitchell 304 Reel Kit, inexpensive spinning kit without rod.

Pop-Out Net, a collapsible landing net that fits securely in the rod handle. Two new Langley spin rods and two fly rods are equipped with the unique Pop-Out Net.

Collapsible Canvas Boat, handy for pond fishing. Porto Co.

Oxy-Charger Minnow Bucket, holds 10 quarts, galvanized, air pressure chamber charges water. By Old Pal.

Floating Minnow Bucket, holds 8 quarts, floats. By Old Pal.

Air Feeder Minnow Bucket, galvanized with detachable cover. Holds 10 quarts. By Old Pal.

Elevator Minnow Bucket, nonfloating, holds 10 quarts. By Old Pal.

Bait Box, one-piece, seamless steel, leakproof box that fits on the belt, carries any kind of live bait, 6″×3 1/2″×2″ deep. By Old Pal.

Bait Box, kidney-shaped container that fits on belt. By Old Pal.

Fiber Bait Bucket, round fiber container suitable for many kinds of live bait. By Old Pal.

Bait boxes, especially good for worms. Hold 2 quarts, fiber. By Old Pal.

Plastic Spin Kit, unusual locking arrangement makes it possible to open either side. Very handy. By Old Pal.

Pete Henning Tackle Box, corrosion-proof, noiseless, floating, tough tackle box with 3 trays. Dimensions: 15 1/4″×6 1/2″×6 3/4″ deep. By Plano.

Plas-Tak, a fine, small utility or spinning box. By Plano.

Transparent Utility Box. By Plano.

Nylon Fish Stringer, rustless, 100 per cent nylon, durable. By Hamel.

Hook Disgorger, floats, almost unbreakable. By Hamel.

Res-Q-Pak, self-inflating life preserver, size of cigarette pack, clips to belt or clothing. Will support 250 pounds in water. Made by Muter Co., 1255 S. Michigan Ave., Chicago 5, Ill.

Go-Kooler, a feather-light cooler made of Dylite with many uses. Inside dimensions are 11 3/4″× 7 1/4″×9 1/2″. Keeps beer, food cold. Also keeps fish fresh on way home. Also can serve as baitkeeper. Very inexpensive. Also available: a Dylite minnow bucket, both by Weber.

Rod Holders, in clamp-on or screw-on models, excellent to hold extra rods while trolling. By Minton.

Floater-Bubble, excellent device for fishing hard-to-reach waters. Opens up many new places to bass fishermen. By Pueblo Tent and Awning Co., Pueblo, Colo.

Spinning Tackle Box, a sturdy plastic box with removable dividers. By Garcia.

Protective Reel Case, leather bag keeps reel clean. By Garcia.

Tortue Pocket Spool Dispenser, handy for making leaders, tippets, or droppers in the field. By Rockland.

Nimrod Camper Trailer, a light, compact, and sturdy trailer that folds out and provides a camp anywhere in about 10 minutes. Sleeps 4. Excellent for bass fisherman who likes to travel, explore. Canvas "porch" available. Follows well. Moderately priced. By Nimrod Trailer Company, 2530 Spring Grove Ave., Cincinnati, Ohio. Also—it's possible for many fishermen to build similar

camper trailers at home in home workshops at a cost of less than $200. One company even specializes in camper-trailer plans. For $2 they will send you blueprints for a camper-trailer that sleeps 4 and which is very easy to build. Write to *Outdoor Plans,* Box 504, Cincinnati 44, Ohio.

Here's a good outfit for family bass fishing, camping, etc. See Appendix for list of manufacturers.

For float tripping and fishing remote waters, it's often hard to beat a canoe. Aluminum models best by far. Several companies make them. Check Appendix for a list of manufacturers.

Car-top Carrier, an especially handy item for bass fishermen with small boats is car-top carrier. Many efficient models are on the market today.

Dacron dinghy weighing 33 pounds, is excellent for fishing hard-to-reach waters.

Fishing in the Neversink River in New York's Catskills is Harry Wall. Although the Neversink is a fine trout stream, its lower reaches contain smallmouths.

Chapter 13

THE EAST

Even though almost half of the citizens of America live in this small region, not one who ever buys a fishing license is very far from fairly good bass fishing waters. That's even true for residents of the Bronx or of Long Island, of Philadelphia or of Baltimore. Most waters of the East are heavily fished, of course, but still a good bass fisherman can stir up enough action to make a fishing trip worth-while.

Not all waters of the East are heavily fished, though; remote waters still remain in parts of New York, Pennsylvania, and New England. Many streams, especially, aren't subject to much pressure at all—and it's in these places a serious bass angler might concentrate. The results can be amazing.

Pennsylvania

By any standards, this is a fine bass-fishing state. Through the years suburban development, industrial expansion, and pollution have damaged or completely destroyed many waters. Still a bass fisherman doesn't have any trouble finding pure water in which to cast. And perhaps today even the pollution picture shows signs of improvement.

Pennsylvania has some excellent bass rivers—excellent for float tripping. It would sound strange to many sportsmen, but the best of the float-trip rivers in Missouri and Arkansas can't compare to several rivers in the Keystone State from the standpoint of fishing success alone. And they're just about as picturesque too. Consider, for example, typical three-day floats on four rivers—the Allegheny, the Juniata, the North Branch of the Susquehanna, and the Delaware—which anyone can make. And it's worth any outdoorsman's time to try them.

First the Allegheny. The trip begins at Warren with a first night's camp at Tidioute. President is a good place to camp the second night. The trip ends at Franklin about 66 miles downstream—good small-mouth fishing all the way.

The Juniata trip begins at Ryde, just above Lewistown, and runs as far downstream as Granville for the first night's camp. Muskrat Spring near Mexico is a fine site for a second camp, and it's during the second day's run where some of the hottest bass fishing in the state exists. The float ends at Amity Hall, about 55 miles below Ryde.

Many addicted eastern bass fishermen consider the Susquehanna the greatest river on the Atlantic Seaboard, and that's easy to understand. The river winds alternately through fertile farm country and between high palisades that make it accessible for long stretches only by boat. The scene is always changing, and every mile of it is floatable. A three-day North Branch trip can begin at Sayre with a first-night stopover at Towanda. The second-night camp can be pitched at Wyalusing and the trip finally concluded at Mehoopany. Altogether that's 65 miles—or about 22 miles a day.

An old hand at fishing the North Branch is Paul Failor of the Pennsylvania Fish Commission. He's an excellent bass fisherman, and he uses only his own homemade, deerhair floating bugs. One deadly trick he employs is to cast the bug and then allow it to drift downstream parallel to the boat. He doesn't give it much motion, and that may be the main part of the secret—because it certainly produces.

A typical Delaware River float trip can begin at Tighe's Boat Livery above Narrowsburg. The first and second night's camp can be made at Masthope and Pond Eddy. The float ends near Milford.

Even in a lifetime of fishing, a fisherman couldn't adequately explore all the tributaries of these four float-trip rivers. In many cases, the tributaries have even better-looking bass waters than the main streams. One specific example is Raystown Branch of the Juniata, which would excite a bass fisherman anywhere in the world. It's about 50 airline miles from Bedford (on the Pennsylvania Turnpike) to Huntington, but it must be at least three times that mileage by way of stream meandering. Practically the entire distance is through sparsely settled country, over fine riffles and deep green pools. There may be some carrying when water levels are low, but just the same it's one of the best canoe-fishing trips in the land.

Charlie Fox of Carlisle, who wrote one of the first and no doubt the best book on light-bait casting for bass, has a list of favorite bass streams which are certainly worth remembering. In order they are the Conodoguinet near Carlisle, the lower Juniata, the Susquehanna near Harrisburg, the New Cumberland, Highspire, and Goldsboro.

The following is a list by counties of the public bass waters of Pennsylvania.

Adams County
Bermudian Creek, Conewago Creek, Conewago Creek (South Branch), Marsh Creek.

Allegheny County
North Park Lake.

Armstrong County
Allegheny River, Crooked Creek Flood Control Reservoir.

Beaver County
Beaver River (Little North Fork), Brady Run Lake, Brush Creek, Connoquenessing Creek, Raccoon Creek Park Lake.

Bedford County
Bobs Creek, Dunning Creek, Gordon Lake, Raystown Branch Juniata River, Wills Creek.

Berks County
Hopewell Lake, Maiden Creek, Ontelaunee Lake, Swatara Creek (Little), Tulpehocken Creek.

Blair County
Frankstown Branch Juniata River, Williamsburg Dam.

Bradford County
Chemung River, Sugar Creek, Susquehanna River (North Branch), Wesauking Lake.

Bucks County
Bristol Pond, Lehigh Coal & Navigation Company Canal, Neshaminy Creek, Neshaminy Creek (Little), Perkiomen Creek (Northeast Branch), Swamp Creek (East), Tohickon Creek, Warren Lake.

Butler County
Connoquenessing Creek, Glade Run, Harmony-Zelienople Sportsmen's Club Lake, Slippery Rock Creek, Wolf Creek.

Cambria County
Harding Dam on Clearfield Creek.

Cameron County
Driftwood Branch.

Carbon County
Harmony Lake, Tippet Swamp.

Chester County
Brandywine Creek.

Clarion County
Allegheny River, Piney Creek, Red Bank Creek.

Clearfield County
Sabula Dam, Sandy Lick Creek.

Clinton County
Bald Eagle Canal, Bald Eagle Creek, Pine Creek.

Columbia County
Fishing Creek.

Crawford County
Canadohta Lake, Clear Lake, Conneaut Lake, Cussewago Creek, Drakes Dam, French Creek, Oil Creek, Pymatuning Reservoir, Sugar Lake.

Cumberland County
Carlisle Water House Dam, Conodoguinet Creek, Susquehanna River.

Dauphin County
Conewago Creek, Susquehanna River, Wildwood Lake.

Erie County
Conneaut Creek, Edinboro Lake, Erie Lake, French Creek, French Creek (South Branch), LeBoeuf Lake.

Forest County
Allegheny River, Tionesta Flood Control Dam.

Fulton County
Cowans Gap Dam, Licking Creek.

Huntington County
Aughwick Creek, Juniata River, Penn Central Dam, Raystown Branch, Standing Stone Creek.

Indiana County
Yellow Creek.

Jefferson County
Red Bank Creek.

Juniata County
Juniata River, Tuscarora Creek.

Lackawanna County
Baylors Pond, Chapman's Lake, Crystal Lake, Deer Lake, Handsome Lake, Newton Lake, Sheridan Lake, Susquehanna River (North Branch).

Lancaster County
Chickies Creek (Big), Chickies Creek (Little), Cocalico Creek, Conestoga Creek, Conowingo Dam, Holtwood Dam, Middle Creek.

Lawrence County
Beaver River (Little, North Fork), Neshannock Creek, Slippery Rock Creek.

Lebanon County
Stracks Dam, Swatara Creek (Little).

Lycoming County
Loyalsock Creek, Lycoming Creek, Pine Creek.

McKean County
Oswayo Creek.

Mercer County
French Creek, Neshannock Creek, Pymatuning Creek, Sandy Creek, Sandy Lake, Shenango River, Shenango River (Little), Wolf Creek.

Mifflin County
Juniata River.

Monroe County
Bradys Pond, Delaware River, Mill Pond No. 1, Naomi Lake, Pocono Summit Lake.

Montgomery County
Macoby Creek, Perkiomen Creek, Perkiomen Creek (Northeast Branch), Perkiomen Creek (Northwest Branch), Ridge Valley Creek, Skippack Creek, Swamp Creek (West).

Montour County
Chilisquaque Creek.

Northampton County
Delaware River.

Northumberland County
Chilisquaque Creek.

Perry County
Buffalo Creek, Juniata River, Shermans Creek, Susquehanna River.

Pike County
Big Tink Pond, Delaware River, Fairview Lake, Pecks Pond, Promise Land Pond, Twin Lakes, Wallenpaupack Lake, White Deer Lake.

Potter County
Oswayo Creek.

Schuylkill County
Sweet Arrow Lake.

Snyder County
Mahantango Creek, Middle Creek, Penns Creek, Pennsylvania Power & Light Company Dam.

Somerset County
Cranberry Glade Lake, Laurel Hill Creek Dam, Youghiogheny Flood Control Reservoir.

Susquehanna County
Comforts Pond, East Lake, Elk Lake (Big), Fiddle Lake, Forest Lake, Fox Pond, Heart Lake, Laurel Lake, Middle Lake, Montrose Lake, Page Lake, Quaker Lake, Susquehanna River (North Branch), Tingley Lake, Upper Lake, Wrighters Lake.

Union County
Buffalo Creek, Laurel Park Dam, Millmont Dam, New Berlin Dam, Penns Creek, White Deer Hole Creek.

Venango County
Allegheny River, French Creek.

Warren County
Allegheny River, Chapman Dam, Conewango Creek.

Washington County
Buffalo Creek, Chartiers Creek (Little), Little Chartiers Creek Dam, Ten Mile Creek, Wheeling Creek (Enslow Fork).

Wayne County

Beach Lake, Como Lake, Coxtown Lake, Delaware River, Elk Lake, Hickory Lake (Little), Keens Pond, Long Pond, Sly Lake, Woods Pond (Upper).

Westmoreland County

Bridgeport Dam, Keystone Coal & Coke Company Reservoir.

Wyoming County

Carey Lake, Chamberlin Pond, Mud Pond, Oxbow Lake, Susquehanna River (North Branch), Tunkhannock Creek, Winola Lake.

York County

Bermudian Creek, Conewago Creek, Conewago Creek (Little), Susquehanna River.

Maryland

This is an eastern state with considerable fishing pressure—but which still contains good bass waters. The Potomac, which flows from Hancock to Washington D.C., is one of these. Although fishermen are usually numerous all through the season, it is beautiful smallmouth water. A list of Maryland's principal bass waters follows.

Deep Creek Lake, 3900 acres near Thayersville, has a good bass population, but they are hard to catch. A good "challenge" lake for the most serious anglers.

Herrington Lake (near Oakland).

Tridelphia Reservoir (near Brighton).

Pretty Boy Reservoir (near Hereford).

Loch Raven Reservoir (near Towson), another lake with bass which are sometimes hard to catch in any numbers. Few lunkers taken here occasionally by jigging.

Conowingo Dam (near Conowingo).

Garland Lake (near Denton).

Linchester Lake (near Preston).

Smithville Lake (near Smithville).

Wye Pond (near Wye Mills).

Add also the following rivers which contain smallmouths: Casselman River near Grantsville, Savage River near Bloomington, Beaver Creek near Hagerstown, Octoraro Creek near Richardsmere, Deer Creek in Harford County.

Also, on the Delamarva Peninsula (which separates Chesapeake Bay from the Atlantic and which includes parts of Delaware and Virginia as well as Maryland) are about 50 ponds which range from public to semiprivate to private. All offer pretty fair bass fishing, especially bass bugging, in settings with a southern accent. Motors not allowed on most of these. Boats available for rent on only a few. Accommodations are numerous in the region, especially around Salisbury.

Maine

Half a century ago there were no bass in Maine, but today smallmouths are well established in over 300 lakes. They're more than established, really, because now Maine must rank with the best smallmouth fishing regions in the world. Not only are the bronzebacks plentiful, but enough 6-pounders are taken each year to add a flavor of trophy collecting.

Bass fishing here begins in June, is excellent all through the month, and although it falls off remains fairly good all through the summer. The premium fishing is with fly rod and bugs in early June. Later on it's a case of using live bait or jigging. In August, trolling is often very successful.

Following is a roundup of outstanding Maine smallmouth waters, listed by regions of watersheds.

Grand Lakes and Schoodic Region: This region covers the two counties of Hancock and Washington, an area comparable to that of the states of Rhode Island and Connecticut.

It is a region that is in part easily accessible, while another part is composed of wild lands that are a network of lakes, ponds, rivers, streams, and brooks. Much of this territory is not fished extensively. Fishing throughout the region is very good. The angler who wishes to "discover" new waters will find this area to his liking.

Grand Lake is one of the original homes of the landlocked salmon, but curiously enough, Big Lake, the lake it empties into, is one of the best smallmouth waters in the world.

Among other waters in the area are Junior Lake, Sysladobsis, East and West Musquash Lakes, Little River, Rolfe Brook, Little and Big Walmatogue Streams, Clifford Stream, Scotch Brook, Amazon Stream, and Otter Brook.

A little to the south are the Meddybemps, Cathance Lake, Rocky Pond, and numerous other lakes, ponds, brooks, rivers, and streams. To the west is Nicatous Lake and the Machias Lakes. To the north Spednic Lake, in the Schoodic Chain, is a 23-mile-long body of water that is rated as one of the best of all bass lakes.

Milo-Enfield-Lincoln Region: This region lies just west of the Grand Lake region.

From Enfield, on Route 2 from Bangor, the angler will find Cold Stream Pond, one of the state's most beautiful bodies of water, and an excellent fishing center. A little over 20 miles away is Lake Nicatous, and the region is dotted with numerous smaller ponds which contain bass.

From Milo the angler is but a few miles from Schoodic Lake, famed for bass, Seboeis Lake, and Endless Lake.

Accommodations in the region are excellent. Guides are available throughout the area.

Bangor Region: Radiating from Bangor like spokes from the hub of a wheel are many roads that lead to truly fine fishing waters, most of which are within an hour's drive or so of the Queen City.

On U. S. Route 2, between Bangor and Ellsworth, 28 miles away, are Phillips Lake, also known as Lucerne-in-Maine, Green Lake, Branch Pond, and Graham Lake.

On Route 9 from Bangor are Chemo Pond, Floods Pond, Beech Hill Pond, Molasses Pond, Webb Pond, and numerous other smaller bodies of water affording excellent fishing for bass early in the year.

On Route 15 from Bangor, in the vicinity of Bucksport, 18 miles away, is another group of excellent lakes including Toddy Pond and Lake Alamoosook.

Near Orono, and about 12 miles from Bangor on Route 2, is Pushaw Pond, noted especially for bass fishing.

In fishing this region the sportsman can make his headquarters at Bangor or can obtain excellent accommodations at the various lakes or in the small towns and cities in the vicinity.

Belgrade Lakes Region: This is one of the more compact areas in Maine. By that it is meant that the various lakes in the region are comparatively close to one another, making it extremely easy for the angler to go from one to the other.

The Belgrade region has long been noted for its extremely fine smallmouth bass fishing. In the Belgrade Chain are six lakes: North, East, Great, Long, Salmon, and Messalonskee.

Excellent roads encompass this chain of lakes and accommodations for the angler and summer visitor are excellent.

Kennebec Lakes Region: This is an interesting region that furnishes excellent smallmouth bass fishing in the spring.

In the center of the region lie Cobbosseecontee, Maranacook, Little Cobbosseecontee, and Annabessacook Lakes. Nearby, near Wayne, are Androscoggin and Pocasset lakes. A long chain of smaller lakes affording very fine bass fishing extends through the towns of Readfield, Fayette, and Mount Vernon.

East of the Kennebec, but still a part of this general region, are a series of good fishing waters extending down to the coast. Some of these waters, well known to the angler, are Webber Pond, Three Mile Pond, China Lake, Palermo Pond, Damariscotta Lake, Biscay Pond, St. Georges Pond, Megunticook Lake, and Pemaquid Pond.

Excellent roads and a multitude of sporting camps and hotels dot this area.

Sebago Lake, Long Lake, and Oxford County Region: Sebago Lake, the second largest lake in Maine, is the central point for this region that encompasses a great part of southern Maine. During the summer fine bass fishing is to be had here. What is true of Sebago is, in general, also true of the many other bodies of water that make up the region.

To the north, connected to Sebago by the beautiful Songo River, is Long Lake. In the same region are Brandy Pond, Highland Lake, Woods Pond, Crystal Lake, Thomas Pond, Lake Pennesseewassee, and Moose Pond. A few miles to the west of Sebago is Peabody Pond and Hancock Pond. Toward the east is Panther Pond and Little Sebago. Toward the northwest is beautiful Lake Kezar, a jewel of a lake, nestled in the foothills of the White Mountains. South of Sebago, in York County, lie Bunganut, Crystal, Kennebunk, and Mousam. This region is characterized by a wealth of fine accommodations for the sportsman and vacationer.

It can't be overemphasized that Maine is particularly well suited and ready for handling the visiting bass fisherman. For example, there are over 3000 skilled guides available. License fees are reasonable. And the country is very beautiful.

New York

To the bass fisherman who thinks of New York as Times Square or the steel-and-concrete jungle of Manhattan, a great surprise is in store, because this is a state with more outdoor opportunities than any citizen could explore in several lifetimes. It's a particularly picturesque state in which to go fishing, too, no matter whether it's in the glens and tilled valleys of the Finger Lakes region, in the green and blue Thousand Islands, or in the cool and lonely Adirondacks. There's fishing variety here and there is an abundance of fishing here, but the competition for it sometimes is keen.

Closest to New York City, there is some bass fishing in the Catskills, as for smallmouths in the Delaware River from Deposit to Port Jervis. The lower East Branch of the Delaware has bass and so does the lower Neversink River, which is better known for trout.

Reservoirs of the New York City water-supply system contain bass and are fishable. Among these are the Croton reservoirs between Peekskill and Mt. Kisco, Kensico at the edge of White Plains, and Ashokan west of Kingston. Across the Hudson in Palisades Interstate Park in Orange County are quite a number of small lakes which offer a limited amount of bass fishing. The bass are there, but they're sophisticated. Other bass ponds are located near Oneonta in the Gilbert Lake and Catskill State parks. Add also Gilboa Reservoir on the Schoharie River near Grand Gorge. State parks with fishing waters in Duchess, Columbia and Rensselaer counties include Clarence Fahnestock, Tagkanic, and Tatonic lakes.

The Adirondack highlands which sprawl across the upper eastern third of the state contain some 1500 lakes and ponds of various sizes. Some have trout, some have bass, some have both. And because of continuing fish-management work, the content is always changing.

Lake Champlain has many resorts, boat liveries, and other facilities—as well as better than average smallmouth fishing. Lake George is a good spot too. Sacandaga Reservoir on the Hudson and Sacandaga rivers produced the world's record northern pike, but not so well known is that 10-pound largemouths occasionally are caught here. It's one of the very best bets in the East for a trophy-hunting bass fisherman. And there are other bass-fishing holes in the upper Hudson Valley. Above Riparius, for example, is Schroon Lake and its smallmouths.

There is also scattered but not especially productive smallmouth fishing in the Saranac Lakes region. Much better is Long Lake, a widening in the Raquette River.

The St. Lawrence Valley contains some of the best smallmouth waters in the East. Fishing is the fastest in the Thousand Islands area and then westward into Lake Ontario beyond Cape Vincent. Watertown is an access point to the Thousand Islands. So are Alexandria Bay and Clayton.

There's superb smallmouth fishing in quite a few smaller rivers hereabout, as well as in Black Lake. The rivers include the Indian and Oswegatchie, the Grass and Raquette rivers near Massena, the St. Regis near Hogansburg and the Salmon near Malone, and the Chazy River, which flows into Lake Champlain near Chazy.

Western New York has a vast wealth of bass waters too. Besides Lake Ontario and Erie, its principal waters are the Finger Lakes. All of the Fingers—Skaneateles, Otisco, Owasco, Cayuga, Seneca, Keuka, Canandaigua, Honeoye, Canadice, and Conesus—contain an extraordinary variety of game fishes, including bass. Probably Cayuga, Canandaigua, and Honeoye are the best for bass, however. Much trolling for bass is done in the Finger Lakes. It's possible that jigging would also pay off handsomely.

Lake Oneida near Oneida has smallmouths with curious migrating habits—so it's either feast or famine fishing. Delta Reservoir near Rome also has a few bass. Add also Canadarago Lake near Richfield Springs and Otsego Lake at Cooperstown for smallmouths.

The Niagara River from Buffalo past Niagara Falls to Lake Ontario is excellent for smallmouths. Chantanqua Lake has both largemouths and smallmouths in quantity. And river anglers in western New York frequent the Allegheny near Olean and Salamanca; the Tioga, Canisteo, and Cohocton in the general vicinity of Corning. The Genesee is a good bass river in Allegheny County; float tripping is a possibility.

A bass fisherman can even find suitable waters on Long Island. Lake Ronkonkoma (50 miles from New York City) may be the best bet; it contains largemouths. Artist Lake, between Middle Island and Ridge, Canaan Lake, and Fort Pond also have largemouths. In addition, a prospecting bass fisherman can find dozens of smaller but productive ponds from Mineola almost all the way to Montauk.

New Jersey

Through the years, because of a high and always-expanding population, New Jersey has been in the unenviable position of squeezing the most from every acre/foot of inland fishing water. Most of its ponds and lakes contain bass, but the number of fishermen is extremely high. Still, a good bass fisherman can find plenty of sport here—by trying new methods and new lures, by probing deep waters, and often by fishing at night when the crowds have departed. Frequently he'll be surprised by catching especially large largemouths.

Largest natural lake in the state is Hopatcong a few miles northwest of Dover. Cottages and resorts, docks and amusement parks virtually "consume" its entire 40-mile shore line. But in recent seasons several 8-pound bass have been taken, nearly all of them after dark.

Most of Jersey's lakes and ponds are located in Sussex, Morris, Warren, and Passaic counties. Much of this land is state-owned because a farsighted policy has permitted the state to acquire recreational properties at a much faster rate than most other states. One of the largest state-owned areas is the Stokes State Forest in northern Sussex County. It contains some bass fishing.

Culvers, Owassa, and Kittatinny lakes, Swartswood Lake in Swartswood State Park contain bass. So does the Wallkill River (eastern Sussex County) and Lake Mohawk at Sparta.

There's good smallmouth fishing in the Delaware River from the northwestern corner of New Jersey to Phillipsburg, with good wading most of the way. At Delaware Water Gap it's especially scenic, but below Phillipsburg it's polluted.

Greenwood Lake in Passaic County has bass. There's also bass fishing in Ramapo Lake, Pompton Lakes, and the Pompton River. Musconetcong Lake above Stanhope, Budd Lake between Hackettstown and Netcong, and Mountain Lake in the Jenny Jump State Forest can be fished.

The southern half of New Jersey is flat, and nearly all of its slow-moving rivers which are not polluted contain bass. The Millstone River and Cranberry Brook east of Princeton are good. Also, many streams which drain into Delaware Bay have largemouths in the brackish fringes where fresh water joins the salt. Some of these streams are the Navesink near Red Bank; Manasquan, Toms River and its branches; Mullica and Wading rivers north of Atlantic City; Great Egg and Tuckahoe rivers upstream from Somers Point; Maurice River downstream, from Millville; Cohansey Creek outside of Bridgeton; Salem Creek above Salem; Oldmans Creek above Harrisonville.

New Hampshire

Cool, green, and beautiful, New Hampshire's lofty mountains, rolling hills, valleys, and pasture lands form a scenic setting for some 1300 lakes and ponds and hundreds of miles of brooks and rivers. Deep forests of mixed conifers and hardwoods and high altitude help to condition both air and water, maintaining good temperatures for fun and fishing.

There are well over a hundred lakes and large ponds where the smallmouth bass is king. Thanks to the ideal environment and modern fish management and stocking practices, New Hampshire has an astonishing variety of good fishing possibilities packed into a comparatively small area.

The Granite State is also rich in the "extras"—the things tangible and intangible that add to a memorable fishing vacation. For centuries anglers have declared that "there is much more to fishing than the mere catching of fish," and maybe the truth of this saying accounts for New Hampshire's popularity with disciples of Izaak Walton down through the years. Not the least of the "tangibles" is the hospitality of an experienced host who provides good meals and the comfortable bed that completes the fishing day.

With today's trend to family travel, you see more husband-and-wife fishing teams and more youngsters at the fishing spots. New Hampshire is a "natural" when the whole family wants to go. And if some of the members don't care to fish, there is usually a wide variety of other forms of sport and entertainment close at hand. The scenery and the historic points of interest are always available, of course, and by Memorial Day, May 30, most of the popular roadside tourist attractions have opened their doors.

In the White Mountains zone, the Connecticut River along the western boundary has smallmouths. So do the following: Armington Lake near Piermont; Upper and Lower Baker ponds near Orford; Burns Pond near Whitfield; Tarleton Lake near Piermont.

Stretching across the state, just south of the White Mountains, lies a belt of lakes and ponds that offers variety of fishing from one end of the season to the other—from Sunapee and Mascoma on the west, to Ossipee and Province Lake on the east. Combined, the five largest lakes in this section—Winnipesaukee, Squam, Newfound, Winnisquam, and Sunapee— have well over a hundred square miles of water surface. All have bass except Newfound. Fishing begins on July 1.

Though many of the larger hostelries wait until later in the season, each of these lakes has a number of inns, hotels, motels, and cabin establishments that open their doors as soon as the ice is out. There are boat liveries and launching places, bait and tackle dealers, and guides.

The section is also well supplied with smaller lakes and ponds, some accessible by good roads, others reached by hiking.

In the northwestern part of this section Lake Wentworth and the "border lakes" to the east of Wolfeboro are best known for their bass. Merrymeeting Lake, New Durham, Mascoma Lake, Enfield, Pleasant Lake, New London have bass.

Following are a list of bass waters in the central part of the state:

Blaisdell Lake, Bradley Lake, Cooks Pond, Crescent Lake, Crystal Lake, Crystal Lake, Grafton Pond, Great East Lake, Guiena Pond, Halfmoon Lake, Highland Lake, Kanasatka Lake, Kezar Lake, Knights Pond, Knowles Pond, Kolelemook

Lake, Kusumpe Pond, Lovell Lake, Mirror Lake, Perkins Pond, Places Pond (Sunset Lake), Post Pond, Province Lake, Rust Pond, Silver Lake, Waukewan Lake, Webster Lake, Whitton Pond, Wickwas Pond, Winona Lake.

In spite of its nearness to large centers of population, the southern part of New Hampshire offers an impressive array of fishing waters. Bass are plentiful and offer good sport during the entire summer.

Bass fishermen should not overlook the Ashuelot River between Marlow and Keene; or the Contoocook River from Bennington to Penacook. Although the Merrimack and Connecticut rivers are somewhat polluted, they hold some hefty bass.

A list of southern New Hampshire bass waters follows:

Ashuelot Pond, Ayers Pond, Beaver Lake, Bow Lake, Chesham Pond, Cole Pond (Crescent Lake), Connecticut River (lower part), Contoocook Lake, Contoocook River, Country Pond, Crooked Pond, Frost Pond, Gilmore Pond, Gould Pond, Gregg Lake, Halfmoon Pond, Harvey Lake, Haunted Lake, Highland Lake, Hubbard Pond, Hunts Pond, Island Pond (near Atkinson), Island Pond (near Washington), Jenness Pond, Massabesic Lake, Massasecum Lake, Mendums Pond, Merrimack River, North River Pond, Northwood Lake, Norway Pond, Otter Lake, Pawtuckaway Lake, Phillips Pond, Pleasant Pond, Pleasant Pond, Robinson Pond, Shattuck Pond, Spofford Lake, Suncook Lakes, Thorndike Pond, Willard Pond, Willey Ponds, Winnipocket Lake.

New Hampshire's clear, cool lakes produce classy smallmouths of good size, superior quality, and excellent fighting ability. Although a few anglers prefer to troll, most fishermen take their bass by casting or by still-fishing with live bait. Favorite streamer flies include Micky Finn, red and white bucktail, dark tiger, wardens worry, white marabou, etc. A large brown hackle or bright yellow wet fly sometimes works well. Surface fly-rod bugs of deerhair, or the "popping" cork variety, are excellent at twilight during the summer season, and will lure bass up to 5 pounds or more.

Vermont

This scenically attractive state contains some good bass fishing in spite of its proximity to the eastern centers of population. The fact is, it's invaded by thousands of out-of-state anglers every year and many of them have at least fair success. In many lakes Vermont bass are as cagey as the local citizens,

and it takes some skill to catch them in numbers. A fisherman's best bet, though, is in early October when the smallmouths seem to be the most active of the entire season. There isn't much fishing pressure then, and the color and atmosphere of autumn are magnificent.

Some of the best Vermont fishing is in border waters—in Lake Champlain on the west and the Connecticut River on the east. Both have smallmouths. The Missisquoi River from Richford to Swanton has smallmouths, and below Swanton largemouths begin to appear. Lake Carmi east of Franklin and Fairfield Pond northeast of Albans also have bass.

Add also these waters for bass, mostly smallmouths: the lower reaches of the Lamoille and Winooski rivers; Hinesburg Pond near Hinesburg; Shelburne Pond east of Shelburne, Hosmer Ponds near Lowell; Seymour Lake near Morgan; Wallis Lake near Averill; Lake Groton between Groton and Marshfield; Fairlee and Morey lakes near Ely; the West River between West Drummerston and Brattleboro; Little Otter Creek near Lake Champlain; lakes Bomoseen, Hortonia, and St. Catherine in Rutland County.

Connecticut

This state isn't a promised land for bass fishermen, because it's extremely crowded; fishing waters aren't too plentiful, and fishing pressure is heavy. There's also the ugly matter of pollution in many streams that would otherwise contain good fishing.

A fairly complete list of the best bass-fishing waters would include the following: Wood Creek Pond and Toby Pond near Norfolk; Wononkapook Pond south of Wononskopomuc and Mudge Pond (for largemouths) below Wononkapook in the Berkshires; Tyler Pond west of Goshen; Spectacle Lakes and Hatch Pond east of Kent; Lake Waramaug near New Preston; Bantam Lake between Bantam and Lakeside; Black Rock Pond southwest of Thomaston; Winnemaug Lake near Watertown; Big Candlewood Lake (largest in the state with 6000 acres) near Brookfield; Zoar Lake at Sheldon; Trumbull Reservoir and Beardsley Park Pond near Bridgeport; Black Pond and Beseck Lake near Meriden; Cedar Swamp Pond south of Bristol; Highland Lake southwest of Winsted; Shenipsit Lake between Tolland and Ellington; Bolton Notch Pond and Willimantic Reservoir near Bolton; Wamgumbaug Lake and Columbia Lake near Willimantic; the group of ponds north of Colchester;

Terramuggus and Pocotopaug lakes above East Hampton; Shaw, Pickerel, Basham, and Moodus lakes near Moodus; Gardner's Lake west of Norwich; Powers, Pataganset, and Rogers lakes; Mashapaug northeast of Stafford Springs; Roseland and Alexander lakes near Putnam; Quandsick Reservoir; Long Pond between Old Mystic and North Stonington.

Massachusetts

This is another heavily populated state with some fishing waters but with only fair bass fishing at best. The best fishing often is in privately owned ponds, many of which can be entered by contacting the owner and/or paying a small fee. Most rivers are too polluted for bass fishing.

Berkshire County has more than the state average amount of bass water. Best spots are Lake Potoosuc and Richmond Pond. Other bass waters include: Hoosac Reservoir; Garfield Lake east of Great Barrington; Otis Reservoir and Big Pond just to the north; Lake Mahkeenac; Creenwater, Yokum, Center and Goose ponds southeast of Lee; Ashmere Lake near Dalton; Burnett Pond east of Adams; Lake Wickapoag and other small ponds in Worcester County; Quinsigamond Lake near Worcester; ponds of Myles Standish State Forest near Plymouth.

Rhode Island

This state is not of much consequence as a bass-fishing region. The best sport is available in small ponds where permission to fish must be obtained. There are quite a few "company" ponds and reservoirs built primarily for power- or water-supply purposes. Nearly all of these are open to fishing too.

Delaware

Only a very limited amount of bass fishing is available in Delaware. The ponds of the Delamarva Peninsula have been described in the Maryland section of this chapter.

Chapter 14

THE MIDWEST

Farm ponds throughout the Midwest are natural bass reservoirs. Bass ponds such as this one abound in Ohio.

Outside of the Southeast, which is the land of both the largest bass and the most bass, a fisherman's best bet lies in the Midwest. This is a fertile region, generally, with an abundance of both natural and man-made waters. The man-made waters, usually large water-supply reservoirs, are located close to the centers of population. And the natural waters become more numerous the farther north you travel.

This is also the region of the Great Lakes; at least it shares the Great Lakes with Canada. But in any case, these are the best smallmouth fishing holes in the world. Smallmouths grow larger in a few southern reservoirs, but the numbers of them can't possibly approach the Great Lakes.

No matter where he lives, though, or no matter where he's traveling through the Midwest, an angler is never far from good bass-fishing waters. And in no other region, anywhere, are accommodations so numerous. That includes everything from motels to tackle shops, bait stores and boat docks, to the thousands of outfitters or camp owners from Missouri to Minnesota who cater to bass fishermen alone.

Ohio

Sometimes it's hard to imagine, when passing through Ohio on high-speed turnpikes, that this is a good bass-fishing state. It's good even though it's among the most intensively developed, farmed, industrialized, and most heavily populated of all states. Ohio ranks fifth in population, but only thirty-sixth in size. There are 8 million resident fishermen.

Today there is ten times the amount of impounded water that existed in primitive times, thanks to a vast network of lakes built for flood control, recreation, water supply, industrial supply, or for a combination of these. There is a fine network of rivers, too, but far too many of these have been badly polluted and, it seems, unnecessarily so. Once Ohio had the most progressive conservation bureau in the country (complete liberalized fishing started here; no closed seasons, no bag limits, no legal lengths on any fish) and considerable pollution-abatement work was under way. But in the past few years politics has changed all that, and wildlife conservation in Ohio is on a swift downgrade. Perhaps pressure from sportsmen can effect a change.

Here follows a list of Ohio's public fishing lakes. Accommodations of all types exist on or very near to every one of them. Detailed maps of all of them are available from the Division of Wildlife. Maps show underwater contours, stump areas, channels, locations of roads, dock, concessions, launching sites.

Adams Lake (Adams Co.).

Allen Lake (Hardin Co.).

Atwood Lake (Carroll, Tuscarawas Co.).

Bass Islands Area (Ottawa Co.). This is one of best smallmouth areas in America. Best time is May or June, but actually good all summer. Put-in-Bay is center of operations. Outstanding area for sportsmen.

Bellevue Reservoirs 1, 2, 3, 4 (Huron Co.).

Bellevue Reservoir 5 (Huron Co.).

Berlin Reservoir (Stark, Mahoning, Portage Co.).
Blue Rock (Muskingum Co.).
Brush Lake (Champaign Co.).
Buckeye Lake (Fairfield, Perry, Licking Co.). Good in early spring.
Burr Oak Lake (Morgan, Athens Co.). Probably best bet for big largemouths.
Caldwell, Stewart Hollow Lakes (Ross Co.).
Charles Mill Reservoir (Richland, Ashland Co.).
Chippewa Lake (Medina Co.).
Clearfork Reservoir (Morrow, Richland Co.).
Clendening Lake (Harrison Co.).
Clouse Lake (Perry Co.).
Clyde City Reservoir (Sandusky Co.).
Cowan Lake (Clinton Co.).
Decker Lake (Miami Co.).
Delaware Reservoir (Delaware Co.). Has very *good* fishing and is not too heavily fished by bass anglers.
Delta Lake (Fulton Co.).
East Harbor (Ottawa Co.). Excellent in May but slumps thereafter.
Echo Lake (Miami Co.).
Erie Lake (Ottawa, Erie Co.).
Findlay Reservoir (Hancock Co.).
Findley Forest Lake (Lorain Co.).
Forked Run Lake (Meigs Co.).
Grant Lake (Brown Co.).
Guilford Lake (Columbiana Co.).
Hargus Creek (Pickaway Co.).
Harrison Lake (Fulton Co.).
Hocking Lake (Hocking Co.).
Hoover Reservoir (Franklin, Delaware Co.). Plenty bass, but not too many bass fishermen here.
Hope Lake (Vinton Co.). Good camping area here.
Hosterman Lake (Clark Co.).
Indian Lake (Logan Co.). Good in April, May.
Jackson Lake (Jackson Co.).
Jefferson Lake (Jefferson Co.).
Kelleys Island Area (Erie Co.).
Kiser Lake (Champaign Co.).
Knox Lake (Knox Co.).
Lake Park (Mahoning Co.).
Leesville Lake (Carroll Co.).
Loramie Lake (Shelby, Auglaize Co.).
Lost Creek Reservoir (Allen Co.).
Madison Lake (Madison Co.).
Metzger Lake (Allen Co.).
Milton Lake (Mahoning Co.)
Mogadore Reservoir (Portage Co.).
Mosquito Reservoir (Trumbull Co.). Excellent spring bass fishing in large stump areas.
Mt. Gilead Lakes (Morrow Co.).

Neers Pond (Champaign Co.).
Nettle Lake (Williams Co.).
Nimisila Reservoir (Summit Co.).
Oxbow Lake (Defiance Co.).
Piedmont Lake (Belmont, Guernsey, Harrison Co.).
Pine Lake (Ross Co.).
Pleasant Hill Reservoir (Richland, Ashland Co.).
Portage Lakes (Summit Co.). Plenty good bass here, but requires very skillful angler. Good in fall.
Punderson Lake (Geauga Co).
Pymatuning Reservoir (Ashtabula Co.).
Richwood Lake (Union Co.).
Rocky Fork Lake (Highland Co.).
Roosevelt Lake (Scioto Co.). Good camping nearby.
Sandusky Bay Area (Ottawa, Erie, Sandusky Co.).
Schoonover Lake (Allen Co.).
Seneca Lake (Guernsey, Noble Co.).
Spring Valley (Greene, Warren Co.).
St. Marys Lake (Mercer Co.).
Stonelick Lake (Clermont Co.).
Swift Run Lake (Miami Co.).
Tappan Lake (Harrison Co.).
Van Buren Lake (Hancock Co.).
Van Wert Reservoir (Van Wert Co.).
Vesuvius Lake (Lawrence Co.). Excellent camping facilities here.
Veto Lake (Washington Co.).
White Lake (Pike Co.).
Zepernick Lake (Columbiana Co.).
Ohio's best bass streams would include the following:

Northeastern Ohio

Maumee River (especially Maumee Rapids above Toledo area for smallmouths; Tiffin, Auglaize, and Blanchard rivers. Sandusky River from Old Fort to Upper Sandusky is good too. Add also the Huron and Vermilion rivers near Norwalk in early spring.

Northwestern Ohio

Best bets are the Grand River (Ashtabula County) and the Chagrin in Geauga County. The Grand can be float tripped.

Central Ohio

This is probably Ohio's best region for stream smallmouth fishing. Good waters include Big and Little Darby, Big Walnut, Whetstone, Deer and Blacklick creeks. Also the Olentangy and Licking rivers. The Kokosing and Mohican rivers are extremely fine float-trip rivers, with good camp sites along the way.

Southeastern Ohio

The Muskingum River, plus such tributaries as Wills Creek, Tuscarawas and Walhonding rivers, has bass fishing which is either very good or very bad. It's a matter of season and locating fish. Add also Leading Creek and Shade River in Meigs County; Symmes and Indian Guyan creeks in Lawrence County, Hocking River above Athens.

Southwestern Ohio

Best are Stonelick Creek, East Fork of Little Miami River, Todd Fork, White Oak Creek, Caesar Creek, Rattlesnake Creek (terrific at times), Compton Creek, Rocky Fork Creek below Rocky Fork Lake, Sunfish Creek (for spotted bass) in Pike County, and Paint Creek.

Minnesota

It would be almost impossible to list all the lakes in this land of sky-blue waters which contain either largemouth or smallmouth bass. There are thousands of them. It's even difficult to list all the rivers. This point is certain, though; the entire state is splendid fishing country.

Equally difficult would be the task of selecting Minnesota's *best* bass-fishing waters—but probably the nod must go to the Mississippi for its full length, but mostly upstream from the Twin Cities. It contains unlimited bass fishing, and to get the details is simply to stop in any tackle store or to contact any crossroads "expert" along the way.

There is also premium bass fishing in many lakes of the Quetico-Superior wilderness up along the border near Ely. Basswood Lake is great in springtime, and other, more remote lakes are "hot" all through the summer. Typical of these is McNaught Lake (actually in Ontario) near Ely. This Quetico-Superior country is completely roadless and wild. To fish there is to go by canoe. Outfitters like Bill Rom of Canoe Country Outfitters in Ely can completely arrange trips of any length or duration. He rents everything from canoes and car-top carriers, to tents, food for a planned daily menu, sleeping bags, utensils and even waterproof route maps of the country. There's great adventure here as well as great bass fishing.

Other lakes most often considered among the best in Minnesota include Bad Medicine, Brule, East Bearskin, Greenwood, Little Vermilion, Loon, Rainy, Saganaga, Turtle, all in the northern half of the state. Other lakes which offer at least fair bass fishing are listed as follows, according to general locality.

Grand Marais Area

Caribou Lake, Pike Lake, Mink Lake, Kimball Lake, Devils Track Lake.

Gunflint Trail Area

Hungry Jack Lake, Poplar Lake, Winchell Lake, Brule Lake, Crab Lake, Iron Lake, Round Lake, John Lake, Tom Lake, Gunflint Lake, Saganaga Lake, Ottertrack or Cypress Lake, Knife Lake, Basswood Lake.

Ely-Tower Area

Wolf Lake, Armstrong Lake, Bass Lake, Clear Lake, Battle Lake, Six Mile Lake, Lake Vermillion, Crab Lake, Farm Lake, Moose Lake, Ensign Lake, Basswood Lake, Bear Island Lake, Everett Lake, Twin Lakes, Little Long Lake, Big Lake, Mitchell Lake, Phiffer Lake, Bear Head Lake, Schalam Lake, Camp Lake.

Whiteface River-Alden Lake Area

Alden Lake, Pequaywan Lake, White Lake or Bates Lake, Wolf Lake, Greenwood Lake, Bars Lake, Island Lake, Cadotte Lake.

Cloquet Area

Floodwood Lake, Island Lake, Janet Lake, St. Louis River, Whiteface River, Pike Lake, Caribou Lake, Big Grand Lake, Little Grand Lake, Martin Lake, Long Lake.

Cotton-Central Lakes Area

East and West Bass Lakes, Dodo Lake, Elora Lake, Fig Lake, Murphy Lake.

Finland Area

Lax Lake, Crooked Lake.

Two Harbors Area

Stewart Lake, Thomas Lake.

Hibbing-Virginia-Biwabik Area

Eskquagama Lake, Wynne Lake, Merritt Lake, Crooked Lake, Fig Lake, Murphy Lake, Long Lake, Auto Club Lake, Clear Lake, Lake 14, Lake Leander, Hobson Lake, Dewey Lake, Long Lake, Harriet Lake, Moran Lake, Island Lake, Whitewater Lake, St. Louis River, Kendall Lake, Hacnke Lake, Little Sand, Paradise Lake, Crystal Lake, Island Lake, Beauty Lake, Sand Lake.

Deer River-Grand Rapids-Nashwauk Area

Ball Club Lake, Bass Lake, Bowstring Lake, Cut Foot Sioux Lake, Deer Lake, North Star Lake, Caribou Lake, Grave Lake, Sand Lake, Spider Lake, Merry Lake, Trout Lake, Wabana Lake, Deer Lake, Prairie Lake, Rice Lake, Sugar Lake, Pokegama Lake, Swan Lake, Buck Lake, Wasson Lake.

International Falls-Little Fork-Orr Area

Rainy Lake, Jeanette Lake.

Cook Area

Elbow Lake, Vermilion Lake, Phiffer Lake, Winchester Lake.

Baudette-Lake of the Woods-Northwest Angle Area

Lake of the Woods, Northwest Angle.

Red Lake-Blackduck Area

Blackduck Lake, Turtle River, Rabideau Lake, North Twin Lake, South Twin Lake, Gull Lake.

Bemidji Area

Balm Lake, Dellwater Lake, Big Turtle Lake.

Bemidji-Cass Lake Area

Beltrami Lake, Wolf Lake, Buck Lake, Swenson Lake, Big Lake, Lost Lake, Windigo Lake, Lake 13, Pike Bay, Lake Bemidji, Bass Lake, North Twin.

Leech Lake-Hackensack-Longville Area

Ten Mile Lake, Birch Lake, Grave Lake, Sugar Lake, Big Vermilion Lake, Willow Lake, Birch Lake, Thunder Lake, Upper Trelipe Lake, Inquadona Lake, Island Lake, Roosevelt Lake, Lawrence Lake, Morrison Lake, Leavitte Lake, Sterns Lake, Big Bass Lake, Little Bass Lake, Coffin Lake, Kidney Lake, Milton Lake, Big Sand Lake, Spring Lake, Long Lake, Webb Lake, Woman Lake, Little Boy Lake, Wabedo Lake, Portage Lake, Little Thunder Lake, Michaud Lake.

Brainerd-Whitefish Lake Chain-Emily Area

Gull Lake, Lake Hubert, Cullen Lake, Big Pelican Lake, Whitefish Lake, Ox Lake, Lake Edward, Bass Lake, Cross Lake, Kimball Lake, East and West Twin Lakes, Mississippi River, Little Pelican Lake, Horseshoe Lake, Big Trout Lake, Lower Hay Lake, Sibley Lake, Horseshoe Lake, Pine Lake, Upper Hay Lake, Pillager Lake, Lower Sylvan Lake, Upper Sylvan Lake, Gull River, Crow Wing River.

Little Falls-Motley Area

Shamineau Lake, Lake Alexander, Fish Trap Lake, Mississippi River, Pierz Fish Lake, Green Prairie Fish Lake, Pine Lake, Cedar Lake.

Bay Lake-Deerwood-Aitkin-Mille Lacs Lake Area

Serpent Lake, Round Lake, Pine Lake, Farm Island Lake, Spirit Lake, Cedar Lake, Esquagamah Lake, Hill Lake, Gun Lake, Dam Lake, Long Lake, Mud-Ripple Lake, Elm Island Lake, Lone Lake, Nord Lake, Clear Lake, Sugar Lake, Rock Lake, Turtle Lake, Hickory Lake, Rabbit Lake, Hamel Lake, Round Lake, Hanging Kettle Lake, Sissabagama Lake, Little Pine Lake, Whitefish Lake, Shakopee Lake, Camp Lake, Holt Lake, Smith Lake, Little White Bear Lake.

McGregor-Carlton Area

Big Sandy Lake, Lake Minnewawa, Wilkins Lake, Jenkins Lake, Dam Lake, Long Lake, Horseshoe Lake, Big Lake, Chub Lake, Cole Lake, Eagle Lake, Bob's Lake, Lake 12, Round Lake.

Moose Lake-Burnum Area

Sand Lake, Island Lake, Big Sturgeon Lake, Twin Bear Lake.

Park Rapids Area

Little Elbow Lake, Elbow Lake, Many Point Lake, Portage Lake, Long Lake, Straight Lake, Potato Lake, Eagle Lake, Island Lake, Big Sand Lake, Little Sand Lake, Lake Emma, Lower and Upper Bottle Lakes, Mantrap Lake, Belle Taine Lake, Boulder Lake, Bad Axe Lake, Crow Wing Lake Chain (1st to 11th), Shingobee Lake, Lake George, Little Mantrap Lake, Garfield Lake, Crooked Lake, Lake Itasca, Squaw Lake, Elk Lake, Stocking Lake, Upper Twin Lake, Lower Twin Lake, Blueberry Lake, Spirit Lake, Bad Medicine Lake, Lake Hattie, Tripp Lake, Two Inlets.

Detroit Lakes Area

Silver Lake, Big Cormorant Lake, Upper Cormorant Lake, Salberg Lake, Eunice Lake, Maud Lake, Detroit Lake, Lake Melissa, Lake Sally, Ice Cracking Lake, Rose Lake, Long Lake, Little McDonald Lake, Pelican Lake, Island Lake, Big Pine Lake, Little Pine Lake, Marion Lake, Paul Lake, Pickerel Lake, Cotton Lake, Pickerel Lake, Big Toad Lake, Little Toad Lake, Big Floyd Lake, Little Floyd Lake, Mud Lake, Buffalo Lake, White Earth Lake, Acorn Lake, Strawberry Lake, Big Sugar Bush Lake, Little Sugar Bush Lake, Round Lake, Juggler Lake, Long Lake, Sauers Lake, Graham Lake, Wiemer Lake.

Fergus Falls-Pelican Rapids-Henning Area

Lake Lida, Silent Lakes, Star Lake, Big Mac-Donald Lake, Spirit Lake, Loon Lake, Franklin Lake, Crystal Lake, Lake Lizzie, East and West Leaf Lakes, Ottertail Lake, West Battle Lake, East Battle Lake, Clitherall Lake, Lake Blanche, Crane Lake, Portage Lake, Donald Lake, Ethel Lake, Sybil Lake, Prairie Lake, Jolly Ann Lake, Beers Lake, Swan Lake, Ten Mile Lake, Rose Lake, Stalker Lake, Eagle Lake, Mill Lake, Long Lake, Long Lake, Long Lake, German Lake, South Turtle Lake, Wall Lake, Hoot Lake, Pleasant Lake, Lake Anna, Bass or Elbo Lake, Jewett Lake, Twin Lakes, West Lost Lake, East Lost Lake, Heidelberger Lake, Spitzer Lake, Block Lake, Walker Lake, Bass Lake, Grass Lake, Cow Lake, Crow Lakes, Leek Lake, Otter Lake, Long Lake, Shallow Lake, Sunfish Lake, Wagner Lake, Round Lake, Lone Pine Lake, Eddy Lake, Brackett Lake, Murray Lake, Murphy Lake, Rush Lake, Lake 5, Lake 6, Lake 7, East McDonald Lake, West McDonald Lake, Little Dead Lake, Head Lake, Jeff Lake, Jim Lake, Rice Lake, Alice Lake, Lone Pine Lake, Lilly Lake, Lone Pine Lake, Nitchie Lake, Tonsit Lake, Pickerel Lake, Tenter Lake, Little Bass Lake, Dead Lake (Big), Beers Lake, Anna Battle Lake, Molly Star Lake, Belmont Lake.

Alexandria-Glenwood-Osakis Area

Lake Mary, Victoria Lake, Darling Lake, Maple Lake, Brophy Lake, Oscar Lake, Lake Ida, Lake Geneva, Lake Carlos, Le Homme Dieu Lake, Andrews Lake, Lobster Lake, Blackwell Lake, Mina Lake, South Union Lake, Cowdry Lake, Jessie Lake, Pocket Lake, Burgan Lake, Crooked Lake, Louise Lake, Stony Lake, Big Chippewa Lake, Little Chippewa Lake, Stowes Lake, Moon Lake, Whiskey Lake, Irene Lake, Lake Miltona, Vermont Lake, Villard Lake, Leven Lake, Lake Minnewaska, Pelican Lake, Amelia Lake, Grove Lake, Lake Osakis, Sauk Lake, Little Birch Lake, Big Birch Lake, Fairy Lake, Grant Lake, Latoka Lake, Lake Moses, Smith Lake, North Union Lake, Turtle Lake, Rachel Lake, Lake Aaron, Red Rock Lake, Elk Lake, Moses Lake, Reno Lake, Little Osakis Lake.

Appleton-Ortonville-Morris Area

Big Stone Lake, Pomme de Terre River, Camp Lake, Scandinavian Lake, Gilchrist Lake, Lake Linka, Barrett Lake.

Willmar-Litchfield-Hutchinson Area

Green Lake, Nest Lake, Andrew Lake, Games Lake, Long Lake, Norway Lake, Diamond Lake, Lake Stella, Washington Lake, Manuella Lake, Union Lake, Lake Betty, Clear Lake, Lake Arvilla, Lake Richardson, Dunns Lake, Big Swan Lake, Collingswood Lake, Lake Erie, Lake Minne Bell, Lake Carrie, Eagle Lake, Hoff Lake.

Paynesville-Richmond-St. Cloud Area

Koronis Lake, Rice Lake, Big Lake, Horseshoe Lake, Long Lake, Browns Lake, Eden Lake, East Lake, Grand Lake, Pearl Lake, Goodner Lake, Carnelian Lake, Lake Marie, Lake Caroline, Lake Augusta, Little Rock Lake, Big Spunk Lake, Lower Spunk Lake, Big Watab Lake, Big Fish Lake, Pleasant Lake, Pelican Lake, Two Rivers Lake.

Annandale-Buffalo Area

Big Clearwater Lake, Grass Lake, Bass Lake, Lake Sylvia, Cedar Lake, Buffalo Lake, Lake Ramsey, Lake Summers, Lake Ida, Lake Ann, Lake Emma, Lake Mary, Lake Howard, Lake Waverly, Lake Brooks, Lake Cokato, Lake Camp, Lake Granite, Lake French, Lake Dans, Lake Mud, Lake John, Lake Pleasant, Lake Augusta, Lake Moose, Lake Moses, Lake Marie, Lake Otter, Lake Connelly, Lake Sugar, Lake Swartout, Lake Caroline, Lake Pearson, Lake Long, Lake Looche, Lake Fish, Lake Bertram, Lake Long, Lake Eagle, Lake Silver, Lake Limestone, Lake Indian, Lake Amber, Lake Pulaski, Lake Black, Lake Twin, Lake Lightfoot, Lake Charlotte, Lake Mink, Lake Deer, Lake Constance, Lake Bee Bee, Lake Maple, Lake Mary, Lake Rock.

Pine City-Mora Area

Knife Lake, Ann Lake, Fish Lake, Devils Lake, Lewis Lake, Lake Eleven, Lake Full of Fish, Mud Lake, Pine Lakes, Pokegama Lake, Cross Lake, Grindstone Lake, Rush Lake, Kettle River, St. Croix River, Snake River, Rock Lake, Kenny Lake, McGowan Lake, Lake Ten, Razor Lake, Upper Twin Lake, Lower Twin Lake, Crooked Lake, Little Tamarack Lake, Big Tamarack Lake, McDormitt Lake, Oak Lake, Net Lake, Sturgeon Lake, Island Lake, Kettle River, St. Croix River, Willow River, Tamarack River, Crooked Creek, Big Sand Creek, Bear Creek.

Cambridge-Princeton-Elk River Area

Skogman Lake, Spectacle Lake, Blue Lake, Long Lake, Green Lake, Stanchfield Lake, Big Lake, Elk Lake, Eagle Lake, Big Elk Lake, Lake Briggs, Lake Julia, Rush Lake, Lake Ann, Lake Orono, Little Rock Lake.

Center City-Forest Lake Area

Chisago Lakes, Forest Lake, Big Marine Lake, St. Croix River, Rush Lake, Goose Lake, Fish Lake, Horseshoe Lake, Green Lake.

Minneapolis-Minnetonka Area

Lake Minnetonka, Waconia Lake, Long Lake, Lake Independence, Lake Sarah, Lake Rebecca, Half Moon Lake, Rattail Lake, Lake George, Linwood Lake, Prior Lake, Spring Lake, Fish Lake, Shady Oak Lake, Orchard Lake, Crystal Lake, Medicine Lake, Zumbra Lake, Long Lake, Lotus Lake, Bryants Long Lake, Crooked Lake, Coon Lake, Martin Lake, Christmas Lake, Victoria Lake, Lake Minnewashta, Schauer Lake, Spurzem Lake, Crow River, Eagle Lake, Fish Lake, Weaver Lake, Fawn Lake, Lake Marion.

St. Paul-White Bear Lake Area

White Bear Lake, Bald Eagle Lake, Lake Josephine, Lake Owasso, Lake Gervais, Lake Phalen, Lake Johanna, Turtle Lake, Sucker Lake, Long Lake, Vadnais Lake.

Red Wing-Wabash-Winona Area

Silver Lake, Shady Lake, Lake Pepin, Lake Zumbro, Lake Florence, Zumbro River, Mississippi River, Clear Lake, North Lake, Zumbro River, South Fork Root River, Money Creek, Pine Creek, Main Root River, Main Root River.

Fairbault-Mankato-New Ulm Area

General Shields Lake, French Lake, Lake Mazaska, Cedar Lake, Fox Lake, Clear Lake, Reeds Lake, St. Olaf Lake, Lake Washington, Lake Madison, Lake Ballentyne, Duck Lake, Lake Crystal, Lake Tetonka, German Lake, Lake Jefferson, Saber Lake, Volney Lake, Clear Lake, Greenleaf Lake, Gorman Lake, Beaver Lake, Circle Lake, Emily Lake, Clear Lake.

Albert Lea-Fairmont Area

South Silver Lake, Amber Lake, Hall Lake, Budd Lake, Sisseton Lake, Bass Lake.

Worthington-Slayton-Marshall Area

Bingham Lake, Fish Lake, Des Moines River, Split Rock Lake, Mound Spring Lake, Round Lake.

Nebraska

Nebraska, one of the drier plains states, is far from a great bass-fishing state. Still, it enjoys a unique status. There is considerable bass water but comparatively few bass fishermen—and those few enjoy plenty of sport in semiprivacy.

Dick H. Schaffer, Chief of the Information Division of Nebraska's Game Commission, lists the major bass waters of his state like this:

Medicine Creek Reservoir, about 7 miles north of Cambridge; Harlan Reservoir at Republican City; Long Lake, 30 miles south of Valentine; Hord State Lake near Central City.

The sand pits and bayous on the North Loup River in the Brewster area have consistent fishing that sometimes becomes red-hot. Wellfleet State Lake at Wellfleet is a good bet too. So are the lakes of the Valentine Waterfowl Refuge, 20 miles south of Valentine.

There are 200 or more farm ponds in Dawes and Sioux counties in the area north of U. S. Route 20 between the city of Chadron and the Wyoming border. There are bass in most of them, and permission to fish usually can be obtained.

Other public bass lakes are Red Deer Lake, 20 miles south of Valentine; Smith State Lake, 23 miles south of Rushville; Lewis and Clark Lake in the Santee area.

In addition, there's some bass fishing in the following pay lakes: Rays Valley Lakes, Pleasure Lakes, and Hartford Lakes near Valley; Linoma Beach Lake near Ashland; Venice Lakes and Platte-view Lakes near Venice.

Iowa

Within a few miles of every Iowa citizen there is some kind of fishing water. Altogether there are 15,000 miles of fishable streams, 45,000 acres of natural lakes, 3500 acres of state-owned artificial lakes, plus countless gravel pits, oxbow lakes, small reservoirs, and farm ponds—nearly all of which contain bass. In addition, the state has provided and developed access sites and boat-launching facilities to supplement private installations at all major bodies of water. Iowa isn't a great bass-fishing state, but it's a very good one.

The Natural Lakes of Iowa

Spirit Lake, Dickinson County: Area 5684 acres. Depth 20 to 25 feet. Clear, open water with generally well-defined shores. Glacial boulders numerous on shore line. Many sandy beaches. Numerous small lakes and sloughs connected, providing spawning areas and food sources for game fish. Excellent fishing all lake species. Boats, bait, and cottages available.

West Okoboji, Dickinson County: Area 3939 acres. Maximum depth 132 feet. High, rocky, wooded banks. Water clear and cool. Provides excellent fishing for bass. Recent studies in this lake have revealed that during hot weather the oxygen content of the water is often zero below a depth of 60 feet. As a result, fishing below this depth is unproductive.

Clear Lake, Cerro Gordo County: Area 3643 acres. Maximum depth 20 feet. Saucer-shaped lake, a little over 4 miles long. Water clear and relatively cold. Sand beaches, some wooded and rocky shores. Noted in recent years for outstanding yellow-bass fishing.

Storm Lake, Buena Vista County: Area 3080 acres. Depth 7 to 9 feet. Two hundred eighteen acres dredged 12 to 20 feet. Open-water lake with wind-storms making water roily. Very few rock reefs. Sand bottom limited to adjacent shores. Highly productive of fish.

East Okoboji, Dickinson County: Area 1875 acres. Depth 8 to 24 feet. This narrow lake is about 6 miles long. Forms the outlet of Spirit and West Okoboji. Banks are high and well timbered. Shore line with considerable rocky stretches. Sand bottom in some areas.

Lost Island Lake, Palo Alto County: Area 1260 acres. Depth 12 feet. This lake is almost round and of uniform depth throughout the main body. It is an attractive lake with generally high banks with some timber fringe.

Trumbull Lake, Clay County: Area 1190 acres. Depth 5 feet. This shallow lake is a clear body of water with gravelly shores and generally well-defined wooded banks. Its limited depth makes bass fishing generally poor.

Silver Lake, Dickinson County: Area 1058 acres. Depth 5 to 8 feet. This lake is a beautiful body of water with high, wooded banks. Considerable rocky shore and sandy beaches.

West Swan Lake, Emmet County: Area 1038 acres. Depth 6 to 8 feet. Irregularly shaped lake about 2 1/2 miles long. Banks are sharp and covered with timber. Large marsh inlet at southwest end. Principal fishing, bullheads and northern pike.

Tuttle Lake, Emmet County: Nine hundred eighty-one acres of this lake are in Iowa. Only fair bass.

Black Hawk Lake, Sac County: Area 957 acres. Depth 6 to 7 feet, with 105 acres dredged to 9 to 16 feet. This is an irregularly shaped lake about 2 1/2 miles long.

Five Island Lake, Palo Alto County: Area 945 acres. Depth 3 to 5 feet. Dredged area 9 to 12 feet. This lake, formerly called Medium Lake, is irregularly shaped and about 4 miles long.

North Twin Lake, Calhoun County: Area 569

acres. Depth 6 to 8 feet, with 135 acres dredged to 9 to 15 feet. This is a narrow lake about 2 1/2 miles long.

Center Lake, Dickinson County: Area 264 acres. This little lake in the Great Lakes region is almost overlooked by most anglers. It is a saucer-shaped lake with a maximum depth of about 8 feet.

Marble Lake, Dickinson County: Area 175 acres. This lake is adjacent to Spirit Lake. Provides good largemouth bass fishing during favorable water periods.

Little Spirit Lake, Dickinson County: Area 214 acres.

Swan Lake, Dickinson County: Area 371 acres. A shallow lake.

Twelve Mile Lake, Emmet County: Area 290 acres.

Ingham (Mud) Lake, Emmet County: Area 421 acres.

Little Wall Lake, Hamilton County: Area 273 acres.

Crystal Lake, Hancock County: Area 238 acres.

Lake Cornelia, Wright County: Area 274 acres. One hundred thirty acres have been dredged to 8 to 10 feet.

The Rivers of Iowa

Mississippi—although this is an outstanding bass stream farther north in Minnesota, it's not very productive in Iowa. Some largemouths are taken in pools or backwaters created by various navigation locks and dams. But that's all.

Upper Iowa River and tributaries. This is the most beautiful stream in the state. For long distances it flows through a very deep valley, over a limestone bottom. Upper reaches contain excellent smallmouth water. Good canoe or float-trip stream, except in lowest water stages.

The Turkey River rises in Howard County and is an important smallmouth stream. Much of its course is through limestone rock.

Volga River is a fairly shallow stream with many riffles which begins in Fayette County and then flows 33 miles to meet the Turkey. Fine smallmouth water; good for streamer fly fishing.

The Little Turkey is similar to the Volga, flows through Howard and Fayette counties. Another similar stream is Crane Creek, in same locality, and its tributaries—Otter, Elk, and Roberts creeks.

The Yellow River begins in Winneshiek County and flows 35 miles to meet the Mississippi in Allamakee County near Marquette. It contains small-

mouths—and so do these tributaries: West Fork, Williams, and Suttle creeks.

Other bass streams of significance are Maquoketa River and its tributaries, North Fork of the Maquoketa, Wapsipinicon and tributaries, Cedar River and tributaries in Mitchell County, Little Cedar near Nashua, Shellrock River plus its tributaries the West Fork and Lime Creek, Iowa River in Hancock County, English River, Skunk River, North Skunk River, Des Moines River (an excellent canoeing or float-tripping river except during periods of lowest water), East Fork of the Des Moines (below Tuttle Lake are some productive bass waters), Boone River (also better than average bass water), Raccoon River, South Raccoon, Middle Raccoon, North River, Middle River, South River, and Whitebreast Creek. The last four are only fair at best.

Whereas waterways in the eastern half of Iowa flow into the Mississippi, streams in the western half flow toward the Missouri, which is the state's western boundary. Too often muddy, few of these have any value as bass streams, but here is a list of the "possibles" anyway:

Big Sioux, Rock, Floyd, Little Rock, Otter, Ocheyedan, Little Sioux, Maple, Soldier, Willow, Boyer, Nishnabotna, Nodaway, Platte, Grand, and Chariton. Add also Mill and Tarkio creeks.

Oxbow Lakes

Lake Manawa, 670 acres near Council Bluffs and Missouri River, has largemouths.

Blue Lake in Monona County has 900 acres, but this varies greatly. Largemouths.

Brown's Lake has 840 acres when full, but water level falls frequently and radically. Good bass fishing at times.

Lake Odessa, a 3000-acre shallow pool 5 miles northeast of Wapello in Louisa County. An excellent bet for resident and nonresident bass fishermen alike. Contains lunkers too.

Artificial Lakes

Iowa has 24 artificial lakes from 16 to 640 acres each, well distributed across the state. All have bass fishing which ranges from fair to very good. Quality of sport varies greatly from year to year.

Allerton, Williamson, Swan, Springbrook, Three Fires, Ahquabi, Red Haw Hill, Keomah, Wapello, Lacey-Keosauqua, Macbride, Backbone, Upper Pine, Lower Pine, Beeds, Mill Creek, Union Grove, Darling, Geode, Nine Eagles, Cold Springs, Rock Creek, Green Valley, Not Named.

Illinois

A highly developed (mostly by agriculture) state, Illinois is extremely level in terrain and fairly well endowed with bass-fishing waters. The best fishing occurs in the lakes, and there are accommodations near all of these—if not on the lake itself, in the adjacent communities. Here follows a list of the most important bass waters.

Lake Zurich, Bangs Lake, Wooster Lake, Turner Lake, Crystal Lake, Maple Lake, Weldon Springs, Anderson Lake, Rice Lake, Lake Ramsey, Crab Orchard Lake, Little Grassy Lake, Horseshoe Lake, Lake Murphysboro, Lake Catherine, Channel Lake, Lake Marie, Bluff Lake, Petite Lake, Grass Lake, Fox Lake, Nippersink Lake, Pistakee Lake, Kickapoo State Park, Lake Chautauqua, Red Hills, Lake Argyle.

Missouri

Bass fishing is traditional sport in Missouri, and that's not hard to explain when you consider the abundance of fine fishing waters—impounded and flowing. That's doubly true of the Ozark region which extends over 90 million acres of the state and which includes all that portion of Missouri south of the Missouri River. In this area alone are about 16,000 miles of fishing streams and 100,000 acres of impounded waters.

In a well-developed resort area centered in the northern part of the hill country is the great Lake of the Ozarks. Its coves, peninsulas, and rocky outcrops form a shore line of 1372 miles—one of the longest in the United States. The species of fish caught in its 60,000 acres of water include largemouth black bass, and in the rocky coves of the upper portions of the lake are a few smallmouths.

Lake Taneycomo is located in Taney county, with Branson, Hollister, Forsyth, and Rockaway Beach on its shore line. Recreational facilities are highly developed, and a number of fine Ozark streams are in the immediate vicinity. Nearly all species of game fish are caught here including small and largemouth black bass, crappie, jack salmon, black perch, sunfish, and channel cat.

Created by a dam in Arkansas, Norfork Lake backs up into Missouri for about 8 miles. Fishing has been consistently good for both black and white bass.

In the southeastern area of the Ozarks, Lake Wappapello attracts many fishermen. Black bass are found also in this lake, created by a dam on the St. Francis River.

Clearwater Dam, on the Black River in Reynolds County, has created Lake Clearwater, which extends upstream 6 miles from the dam and covers 1650 acres. It opened to general fishing in 1949 and has been a source of fine catches ever since.

Bull Shoals Lake, newest of the great fishing spots, extends into Ozark and Taney counties of Missouri. This reservoir has an area of 45,000 acres and extends 87 miles from the main dam site in Arkansas. The lake replaces that portion of White River below Lake Taneycomo. About 15,000 acres of coves, arms, and deep water lie in Missouri, including some of the best angling areas.

In north Missouri, Thousand Hills Lake near Kirksville and Lake Paho, in Mercer County, offer fine bass fishing, as do smaller lakes and farm ponds above the Missouri River.

The water systems of the White, Eleven Point, Current, Black, Gasconade, Meramec, and St. Francis rivers comprise the major Ozark streams. The numerous springs of this region, coupled with vast areas of forest, make these waters ideal for smallmouth bass.

Float Trips

Float fishing, which originated in the Missouri Ozarks at the turn of the century, is becoming more popular every year. This unique method of going after fish attracts fishermen from everywhere.

You can float for a half day or two weeks—commercial guides who do all the paddling, campmaking, and cooking are available. Or, if you are an experienced river man, you can float the streams yourself. There are some 25 popular float streams in the Missouri Ozarks, and they're all cold and clear, curving and bent back on themselves. Rapids and "white water" give way to long deep pools, and bold rock cliffs are succeeded by gently sloping gravel bars. The scenery is the equal of any in the nation, and you can drift along at the current's speed all day long and still be only a mile (overland) from where you started that morning.

Where a number of boats are necessary for a large float-trip party, a "commissary" boat—loaded with camp and cooking gear—will be provided. The "commissary" crew works out a schedule whereby it will have the lunch camp set up in advance of your arrival, and at dusk the tents and overnight camp will be ready when the day's fishing is done.

At the end of your trip a truck will be waiting to

load up all equipment and supplies and deliver your party back to its starting point.

In addition to bass, large goggle-eye spice up the fishing and there are possibilities of doing battle with a 12-pound jack salmon. They've been taken up to 17 1/2 pounds. Don't be surprised, either, if you tangle with an occasional channel cat on minnows or a trout while using a fly.

All the fisherman needs to bring along is his tackle. Outfitters usually supply the camp equipment, food, and other essentials. The cost per person for a float trip averages about $15 or $20 per day, but for exact costs and information you'd better write to one or more of the outfitters known to be operating this season.

The major Ozark streams on which floats are conducted, or on which experienced fishermen float themselves, are as follows: Beaver Creek, Big Piney River, Big River, Black River, Bourbeuse River, Bryant Creek, Courtois Creek, Crooked Creek, Current River, Dry Creek, Eleven Points River, Elk River, Flat Creek, Gasconade River, Huzzah Creek, Indian Creek, Jacks Fork, James River, Kings River, Long Creek, Meramec River, Niangua River, North Fork (White River), Osage Fork, Osage River, St. Francis River, Swan Creek, and White River.

The individual taking a float trip should keep the calendar in mind when making plans, so that appropriate clothing will be available. The weather likely will be rather cool at night during spring and fall months. Serviceable clothing is a necessity. Rubber-soled sneakers will make for safety if wading from the shore is contemplated. The item that will come in handy on nights when the moonlight is absent is a small but bright-beamed flashlight.

Indiana

Somehow the Hoosier State always escapes recognition as a good bass-fishing state, which is unfortunate because the northern portion, particularly, is full of good bass waters. These are natural lakes scooped out by glaciers in a prehistoric age. Elsewhere in the state, artificial lakes take up the slack.

Several of Indiana's streams have great potential for float tripping, and on the Tippecanoe, at least, outfitters have facilities for visiting fishermen. Even though it is quite often roily, the Wabash is good for floating too.

A list of major Indiana bass fishing waters follows.

Yellowwood Lake, Freeman Lake, Shafer Lake, Story Lake, Ferdinand Lake, Manitou Lake, Lake Jason, Starve Hollow Lake, Wawasee Lake, Barbee Chain, Dewart Lake, Big Long Lake, Lake-of-the Woods, Twin Lakes, Pine Lake, Geist Reservoir, Lake Maxinkuckee, Pretty Lake, Big Lake, Sylvan Lake, Bass Lake, Clear Lake, Hamilton Lake, Lake James, Chain of Lakes, Crooked Lake, Tippecanoe River, Pigeon River, St. Joseph River, Blue River, Whitewater River, Sugar Creek, Wabash River, oxbow lakes and sloughs of Wabash, Willow Slough Fish and Game Area near Morocco.

South Dakota

This is not a great bass-fishing state, but some good lakes do exist in the eastern third of the state. Bass do exist in several Black Hills lakes, but the fishing for them is poor there and the bass seldom grow to a desirable size. For practical purposes there is no stream fishing. A list of eastern lakes follows.

Lake Traverse, Clear Lake, Roy Lake, Elm Lake, Pickerel Lake, Enemy Swim, Cottonwood Lake, Pelican Lake, Lake Louise, Lake Byron, Lake Poinsett, Lake Madison, Marindahl Lake, Fort Randall Reservoir, Angostura Reservoir.

North Dakota

Bass fishing in this prairie state is very spotty and unpredictable. Nearly all of the state's waters are shallow, cold, subject to roiliness until late summer, and also subject to winter kills. The following is a list of lakes which contain or have once contained bass. It *isn't* a recommendation to fish any of them. Frequently no accommodations exist nearby.

Lake Odland, Cedar Lake, North Lemmon Lake, Raleigh Reservoir, Dickinson Reservoir, Benet Lake, Heart Butte Reservoir, Danzig Reservoir, Welk Lake, Bald Hill Reservoir, Lake Elsie, Homme Dam, Kadrmas Lake, Lake Ilo.

Michigan

There's a common saying in Michigan Chamber of Commerce circles that the Wolverine State was attracting tourists before many others were attracting settlers. And it's not idle talk. The state has been in the holiday business since before the War Between the States. They can thank their jack-pine woodlands, their lakes scooped out by glaciers, their beaches and waterways, and most of all their splendid fishing.

Yet, even in this state, with unlimited outdoor possibilities, one region—the Upper Peninsula—is outstanding. It's a kind of promised land for sportsmen and their families. It's a chunk of real estate, free from hay fever, the size of Massachusetts, Rhode Island, Connecticut, and Delaware combined. It separates Lake Superior from lakes Michigan and Huron. If you like cold statistics, it contains 4303 inland lakes, 12,406 miles of streams, 1723 miles of shore line on the Great Lakes, and only a few more people than are necessary to take good care of the annual summer visitors.

The UP is a happy blend of civilization and wilderness. The centers of well-manicured towns, for example, are only a few minutes away from lonely lakes. There are a few cottages and camps, but not too many of them to spoil the atmosphere that most anglers prefer. There are fancy resorts, plain resorts, public camp sites, and vast areas (83 per cent of the total, in fact) of unbroken forests. It's an evergreen playground, really, that caters mostly to family groups.

The first tourists came to the first resort on the UP by horse and carriage from St. Ignace to jewel-like Brevoort Lake. The accommodations now are more modern, the lake as lovely as ever. And it still has a respectable population of bass. Farther west are Millecoquins and Millekokia lakes, both good fishing—as are dozens of others in the region thereabouts. Still farther west are the Manistique Lakes, best known for walleyes.

Also a part of Mackinac County are a number of islands—Mackinac, Bois Blanc, and Les Cheneaux. Mackinac is a picturesque, somewhat quaint summer resort that's surely worth a visit, but boasts nothing special in the outdoor line. It's a different story around the other islands, though. The waters around Bois Blanc have plenty of bass, and it's hard to match the smallmouth fishing around the Cheneaux archipelago.

North of Mackinac and farthest east of the UP counties is Chippewa, with 294 miles of rocky, broken, Great Lakes shore line, 169 lakes, and 800 miles of streams. Once the stomping grounds of Algonquin Indians, it's now patronized by anglers in wholesale lots.

Offshore and to the east is Drummond Island, surrounded by some of the most fertile fishing water in America—especially for large smallmouths. It's a lonely, almost bleak bit of land, but it contains plenty of camps for fishermen. Neebish and Sugar islands are also situated in the center of good fishing waters.

Trout Lake has good angling and so has Caribou Lake near Raber. The state park near Brimley has splendid facilities for public camping.

West of Chippewa County is Luce County on Lake Superior. Altogether, the county boasts about 571 inland lakes and 658 miles of streams. Not the least known of these is the Two Hearted—because of the caliber of its fishing and because it's the scene of an early Hemingway tale. Some of the best fishing usually occurs in the Manistique Lakes, but here is country that an adventurous angler with car-top boat or trailer can explore much farther. Many a woodland pond hereabout never sees an angler from one season to another, and many contain bass.

Farther west along Lake Superior is Alger County and the spectacular Pictured Rocks Country. A quick tabulation shows 81 miles of Superior shore, 253 lakes, and 699 miles of stream—more water, really, than exists altogether in many states. Some specific places to try are the Au Train River, Au Train Lake, and Trout, Long, Ready, and Lost lakes.

Next county, still moving westward, is Marquette, largest in the state. Besides 68 miles of Lake Superior boundary, it has the most lakes (835) and most miles (1906) of streams. It would take a lifetime to sample only the best fishing waters.

Largest lake is Michigamme in the western part, and it's good for bass. Ives and Independence lakes near Big Bay are hot spots as are Goose, Teal, Bass, Kawbowgam, Deer, Silver, Mountain, and Pine lakes.

There is excellent fishing for bass in the Princeton, Gwinn, and Little system of lakes. Budget-priced accommodations are available at most lakes and towns in the area. A public camp site is located on the nearby 333,000-acre Escanaba Game Area.

Baraga County comes next. It's a typical northern Michigan region of clean forests, cold rivers, and atmosphere that's likely to make old fishermen feel like young fishermen. The box score reads 206 lakes and 696 miles of streams—plus Keweenaw and Huron bays of Lake Superior. Best lake fishing is in Vermillac, King, Drummond, Ned, Fence, and Cliff lakes.

Houghton County is located at the base of a small peninsula that points northward into Lake Superior. In the heart of Michigan's Copper Country, it's the kind of place people can get genuinely excited about in travel folders. There are 197 lakes and 923 miles of streams.

Portage Lake near Chassell is good. There is also excellent fishing all around Kenton and Sidnaw, especially in Perch Lake. Other good lakes are Bob, Otter, Gerald, Roland, Rice, Norway, and Mud.

Keweenaw County is Michigan's smallest and northernmost. It's almost surrounded by Lake Superior but nonetheless contains 125 lakes and 275 miles of streams. Lac la Belle in the center of the county is a fine producer of bass. Lake Fanny Hooe is a good one, and so are Manganese, Breakfast, and Schlatter lakes.

One of our wilderness national parks—Isle Royale—lies just 50 miles offshore from the Keweenaw Peninsula. It's about 9 by 45 miles long. There's splendid fishing all around this remote island, and boats leave from Houghton three times a week. Reservations should be obtained in advance.

They call Ontonagon County the "Jewel of the Porcupines" because of the Porcupine Mountains rather than because it contains more quill-pigs than any other section of the UP. The best of the lake fishing is concentrated in lovely Lake of the Clouds, Gogebic, Mirror, and Bond lakes. These are bass waters that hold up all summer long. The waters remain cool enough, even during dog days, to keep the fish active when they're on a hunger strike farther south.

There are 1200 miles of streams and 488 named lakes in Gogebic, the county farthest west on the UP. The area around Watersmeet in the southeastern part of the county has almost as much water as land. In June there's fast fishing in lakes like Tamarack, Duck, Crooked, Sucker, Cisco, and Lac Vieux Desert.

Gogebic Lake is an especially fine resort and cottage area, but it also has a fine, 361-acre state park with public campgrounds, etc. The lake itself is fine for bass.

East of Gogebic is Iron County with 528 lakes and 902 miles of streams. There's bass fishing in the reservoirs created by power dams on the Paint and Michigamme rivers near Crystal Falls. There are public camping grounds and facilities on Fortune, Chicaugon, and Runkel lakes.

Another good fishing area is located around Iron River and to the southwest of the town—as in Sunset and Pickerel lakes.

Dickinson County has 125 inland lakes and 647 miles of streams.

A fisherman can find some bass in the Hamilton Lakes around Loretto. There's good bass fishing and a county park on Lake Antoine. The same is true of a series of small lakes between Felch and Ralph.

Menominee County is a busy and prosperous place, and much of the prosperity comes from taking good care of vacationists and visiting fishermen. The Big Cedar River at times has the finest smallmouth fishing you can find. There's some good bass in the small lakes east of Stephenson and Ingalls.

Delta County, Michigan, and Escanaba, the county seat, are known all over the world for the fabulous smelt runs—if not for the excellent sport fishing in the region. Big and Little Bay de Noc contain smallmouths. Boats, motors, guides, and all sorts of accommodations are available out of Escanaba, Gladstone, Rapid River, Stonington, Nahma, Sac Bay, Garden, and Fairport.

Besides the sheltered waters off of Lake Michigan, Delta County boasts of 148 inland lakes and 514 miles of streams.

Schoolcraft is the least developed of Upper Peninsula counties. It contains vast areas of beautiful birch, beech, and coniferous forest, and therefore it's superb camping country. An especially choice section for camping is that west of Steuben where the woods conceal a whole network of small, blue lakes. They contain bass—large and smallmouths. There's a similar network of lakes and ponds in the north central part of the county.

Indian Lake near Manistique is the county's largest of 320 inland lakes. Its shore line contains every sort of accommodation, including a fine state park with camping facilities.

Lower Michigan

Michigan has over 3000 miles of shore line along four Great Lakes alone, plus 30 major river systems. Of course, all this means bass fishing that rates with the best in the land.

In parts of southern Michigan, pollution and industrial development has taken a heavy toll of good fishing waters—but others still remain within easy reach of Detroit and the other motor cities. For example, there are Gun and Thornapple lakes in Barry County, Black and Spring lakes in Ottawa County. The Irish Hills lakes have good fishing early in the spring, but it deteriorates later on. Bass fishing in Lake St. Clair, between Lake Erie and Lake Huron, is much more consistent the year round.

Two lake "areas," the first extending from Lapeer and near Flint to Hillsdale and Coldwater, and the second from near Greenville to the Indiana line, contain bass.

The northern part of Michigan's lower peninsula has hundreds of excellent bass lakes—which contain both largemouths and smallmouths. A partial list of the best lakes would have to include these: Clam, Elk, and Torch lakes in Antrim County; Big Platte Lake in Benzie County; Black, Burt, and Millet lakes and Indian River in Cheboygan County; Elk

Lake in Grand Traverse County; Torch Lake in Kalkaska County; Lake Leelanau in Leelanau County; Hamlin and Pere Marquette lakes in Mason County; Bear Lake in Muskegon County; Pentwater Lake in Oceana County; Houghton and Higgins lakes; Grand Lake in Presque Isle County; Lake Avalon in Montmorency County; Lake Margrethe near Grayling.

The Muskegon, Manistee, and Au Sable rivers are well known nationwide as topnotch trout streams, but the lower reaches of all three contain small-mouths in surprising numbers.

Somehow most of Michigan's bass fishing holds up well all through the hot months, but it's always best immediately after the season opens—and that's usually in the middle of June. Probably the best advice for a visiting angler is to try new lures and new techniques; I've found that this is especially true where fishing pressure is heaviest. In the sandy, glacial lakes especially, the bass tend to loiter in small confined areas right on the bottom. Find these by drifting and casting or by drifting and dunking live bait as you go. Night crawlers drifted or rather thumped along the bottom are deadly. So are crayfish, lampreys, leeches, and hellgrammites.

Wisconsin

Any angler, resident or nonresident, is lucky to find himself in Wisconsin because this is not only a beautiful pine-balsam-and-birch state, but it also contains 8676 lakes and enough waterways to stretch a couple of times around the earth. Bass are almost everywhere.

There are all kinds of lakes—deep ones such as Big Green, which drops off 300 feet beneath the surface, and big ones like Winnebago with its 137,708 surface acres. There are small clear "kettle" lakes located in the terminal moraines. And there are lakes with rocky shore lines and gravel bottoms too. Since virtually all contain bass, a bass fisherman can hardly go wrong—no matter where he finds himself in this attractive vacationland.

Maps showing size, depths, bars, weed beds, and principal roads are available for about 800 lakes. They can be obtained from the conservation department and are certainly worth while.

Far too little emphasis has been placed on Wisconsin's wonderful streams, many of which are great for float tripping. The Chippewa is excellent, as is the entire Chippewa Flowage-Hayward lakes region. So is the Flambeau, the Wisconsin, the Fox, Wolf, Black, St. Croix, and the Namakagon. Autumn

floating may mean carrying occasionally across shallow riffles, but otherwise it's productive and a magnificent experience when both the weather and the color are at their best.

The Mississippi River from La Crosse to Red Wing, Minnesota, is outstanding bass water too. It isn't hard to find anglers who consider it the most consistent in the country. Plenty of boats for rent along the way.

In few places are there more, better, or a greater variety of accommodations than in northern Wisconsin. They're numerous, but not too numerous to spoil the wilderness atmosphere. American-plan resorts are especially popular in this country, particularly in the Hayward, Rhinelander, Tomahawk, Lac du Flambeau, Boulder Junction, Ladysmith, and Spooner areas.

A list of all Wisconsin's lakes which contain bass would consume too much space. The following list, by counties, includes all bass lakes of more than 50 acres each.

Adams County

Flowage Lake, Goose Lake, Jordan Lake, Mason Lake, Millpond Lake (Friendship), Parker Lake, Patricks Lake, Van Kuren Lake.

Ashland County

Augustine Lake, Bear Lake, Beaver Dam, Beaver Lake, Butternut Lake, Caroline Lake, Carrol Lake, Cycle Lake, Dry Lake, East Twin Lake, English Lake, Eureka Lake, Gallilee Lake, Gordon Lake, Hay Lake, Hoffman Lake, Honest John Lake, Kakagon Slough, Little Clam Lake, Leland Lake (Long), McLaren Lake, Meader Lake, Mellen Flowage Lake, Mineral Lake, Pelican Lake, Spider Lake, Spillberg Lake, Summit Lake, Tea Lake, Torrey Lake, Torch Flowage Lake (Dead Horse), Upper Clam Lake.

Barron County

Bass Lake, Bear Lake, Beaver Dam, Big Butternut Lake, Big Sand Lake, Bolger Flowage Lake, Bryer Lake, Chetek Lake, Desair Lake, Devils Lake, Dietz Lake, Duck Lake, Echo Lake, Granite Lake, Hemlock Lake, Horseshoe Lake, Horseshoe Lake, Island Lake, Kirby Lake, Little Sand Lake, Long Lake, Loon Lake, Lower Turtle Lake, Mirror Lake (Pipe), Montanis Lake, Moon Lake, Mud Lake, Pipe Lake (Sylvan), Pokegama Lake, Poskin Lake, Prairie Lake, Red Cedar Lake, Rice

Casting to the edge of weed beds at Ghost Lake, near Hayward, Wisconsin.

Lake, Scott Lake, Stump Lake, Tabor Lake, Thirty Lake, Tuscobia Lake, Twin Lake, Upper Turtle Lake, Upper Vermillion Lake, Vermillion Lake, Wickert Lake (Scott).

Bayfield County

Atkins Lake, Bass Lake, Bass #1 Lake (Cisco), Bass #2 Lake (Esox), Bass #4 Lake (Andanta), Bass Lake, Basswood Lake, Bellvue Lake, Bismark Lake, Bladder Lake, Bluebird Lake (Hildur), Bony Lake, Buffalo Lake, Cable Lake, Chenequa Lake (Five), Chippewa Lake, Cisco Lake, Coffee Lake, Cranberry Lake, Crooked Lake, Crystal Lake, Deep Lake, Dells Lake, Delta Lake, Diamond Lake, Drummond Lake, Duck Lake, Eagle Lake (Wiehe), East Lake (Tahkodah), Ellison Lake, Five Island Lake, Fourth Dells Lake, Ghost Lake, Hammel Lake, Iron River Flowage Lake, Iron Lake, Island Lake, Jackson Lake, Kelly Lake, Kern Lake, Little Spider Lake, Long Lake, Lower Eau Claire Lake, McGary Lake, McLeod Lake, Marengo Lake, Middle Eau Claire Lake, Millpond Lake, Mud Lake, Mullenhoff Lake, Muskie Lake (White Bass), Namekagon Lake, North Lake (Bow), Nothing Lake, Owen Lake, Patsy Lake, Perch Lake, Perry Lake, Pest House Lake (Amek), Pickerel Lake, Pigeon Lake, Pike Lake Chain (Buskey Lake, Crow Lake, Eagle Lake, Flynn Lake, Hart Lake, McGary Lake, Millicent

Lake), Pike Lake, Porcupine Lake, Price Lake, Ruth Lake, Sand Bar Lake, Shunenberg Lake, Siskowitt Lake, Smith Lake, Spider Lake, Star Lake, Swede Lake (Sweet), Taylor Lake, Tomahawk Lake, Turtle Lake, Twin Lake (East), Twin Bear Lake, Upper Eau Claire Lake, Wilapiro Lake.

Burnett County

Austin Lake, Bashaw Lake, Bass Lake, Bass Lake, Bass Lake, Bass Lake, Bear Lake, Benoit Lake, Big Bear Lake, Big Doctor Lake, Big McKenzie Lake, Big Sand Lake, Big Wood Lake, Birch Island Lake, Birlingame Lake, Blomers Lake, Bonner Lake, Briggs Lake, Buck Lake, Buffalo Lake, Cadotte Lake, Clam Lake, Clam Lake (Upper), Clam River Flowage, Clear Lake, Connors Lake, Cranberry Lake, Crooked Lake, Crooked Lake, Deer Lake, Des Moines Lake, Devils Lake, Doctor Lake, Duboy Lake (Dubois), Dunham Lake, Eagle Lake, Eagle Lake, Faulk Lake (Love), Fernstad Lake, Fish Lake, Gaslyn Lake, Goose Lake, Green Lake, Ham Lake, Hanscome Lake, Hayden Lake, Holmes Lake, Johnson Lake, Lang Lake, Lily Lake, Lipsett Lake, Little Bear Lake, Little McGraw Lake, Little Pokegama Lake, Little Trade Lake, Little Wood Lake, Little Yellow Lake, Long Lake, Long Lake, Loon Lake, Loon Lake, Loon Lake, Lower Twin Lake,

Lucerne Lake, McGraw Lake, Middle McKenzie Lake, Minerva Flowage Lake, Miniture Lake, Minnie Lake, Mud Hen Lake, Nicaboyne Lake, North Sand Lake, Oak Lake, Phernetton Lake, Pine Lake, Pine Lake, Point Lake, Pokegama Lake, Poquettes Lake (Long), Rice Lake, Rice Lake, Rice Lake, Rooney Lake, Round Lake, Sand Lake, Shoal Lake, Spencer Lake, Spirit Lake, Staples Lake, Tabor Lake, Taylor Lake, Trade Lake, Tucker Lake, Twenty-Six Lake, Viola Lake, Warner Lake, Webb Lake, Yellow Lake.

Calumet County

Winnebago (see Winnebago County).

Chippewa County

Axe Handle Lake, Bass Lake (Round), Bloomer Millpond, Bob Howe Lake, Chain Lake, Chippewa Flowage, Cornell Lake, Cornell Flowage, County Lake, Finley Lake, Fisher River, Hallie Lake, Henneman Lake, Holcombe Lake, Jims Lake, Jim Falls Flowage, Jump River, Larrabee Lake, Long Lake, Loon Lake, Marshmiller Lake, Pike Lake, Pine Lake, Popple Lake, Round Lake (Bass), Salisbury Lake, Sand Lake, South Shattuck Lake, Wissota Lake.

Clark County

Arbutus Lake, Black River Flowage, Greenwood Flowage, Humbird Pond, Mead Flowage, Sherwood Lake, Snyder Pond, Willard Lake (Rock Dam).

Columbia County

Long Lake, Mason Lake (see Adams County), Park Lake, Swan Lake, Wisconsin Lake.

Dane County

Bass Lake, Belleville Millpond, Crystal Lake, Fish Lake, Grass Lake, Kegonsa Lake, Koshkonong Lake (see Jefferson County), Masomanie Millpond, Mendota Lake, Monona Lake, Mud Lake, Mud Lake, Rice Lake, Waubesa Lake, Wingra Lake.

Dodge County

Beaver Dam, Emily Lake, Fox Lake, Lost Lake, Neosho Pond, Sinissippi Lake.

Door County

Clarks Lake, Europe Lake, Forrestville Pond, Kangaroo Lake.

Douglas County

Alexander Lake, Amnicon Lake, Bardon Lake (Whitefish), Bass Lake, Bass Lake, Beauregard Lake, Bond Lake, Chain Lake (Lower and Upper), Cranberry Lake, Crotty Lake, Crystal Lake, Dowling Lake, Flat Lake, Gander Lake, Gordon Lake, Grover Lake, Harriet Lake, Leader Lake, Little Amnicon Lake, Little Sand Lake, Loon Lake, Lower Chain Lake, Lund Lake, Lyman Lake, McDonald Lake, Minnesuing Lake, Mud Lake, Mulligan Lake, Nebagamon Lake, Person Lake, Red Lake (Stafford), Round Lake, St. Croix Lake, Sabin Lake, Sand Lake, Sauntry Pocket, Simms Lake, Snake Lake, Steele Lake, Sullivan Lake, Twin Lake, Twin Lake, Two Mile Lake (Half Way), Upper Ox Lake, Webb Lake.

Dunn County

Colfax Pond, Eau Gaile Lake, Elk Lake, Menomin Lake, Tainter Lake.

Eau Claire County

Altoona Lake, Dells Millpond, Dells Pond, Eau Claire Lake, Half Moon Lake.

Florence County

Anna Lake, Boot Lake (Shadow), Elwood Lake, Emily Lake, Fisher Lake, Halsey Lake, Keyes Lake, Lake of Dreams, Lost Lake, Pine River Flowage, Price Lake, Railroad Lake (Cosgrave), Sand Lake, Sealion Lake, Spreadeagle Chain (Bass Lake, East Lake, Long Lake, Middle Lake, North Lake, West Lake), West Bass Lake.

Fond du Lac County

Crooked Lake (see Sheboygan County), De Neveu Lake, Fifteen Lake, Forest Lake, Long Lake, Mauthe Lake, Round Lake, Twin Lake, Wolf Lake.

Forest County

Ada Lake (see Langlade County), Arbutus Lake, Bass Lake, Birch Lake, Bradley Lake, Butternut Lake, Crane Lake, Deer Lake, Franklin Lake, Gordon Lake, Ground Hemlock Lake, Harmony

Lake, Kentuck Lake, Laona Mill Pond, Laura Lake (Camp 9), Lily Lake, Lima Lake, Little Long Lake, Little Rice Lake, Little Sand Lake, Little Star Lake, Long Lake, Lost Lake, Lucerne Lake, Mud Lake, Pat Shay Lake, Pickerel Lake, Pine Lake, Popple Lake, Range Line Lake, Roberts Lake, Ross Lake, Scattered Rice Lake, Silver Lake, Trump Lake (Long), Van Zile Lake, Wabikon Lake, White Deer Lake, Windfall Lake, Woodbury Lake.

Green Lake County

Big Twin Lake, Green Lake, Kingston Millpond, Little Green Lake, Puckaway Lake, Spring Lake, Spring Lake.

Iowa County

Avoca Lake.

Iron County

Bearskull Lake, Big Martha Lake, Big Muskie Lake, Big Oxbow Lake, Big Pike Lake, Big Pine Lake (Wilson), Birch Lake, Black Lake, Catherine Lake, Cedar Lake, Charmley Lake (Charmley), Clear Lake, Crystal Lake, East Cramer Lake, Echo Lake, Ess Lake, Evelyn Lake, Fat Lake, Ferry Lake, Fischer Lake, Flambeau Flowage Lake, French Lake, Grant Lake, Hewitt Lake (High), Island Lake, Lake of the Falls, Lavinia Lake, Little Island Lake, Little Pike Lake, Long Lake (Pork and Beans), McDermott Lake, Mercer Lake, Minnow Lake (Artificial), Moose Lake, Mud Lake (Bass), Nine Lake, O'Brien Lake, Owl Lake, Pardee Lake, Payment Lake, Pleasant Lake, Randall Lake, Rice Lake, Sand Lake (Clear), Sandy Beach Lake, Sardine Lake, Six Lake, South Bass Lake (Beauty), Spider Lake, Springstead Lake, Stone Lake, Tank Lake (Grand Portage), Trude Lake, Turtle Flowage, Wilson Lake.

Jefferson County

Blue Spring Lake, Golden Lake (see Waukesha County), Hope Lake, Koshkonong Lake, Lower Spring Lake, Ripley Lake, Rock Lake, Rome Millpond Lake, Waterloo Pond.

Juneau County

Beaver Flowage, Castle Rock Flowage, Kingston Flowage, Mauston Pond Lake (Decorah), Meadow Valley Lake, Necedah Lake, Petenwell Flowage.

Kenosha County

Benedict Lake, Camp Lake, Center Lake, Cross Lake, Dyer Lake, Elizabeth Lake, George Lake, Hooker Lake, Marie Lake, Paddock Lake, Powers Lake, Rock Lake (Marshall), Silver Lake.

Kewaunee County

East Alaska Lake, Engledinger Lake (Bolt).

La Crosse County

French Slough, Neshonoc Pond, Round Lake.

Langlade County

Ada Lake, Bass (Moccasin) Lake, Big South Twin Lake, Black Oak Lake, Boulder Lake, Camp Lake, Deep Woods Lake, Duck Lake, Dynamite Lake, Echo Lake (Otter), Enterprise Lake, Greater Bass Lake, Jack Lake, Loon Lake, Lower Bass Lake, Lower Clear Lake, Post Lake, Rolling Stone Lake, Sawyer Lake, Spring Lake (Fisher), Summit Lake, Upper Clear Lake, White Lake.

Lincoln County

Alice Lake, Bass Lake, Big Somo Lake, Clara Lake, Clear Lake, Crystal Lake, Deer Lake, Echo Lake, Halfmoon Lake, Harrison Lake, Hilderbrand Lake, Hilts Lake, Horn Lake, Jersey City Flowage, Long Lake, Muskellunge Lake, Nokomis Lake (see Oneida County), Otter Lake, Pesobic Lake (Lake View), Pickerel Lake, Pine Lake, Road Lake, Rodd Lake, Seven Island Lake, Silver Lake, Skanawan Lake, Spirit River Flowage, Squaw Lake, Tug Lake, West Twin Lake.

Manitowoc County

Big Pigeon Lake, Cedar Lake, Long Lake, Silver Lake, Wilke Lake.

Marathon County

Bass Lake, Big Bass Lake, Big Eau Pleine Reservoir, Crooked Lake, DuBay Lake, Go To It Lake (Norrie), Half Moon Lake, Mosinee Flowage, Pike Lake, Schofield Flowage, Sunflower Lake (Mayflower), Wadley Lake (Shanty Town), Wausau Lake (Flowage).

Marinette County

Big Newton Lake, Coleman Lake, Eagle Lake, Elbow Lake, Frieda Lake, Gilas Lake, Glenn Lake, Grass Lake, Hilbert Lake, Johnson Falls Flowage, Julia Lake, Left Foot Lake, Lindquist Lake, Little Newton Lake, Long Lake, Mary Lake, McCaslin Lake, Moon Lake, Morgan Lake (Sullivan), Mountana Lake, Niagara Flowage, Noquebay Lake, Oneonta Lake, Sturgeon Falls Flowage.

Marquette County

Buffalo Lake, Comstock Lake, Crystal Lake, Harrisville Mill Pond, Kinney Lake (Williams), Lawrence Lake, Moon Lake (Birch), Montello Lake, Mud Lake, Turtle Lake, White Lake, Wood Lake.

Monroe County

Perch Lake, Tomah Lake.

Oconto County

Anderson Lake, Archibald Lake, Bass Lake, Bear Lake, Berry Lake, Big Horn Lake, Big Maiden Lake, Big Squaw Lake, Boot Lake, Chain Lake, Chute Pond, Cooley Lake, Crooked Lake, French Lake, Funk Lake (Beaver), John Lake, Kelly Lake, Lee Lake (Leigh), Little Bass Lake, MacHolm Lake, Moshawquit Lake, Munger Lake, Neltigan Lake, Oconto Falls Pond, Paya Lake, Pickerel Lake, Pine Lake, Reservoir Pond, Rice Lake, Rost Lake, Shay Lake, Star Lake, Surprise Lake, Turtle Lake, Ucil Lake, Waubee Lake, Wescott Lake, Wheeler Lake, Wheeler Pond, White Lake, White Potatoe Lake.

Oneida County

Aldridge Lake, Alva Lake, Baker Lake, Bass Hatchery, Baycat Lake (Alice), Bear Lake (Harriet), Bearskin Lake, Big Lake, Big Carr Lake, Big Fork Lake, Big Moccasin Lake, Big Stone Lake, Birch Lake, Bird Lake, Blue Lake, Bobcat Lake, Boglar Lake (McKenna), Boom Lake (Rhinelander Flowage), Booth Lake, Brown Lake, Buck Lake, Buckskin Lake, Buffalo Lake, Burnham Lake, Burrows Lake, Camp 21 Lake, Carroll Lake, Chain Lake, Clear Lakes (4), Clearwater Lake, Columbus Lake, Crescent Lake, Crooked Lake, Crystal Lake (Anderson), Dam Lake, Deer Lake, Denton Lake, Diamond Lake, Dog Lake (Deer), Dorothy Lake (Dougherty), East Horsehead Lake, Fawn Lake, Fifth Lake, Flannery Lake, Four Mile Lake, Franklin Lake, Fuller Lake, Garth Lake, George Lake, Gilmore Lake (Silver), Ginty Lake, Goodyear Lake, Great Bass Lake, Greater Bass Lake, Hancock Lake, Hasbrook Lake, Hodstradt Lake, Horsehead Lake, Island Lake, Jenny Weber Lake, Julia Lakes, Kathan Lake, Katherine Lake, Kawaguesage Lake, Kechewaishke Lake, Lee Lake (Leigh), Little Bearskin Lake, Little Fork Lake, Little Tomahawk Lake, Lone Stone Lake, Long Lakes (5), Lost Lake, Lower Kaubeshine Lake, Lucille Lake (Tanka), Lugh Lake, McCormick Lake, McNaughton Lake (Helen), Madeline Lake, Malby Lake, Manson Lake, Maple Lake (Dog), Margaret Lake, Marrion Lake (Miller), Maud Lake, Medicine Lake (Laurel), Mercer Lake, Mildred Lake, Mill Lake, Miller Lake, Minocqua Lake, Moens Lake, Mosquito Lake, Mud Lake (Crystal), Mud Lake, Muskellunge Lake, Nawaii Lake (Mid), Nokomis Lake, North Nokomis Lake, North Pelican Lake, North Two Lake, Oatmeal Lake, Ogemaga Lake, Ole Lake, Oneida Lake, One Stone Lake, Oscar Jenny Lake, Oswego Lake (Clear), Pelican Lake, Pickerel Lake, Pickerel Lake, Pier Lake, Pine Lake, Pine Lake (Round), Pine Lake, Planting Ground Lake (Mud), Rainbow Flowage Lake, Range Line Lake, Rice Lake, Round Lake, Sand Lake, Seven Mile Lake, Shepard Lake, Shishebogama Lake, Skunk Lake (Sunshine), Snowden Lake, South Two Lake, Spirit Lake, Squash Lake, Squaw Lake (Oneida), Squirrel Lake, Starvation Lake (Arbutus), Stella Lake, Stone Lake, Sunday Lake, Swampsauger Lake, Tamarack Lake, Third Lake, Thompson Lake, Thunder Lake, Thunder Lake, Tomahawk Lake, Tom Doyle Lake, Townline Lake, Townline Lake, Two Sister Lake, Virgin Lake, Vensus Lake, Whitefish Lake, Willow Lake, Willow Reservoir, Windpudding Lake, Wolf Lake, Woodcock Lake, Yawkey Lake.

Pepin County

Bear Lake, Dead Lake, Nine Mile Slough Lake, Silver Birch Lake.

Pierce County

Dead Lake, Hunters Lake, Goose Lake, Mud Lake, Pepin Lake (see Pepin County).

Polk County

Apple River Flowage Lake, Balsam Lake, Bass Lake, Bear Trap Lake, Big Lake, Big Butternut

Lake, Horseshoe Lake, Big Horseshoe Lake, Blakes Lake, Bloom Lake, Bone Lake, Cedar Lake, Church Pine Lake, Clara Lake, Dahl Lake, Deer Lake, Diamond Lake, East Lake, Footes Lake, Garfield Lake, Goose Lake, Greenquist Lake, Half Moon Lake, Horse Lake, Johnson Lake, Kenabee Lake, Lamount Lake, Largin Lake, Little Butternut Lake, Little Round Lake, Long Lake, Long Lake, Long Trade Lake, Loveless Lake, Mud Lake, North Pipe Lake, North Twin Lake, Peaslee Lake, Pike Lake, Pine Lake, Pipe Lake, Poplar Lake, Rice Lake, Round Lake, Round Lake (Big), Sand Lake, Straight Lake, Swede Lake, Wapogasset Lake, Ward Lake, White Ash Lake, Wild Goose Lake, Wolf Lake.

Portage County

Emily Lake, Lime Lake, McDill Pond (Plover River, Mill Pond), Pickerel Lake, Skunk Lake, Sunset Lake, Thomas Lake, Three Lake, Washburn Lake, Wisconsin River Flowage, Wolf Lake.

Price County

Bass Lake, Big Pine Lake, Blockhouse Lake, Butternut Lake, Cochran Lake, Cranberry Lake, Crane and Chase Lake, Davis Lake, Deer Lake, Duroy Lake, Elk Lake, Gates Lake, Granger Lake, Grassy Lake, Hultman Lake, Kabol Lake, Lac Sault Dore Lake, Le Tourneau Lake, Long Lake, Lower Price Lake, Middle Price Lake, Musser Flowage Lake, Newman Lake, Patterson Lake, Phillips Flowage (Wilson Creek), Pike Lake, Rice Lake (Amik), Riley Lake, Round Lake, Sailor Creek Flowage, Schnur Lake (Snore), Sixteen Lake (Mytrie), Spirit Lake, Stone Lake, Thompson Lake, Turner Lake, Worcester Lake.

Racine County

Bohners Lake, Browns Lake, Eagle Lake, KeNong Go Mong Lake (Long), Long Lake, Minister Lake (Waubese), Rockland Lake (Frieda), Tichigan Lake, Wind Lake.

Richland County

Cazenovia Millpond, Lawson Pond.

Rock County

Clear Lake, Gibbs Lake.

Rusk County

Amacoy Lake, Bass Lake, Big Falls Flowage, Boot Lake, Cedar Rapids Flowage, Chain Lake, Clear Lake, Fish Lake, Ladysmith Flowage, Little Falls Flowage, Little Rice Lake (Fireside), McCann Lake, Mud Lake, Pine Lake, Port Arthur Flowage, Potato Lake, Pulaski Lake, Sand Lake, Skinner Lake, Thornapple Flowage.

St. Croix County

Apple River, Bass Lake, Brushy Mound, Burkhardt Flowage, Cedar Lake, Dry Dam, Hatfield Lake, Maltalieu Lake, Middle Flowage, Oak Ridge, Perch Lake, St. Croix River, Squaw Lake, Twin Lake.

Sauk County

Delton Lake, Devils Lake, Lower Mirror Lake, Upper Mirror Lake, Wisconsin Lake (see Columbia County).

Sawyer County

Ashegon Lake, Barber Lake, Barker Lake, Beaver Lake, Benet Lake, Big Lac Court Oreilles Lake, Big Ole Lake, Big Round Lake, Big Sand Lake, Big Sissabagama Lake, Big Spider Lake, Billy Boy Flowage, Black Lake, Black Dan Lake (McDonald), Blaisdell Lake, Blueberry Lake, Brunet Flowage, Callahan Lake, Chetac Lake, Chief Lake, Chippewa Flowage, Chippewa River, Chippewa River (West Fork), Christy Lake, Clear Lake, Connors Lake, Couderay Lake, Crane Lake, Durphee Lake, Evergreen Lake, Fishtrap Lake, Ghost Lake, Grindstone Lake, Gurno Lake, Ham Lake, Hayward Flowage, Hegemeisters Lake, Helane Lake, Hunter Lake, Indian Lake, Island Lake, Johnson Lake, Little Lac Court, Little Ole Lake, Little Round Lake, Little Sand Lake, Little Sissabagama Lake, Little Spider Lake, Lost Land Lake, Lovejoy Lake, Lower Clam Lake, Mason Lake, Moose Lake, North Lake, O'Pines Lake (Swamp), Pac-wa-wong Lake, Patsy Lake, Perch Lake (Siren), Pickerel Lake, Placid Lake, Raddison Flowage, Reed Lake, Smith Lake, Spring Lake, Squaw Lake, Star Lake, Summitt Lake, Teal Lake, Tiger Cat Flowage, Upper Twin Lake, Whitefish Lake, Wilson Lake, Windigo Lake.

Shawano County

Big Lake, Island Lake (Park), Lily Lake, Long

Lake, Loon Lake, Lulu Lake, Mud Lake, Pensaukee Lake, Pine Lake, Shawano Lake, Shroenrock Lake, White Clay Lake.

Sheboygan County

Big Elkhart Lake, Crooked Lake, Crystal Lake (Cedar), Elien Lake, Franklin Millpond, Johnsonville Pond, Little Elkhart Lake, Random Lake, Richardson Pond.

Taylor County

Diamond Lake, Duchien Lake, Grassy Knoll, Hulls Lake, Isadore Lake, Jump River Flowage, Kathryn Lake, Mondeaux Flowage, Moon Lake, North Harper Lake, North Spirit Lake, Rib Lake, Sacketts Lake, Skinner Lake, South Harper Lake, Spirit Lake, Wood Lake, Yellow River.

Trempealeau County

Independence Lake, Marinuka Lake, Trempealeau Pond.

Vilas County

Adelade Lake, Alder Lake, Allequash Lake, Alma Lake, Amik Lake (Rice), Annabelle Lake, Anvil Lake, Apeekwa Lake (Pine and Little), Armour Lake, Arrowhead Lake (Little Star), Aurora Lake (Rice), Averill Lake (Mud), Ballard Lake, Beaver Lake, Belle Lake, Big Lake, Big Arbor Vitae Lake, Big Bass Lake, Big Crooked Lake, Big Crooked Lake (Clear), Big Gibson Lake, Big Kitten Lake, Big Muskellunge Lake, Big Portage Lake, Big Sand Lake, Bills Lake, Birch Lake, Bittersweet Lake (Bass), Black Oak Lake, Bolin Lake, Bolton Lake, Boot Lake, Boulder Lake, Brandy Lake (Cecilia), Broken Bow Lake (Little Crooked), Camp 12 Lake, Carlin Lake, Carpenter Lake, Catfish Lake, Cedar Lake (Mink), Circle Lily Lake, Clair Lake, Clear Lake, Cochran Lake, Constance Lake, Content Lake, Corrine Lake, Crab Lake (Musky), Cranberry Lake, Crampton Lake, Crawling Stone Lake, Crystal Lake, Day Lake, Dead Pike Lake, Deer Lake, Deerskin Lake, Devine Lake (Dollar), Diamond Lake, Dollar Lake, Donahue Lake, Dorothy Dunn Lake, Duck Lake, Dunn Lake, Eagle Lake, Edith Lake, Erickson Lake, Escanaba Lake (Rock), Fallison Lake (Long), Fence Lake, Finley Lake, Finger Lake, Fishtrap Lake, Flora Lake, Forest Lake, Found Lake, Frank Lake (Bear), Frost Lake (Mud), George Lake, Grassy Lake, Gunlock Lake, Hardin Lake, Harris Lake, Haskell Lake, Heart Lake, Helen Lake, High Lake, Horsehead Lake, Hunter Lake, Ike Walton Lake, Imogene Lake, Indian Lake, Irving Lake, Island Lake, Jag Lake, Jenny Lake, Jerms Lake, Johnson Lake, Jones Lake, Jute Lake, Katinka Lake, Kentuck Lake, Kenu Lake (Ethyl, Alice), Kildare Lake (Pine), Lac du Flambeau Lake, Lac du Lune Lake (Island), Lac Vieux Desert Lake, Landing Lake (Charlotte), Laura Lake, Little Arbor Vitae Lake, Little Bateau Lake (Bass), Little Bear Lake, Little Crab Lake, Little Crawling Stone Lake, Little Crooked Lake, Little Horsehead Lake, Little Muskie Lake, Little Portage Lake, Little Presque Isle Lake, Little St. Germain Lake, Little Sand Lake, Little Spider Lake, Little Star Lake, Star Lake, Little Trout Lake, Lone Pine Lake, Lone Stone Lake, Lone Tree Lake, Long Lake, Long Lake (Interlaken), Lost Canoe Lake, Lost Lake, Lower Buckatabon Lake, Lower Gresham Lake, Lower Nine Mile Lake, Lower Sugarbush Lake, Lynx Lake, Mamie Lake, Manitowish Lake, Mann Lake, Manuel Lake (Manna), Marshall Lake, McCollough Lake, McLeod Lake, Mermaid Lake, Meta Lake, Mid Ellerson Lake, Middle Gresham Lake, Middle Sugarbush Lake, Mill Lake, Minette Lake (Bass), Minonk Lake (Oscar), Mitten Lake, Moccasin Lake, Morton Lake, Moss Lake (Mud), Murphy Lake, Muscallunge Lake, Muskesin Lake (Bass), Nebish Lake, Nelson Lake, Nixon Lake, No Mans Lake, North Turtle Lake, North Twin Lake, Oswego Lake, Otter Lake, Oxbow Lake, Pallette Lake, Palmer Lake, Papoose Lake, Partridge Lake, Pickerel Lake, Pine Island Lake, Pioneer Lake, Plum Lake, Pokegama Lake, Presque Isle Lake, Rainbow Lake, Range Line Lake, Razorback Lake, Rest Lake, Rice Lake, Roach Lake, Rock Lake (Yolanda), Ross Lake, Ross Allen Lake, Round Lake (Sunset), Round Lake, Rudolph Lake, St. Germain Lake, Salsich Lake, Sanborn Lake, Sandford Lake, Scattering Rice Lake, Seventeen Lake, Sherman Lake, Silver Lake, Snipe Lake, South Turtle Lake, South Twin Lake, Sparkling Lake (Silver), Spectacle Lake, Spider Lake, Star Lake, Starrett Lake (Bear), State Line Lake, Stearns Lake, Stone Lake (Fawn), Sugar Maple Lake (Bass), Sunfish Lake, Sunset Lake, Tamarack Lake, Tambling Lake (Little Bass), Tellefson Lake, Tenderfoot Lake, Tepee Lake, Tippecanoe Lake (Island), Toulish Lake (Stellnack), Towanda Lake (Bass), Trilby

Lake, Trout Lake, Twin Island Lake, Upper Buckatabon Lake, Upper Gresham Lake, Upper Sugarbush Lake, Vandercook Lake (Crane), Van Viet Lake, Verna Lake, Watersmeet Flowage, West Bay, West Ellerson Lake, Whitches Lake (Witches), White Birch Lake, Whitefish Lake, White Sand Lake, White Sand Lake, Whitney Lake (Harrington), Wildcat Lake, Wild Rice Lake, Wishow Lake, Wolf Lake, Wyandock Lake, Yellow Birch Lake.

Walworth County

Benedict Lake (see Kenosha County), Beulah Chain (Upper, Round, Lower, Mill), Booth Lake, Como Lake, Comus Lake, Delavan Lake, East Troy Lake (Army), Geneva Lake, Lauderdale Chain (Green, Middle, Mill [Lauderdale]), Loraine Lake, Lulu Lake, Pell Lake, Pleasant Lake, Potters Lake, Trapp Lake (Tripp), Turtle Lake, Wandawega Lake (Otter), Whitewater Lake.

Washburn County

Balsam Lake, Bass Lake, Bean Lake, Bear Lake, Beaver Lake, Big Bass Lake, Big Casey Lake, Big Dugen Lake, Big Ripley Lake, Birch Lake, Cable Lake, Carassy Lake, Chicog Lake, Chippenaze Lake, Cyclone Lake, Deer Lake, DeRosier Lake, Devils Lake, Dunn Lake, Ellsworth Lake, Fenton Lake, Gilmore Lake, Goose Lake, Goose Lake, Gull Lake, Harmon Lake, Hay Lake, Herbert Lake, Hointville Lake, Horseshoe Lake, Island Lake, Kekegama Lake, Kimball Lake, Lakeside Lake, Lazy Island Lake, Leach Lake, Leesome Lake, Lincoln Lake, Little Bass Lake, Little Cable Lake, Little Devils Lake, Little Gilmore Lake, Little Long Lake, Little Sand Lake, Little Spider Lake, Long Lake, Loon Lake, Loyhead Lake, Lower Kimball Lake, Lower McKenzie Lake, Mac Lake (Stance), Mac Crea Lake, McKinley Lake, Mac Lain Lake, Mathews Lake, Middle Kimball Lake, Miles Lake, Monda Lake (Monday), Mud Lake, Nancy Lake, Nancy Flowage, Nick Lake, Noltz Lake, North Twin Lake, Nyes Lake, Oak Lake, Pavis Lake, Pear Lake, Pokegama Lake, Potato Lake, Rice Lake, Rocky Ridge Lake, Sand Lake, Scovils Lake, Seynore Lake, Shell Lake, Silver Lake, Skunk Lake, Sleepy Eye Lake, Slim Lake, Slim Creek Flowage, South Twin Lake, Spider Lake, Spooner Lake, Spring Lake, Spring Lake, Stone Lake, Sugar Bush Lake, Taylor Lake, Tranus Lake, Trego Flowage, Upper Kimball Lake, Whalen Lake, Yeckout Lake, Yellow River Flowage.

Washington County

Bark Lake, Big Cedar Lake, Druid Lake (Ashippin), Five Lake, Friess Lake, Green Lake (Schwin), Little Cedar Lake, Lucas Lake, Silver Lake, Smith Lake (Drickens), Wallace Lake.

Waukesha County

Ashippun Lake, Beaver Lake, Big Muskego Lake, Crooked Lake, Denoon Lake, Eagle Spring Lake, Fowlers Lake, Golden Lake, Keesus Lake, La Belle Lake, Little Muskego Lake, Lower Nashotah Lake, Lower Nemabbin Lake, Lower Phantom Lake (Hewitt), Moose Lake (Mouse), Nagawicka Lake, North Lake, Oconomowoc Lake, Okauchee Lake, Pewaukee Lake, Pine Lake, Saylesville Millpond, School Section Lake, Silver Lake, Spring Lake, Upper Genesee Lake, Upper Nashotah Lake, Upper Nemabbin Lake, Upper Phantom Lake.

Waupaca County

Bear Lake, Campbell Lake, Clintonville Pond, Columbian Lake, Crystal Lake, Grahm Lake, Hicks Lake (Sunset), Iola Millpond, Long Lake, Manawa Millpond, Marion Millpond, Partridge Lake, Partridge Crop Lake, Rainbow Lake, Round Lake, Silver Lake, Spencer Lake, Stratton Lake, Taylor Lake, Weyauwega Lake, White Lake.

Waushara County

Aurorahville Pond, Big Silver Lake, Bing Lake, Fish Lake, Gilbert Lake, Hills Lake, Johns Lake, Koosle Lake (Kossel), Little Hills Lake, Little Silver Lake, Long Lake, Mt. Morris Lake, Norwegian Lake, Pearl Lake, Pine Lake, Pleasant Lake, Porters Lake, Round Lake, Twin Lake, Upper White River Millpond, White River Flowage, Wilson Lake.

Winnebago County

Butte des Morts Lake, Poygan Lake, Winnebago Lake, Winneconne Lake.

Wood County

Nepco Lake, Wazeecha Lake.

Chapter 15

THE SOUTHEAST

This is the most important and productive bass-fishing region in the world. An angler can find himself anywhere in the Southeast and practically never be more than a few minutes away from good bass waters—and from big bass.

Many of the very best bass waters—the lakes which contain the lunkers—have already been described in Chapter 7. This chapter, then, is a summary of as many bass-fishing opportunities as can be compiled into the space available.

Tennessee

Here is a state of widely contrasting waters—from giant reservoirs to shallow, eerie earthquake ponds such as Reelfoot Lake—but except for the cold mountain streams in between, there are few waters which do not contain bass. All three species of bass are present in Tennessee waters: largemouth, smallmouth, and spotted. The largemouth is the most common black bass in ponds and lakes. Managed farm ponds, state-owned lakes managed by the Game and Fish Commission, and practically all of the lakes and reservoirs of the state are popular largemouth fishing areas. Reelfoot Lake has long been an unusually good spot for largemouth bass. While the larger, slower rivers provide some largemouth fishing, the lakes and ponds offer the most reliable fishing areas . . . March to November.

The smallmouth bass in Tennessee is a prize regardless of where he is caught. Originally the smallmouth was almost exclusively a stream fish in Tennessee, but with the impounding of some of our smallmouth streams into lakes, he has taken on new and larger proportions. The smallmouth may be found in many streams throughout that part of Tennessee east of Kentucky Lake. More of the better streams are found in middle Tennessee. Among the eastern Tennessee streams providing better smallmouth fishing are the Powell and Clinch rivers above Norris Lake, Holston River, Little River, and several smaller streams in Monroe County. The larger streams on the Cumberland Plateau also support some smallmouth. In middle Tennessee almost every clean stream that flows the year round is inhabited by smallmouth. Among the better of these are Elk, Upper Duck, Caney Fork, Collins, Stones, Harpeth, and Buffalo rivers and many of their tributaries.

For larger smallmouth, some weighing from 5 to 10 pounds, the fisherman should go to certain lakes. Dale Hollow and Center Hill lakes have produced record smallmouth regularly since they were impounded. Norris Lake and Watauga Lake also have produced many outstanding fish. The best smallmouth fishing, on either streams or lakes, is during the spring and fall months.

The Kentucky or spotted bass is less abundant than either the largemouth or smallmouth but may occur in any lake or stream. Although sometimes associated with the smallmouth, it is common in the clearer streams of western Tennessee, such as the headwaters of the Obion, Hatchie, Loosahatchie, and Wolf rivers. Harpeth River in middle Tennessee also has large numbers of this species. The larger Kentuckys are usually taken from lakes. A list of major fishing lakes follows.

Chickamauga Lake: Chickamauga Lake on the Tennessee extends 59 miles upstream from near Chattanooga and covers 34,500 acres. Largemouth bass is the predominant game fish.

Cherokee Lake: Cherokee is a storage lake on the Holston River, near Morristown, Tenn. It extends 59 miles and covers an area of 31,000 acres. Cherokee Lake is excellent bass water.

Douglas Lake: Douglas is a storage lake on the French Broad River. It has a length of 43 miles and cover 31,000 acres. It is near Dandridge (pop. 446), Tenn., and 30 miles east of Knoxville, and 20 miles north of Gatlinburg, headquarters city of the Great Smoky Mountains National Park. Principal game fish is the largemouth.

Fort Loudoun Lake: Fort Loudoun is on the main channel of the Tennessee. It extends 55 miles upstream to Knoxville, Tenn., and covers 14,500 acres.

Great Falls Lake (Rock Island): The only lake of the TVA system not in the Tennessee River Valley, is located on Caney Fork River, a tributary of the Cumberland, near McMinnville. It has been in existence since 1916, has an area of 2270 acres, and is 22 miles long.

Hales Bar Lake: This one is on the main channel of the Tennessee River just below Chattanooga. It's 40 miles long and covers 6000 acres.

Kentucky Lake: Kentucky Lake, on the main channel of the Tennessee, extends from near the Mississippi state line entirely across the state of Tennessee to Gilbertsville, Ky., a distance of 184 miles. It covers 158,300 acres and has a ragged shore line of 2380 miles. It covers more area and has a longer shore line than any other man-made lake in the United States. Excellent bass water.

Norris Lake: First of the TVA-created lakes, Norris has been an attraction to thousands of fishermen since it was filled in the summer of 1936. It is located in Tennessee 25 miles north of Knoxville, is easily accessible, and is in use the year round.

Pickwick Lake: Pickwick Lake extends 53 miles along the Tennessee from the dam at Pickwick Landing to Wilson Dam in Alabama. About 10 miles of its length lies in Tennessee. Largemouth bass are the chief attractions for the angler.

Watts Bar Lake: One of the main-stream links of the Tennessee system, Watts Bar Lake covers an area of 38,000 acres and is 74 miles long. The largemouth bass supports most of the sport fishing.

Fontana Lake: Fontana Dam is located in a wooded mountain region on the Little Tennessee River 68 miles from Knoxville, Tenn. It is a storage dam on a tributary of the Tennessee River system, forming a lake 30 miles long.

Dale Hollow Lake: One of the newest recreational areas in the north Cumberland Mountains of Tennessee is Dale Hollow Lake, covering about 40,000 acres. This clear body of water was recently impounded by U. S. Army engineers on the Obey River, near where it empties into the Cumberland River near Celina. First opened to fishing in October 1944, it provides the best sustained bass fishing in Tennessee. It can be approached through the towns of Celina or Livingston.

Reelfoot Lake: During the great earthquake of 1811 forest lands sank beneath the surface and the Mississippi River poured in, bringing almost every variety of fish known to inland waters. This later became known as Reelfoot Lake. Many of the submerged trees died, leaving the lake filled with stumps, forming one of the finest natural fish hatcheries in the world. The lake is teeming with largemouth bass and approximately 27 other species.

Center Hill Lake: A 40,000-acre impoundment on the Caney Fork River near Smithville. Plentiful facilities all around. Plenty of bass.

South Holston Lake: Good bass lake near Bristol, opened to fishing in 1952.

Watauga Lake: Good bass lake covers 6400 acres, is 17 miles long, in Cherokee Forest area near Elizabethton.

Parksville Lake: Between Ocoee and Ducktown, this lake has 1900 acres and 18 miles of shore line.

Davy Crockett Lake: Lake contains 900 acres and is located 9 miles from Greeneville on the Nolichucky River.

Cheatham Lake: Long and narrow reservoir on Cumberland River just west of Nashville. Numerous boat docks, facilities.

Old Hickory Reservoir: About 25,000 acres on the Cumberland Reservoir just east of Nashville.

Woods Reservoir: Located near Estill Spring, one boat dock.

Boone Lake: Good fishing water in extreme northeastern corner of state. Many good facilities nearby.

Fort Patrick Henry Lake: Good bass fishing near Kingsport on South Fork of Holston River.

Bedford Lake: Bedford County, near Normandy and about 14 miles east of Shelbyville. 47 acres. Boat dock, fishing pier, bait, and boats. This lake is noted for its catches of large bass. Two largemouths weighing more than 13 pounds each have been taken.

Brown's Creek Lake: Henderson County, in the Natchez Trace Forest, about 9 miles northeast of Lexington. 167 acres. Boat docks, boats, and bait.

Burgess Falls Lake: White and Putnam counties, 7 miles south of Cookeville toward Sparta. Noted for big largemouth bass in the lake and smallmouths below the dam.

Carroll Lake: Carroll County, about 3 miles south of McKenzie, 8 miles north of Huntingdon, on State Highway 22. 100 acres.

Fisherville Lake: About 20 miles east of Memphis, western edge of Fayette County, on Macon Road. 177 acres.

Humboldt Lake: Crockett County, 4 miles west of Humboldt, 87 acres. Excellent for both fishing and other recreation.

Laurel Hill Lake: 14 miles west of Lawrenceburg on the Natchez Trace (U. S. Route 64). 327 acres.

Maple's Creek Lake: Southeast corner of Carroll County, in the Natchez Trace Forest, between Lexington and Huntingdon. About 90 acres.

Marrowbone Lake: Davidson County, about 20 miles north of Nashville. 60 acres. Boats, trolling motors, boat dock, bait, and tackle.

Kentucky

Every season is bass-fishing time in Kentucky, with many types of fishing methods to suit every fisherman. At one time only the warmer months attracted anglers to this state. However, with the completion of five major lakes, one of them the largest man-made lake in the world, Kentucky fishing has taken on new aspects. Five impoundments, augmented by more than 14,000 miles of running water and over 100,000 farm ponds, have lured fishermen from everywhere to the fine facilities offered here.

Fall fishing in Kentucky is excellent in streams and lakes as well. When cooler weather arrives bass may be taken from all lakes and streams and offer more vigorous fights, perhaps, than at any other period.

Winter fishing is good for bass, even on very cold days. They may be taken by the sure-fire method of jigging which involves dangling a triple hook, baited with night crawlers, in the murky to muddy waters alongside the banks.

In the spring, of course, fishing breaks out all over. Bass are on a rampage during this three- or four-month period. Jump fishing is becoming more popular in this state, and even on the hottest days full catches of bass are made by this method.

In late June and on through the summer, when the shad become two or three inches in size and school up by the thousands, the greedy bass gets his dinner in easy fashion. He locates a school, plows through it, and scoops up the shad. The fisherman, watching for these ripples in the water, casts his plug and often pulls in a whopper.

Kentucky Lake, in the western part of the state, is the largest man-made lake in the world with 2380 miles of shore line. It is comparatively shallow and offers good fishing the year round. All three species of black bass may be taken from these waters. Facilities around this lake are excellent.

Lake Cumberland is the newest in a series of Kentucky lakes. It lies wholly in Kentucky and is 105 miles long. A deep lake, its bass population has been found to be among the greatest of any lake in the nation. Since it is a young lake, not so many large bass have been taken from it as from other lakes, but in numbers the yearly catch is greatest of all. Because of its depth (it averages 91 feet) this lake is becoming the best bass-fishing lake in this section of the nation. One fisherman once caught 97 bass in one morning.

Dale Hollow lies in the extreme south-central section of the state and has long been known for the huge bass caught there. Casting the banks in the early spring and fall produces most of the bass although bait fishermen may catch them on minnows. The catch per day may not be so great as in other lakes, but the average size of the bass taken from this lake probably is greater than from any other.

Herrington Lake, in central Kentucky, has offered good fishing for more than 35 years. This is the oldest major impoundment in the state. It is 31 miles long and is comparatively deep. Catches of black bass are good there periodically, and, like Dale Hollow, some very large bass are taken.

Dewey Lake, in the eastern part of the state, is smaller but bass fishing is good.

More than 100,000 farm ponds produce good bass and bluegill fishing throughout the year, and, for the fisherman who has but a limited time to fish, they offer some of the very best fishing.

Kentucky has more miles of running water than any other state in the union. It should not be said that all the stretches of all these streams offer good fishing. But Kentucky does have as many miles of fishable waters as any other state, and some of them can't be beat for bass.

Triplett and Kinniconick in the eastern section of the state are well known in their vicinities. Green River, in the southeastern section, is great. Barren River and Gasper are outstanding among the streams in the south-central section.

Kentucky surely has more good smallmouth bass waters than any other state. Many of its streams are swift and clear. These are ideal places for the smallmouth to live, and strings of fish taken from them attest the fact that the population of this species is good.

It is impossible to list all those streams which have proved their worth as fishing waters, but listed herewith are some of the better known and more heavily fished streams.

In the southwestern section there are the Cumberland, Ohio, Mississippi, Tennessee, and Blood rivers, plus many smaller rivers and creeks.

In the south-central section may be found the Green, Red, Gasper, Barren, and Nolin rivers and numerous smaller streams.

The Ohio and Salt rivers and many smaller streams are found in the Louisville area.

In the north-central section, fishermen may visit Kentucky, Licking, and Little Kentucky rivers and famous old Elkhorn Creek.

Right in the heart of the Bluegrass, in addition to the Kentucky and Licking rivers, there are the Chaplin, Red, and Rockcastle rivers and numerous smaller streams.

Along the eastern fringe of the state are the Big Sandy, Licking, and branches of the Kentucky River and innumerable fine mountain streams.

Slightly to the north of this section are forks of the Licking, Ohio, and Red rivers, and famous Kinniconick and Triplett creeks and other small streams.

In the southern section of the state, and slightly to the east, Laurel, Cumberland, Rockcastle, and branches of the Kentucky River and many smaller streams may be found.

Because of the vast number of fine, relatively undisturbed smallmouth streams, the writer considers Kentucky the finest bass float-trip region in America. Below are listed some of the famous float-fishing streams in Kentucky and available information as compiled by the staff of *Happy Hunting Ground* magazine.

North Fork of Kentucky (May and June, September and October): Upper portion riffles in summer. Boat must be carried. Abounds in largemouth and smallmouth bass and some musky.

Places to put in or take out boat—Route 28 from Chavies to Breathitt County line; Route 1570 to Barrwick and Wolfcole; Route 1110 to Haddix; Route 15 to Jackson and Route 731 to Mt. Carmel Bible School. All in Breathitt County. In Lee County at Airdale Bridge 12 miles east of Beattyville on gravel road known as Airdale Bridge Road (12-mile section no riffles, all back waters). Stream has some 75 miles of fishing water.

Middle Fork of Kentucky (May and June, September and October): Upper portion has many riffles and in summer months boat must be carried over these. Buckhorn Dam only large obstacle. Float to this area or from below dam. Abounds with large-mouth and smallmouth bass as well as muskies.

Starting at Confluence, Leslie County Hi-ways 421 and 257 to Buckhorn Dam: Buckhorn through small portion of Perry County: Hi-way 28 through Breathitt County to Athol on Hi-way 315; Lymons Creek bridge 20 miles southeast of Beattyville, on Hi-way 52 to St. Helens, on Hi-way 52. Stream has some 90 miles of fishing water.

South Fork of Kentucky (May, June, and August): Upper portion has many riffles and in summer boat must be carried over these (through Clay, Owsley, and Lee counties) from Oneida to Crane Creek; to Rocky Branch; to Sexton Creek; to Lower Wolf Creek; to Fish Trap Branch; to Booneville; to Beattyville. Stream has 56 miles of fishing water. Largemouth and smallmouth bass and some musky.

Green River (early spring, late summer, and fall): Upper portion riffles. Boat must be carried in summer. Lower section has several dams, boats must also be carried except for two locks. Upper section noted for all three species of black bass and redeye. Lower section same and also walleye and mammoth musky. 354 miles of fishing water.

Starting at Green River Bridge on Hi-way 198 to Liberty; Roberts Ford Hi-way 35; Dunnville at iron bridge 1/4 mile off Hi-way 35, all in Casey County. Beech Grove, Adair County, Hi-way 76; Neatsville, Adair County, Hi-way 76; Fisherford, Adair County, rural road; Taylor County Hi-way 55; Roachville, Taylor County, rural road; Bluff Boone, Green County, rural road; Sardin Ford, Green County, ball park in Greensburg; Berry Bridge, Green County on Burma Road; Well Ferry Bridge, Green County Hi-way 881; Sidebottom ford, Green County off Hi-way 88 near Bucknerville; Little Barren River, Hart County, Derfies; 300 Springs, Hart County, off Hi-way 31-E at Canmer; Munfordville, Hart County, 31-W; Hart County Park in Hart County; Dennison Ferry, Mammoth Cave National Park, Edmonson County; Mammoth Cave Ferry near Headquarters of Mammoth Cave National Park; Lock #5, Warren County, Hi-way 185; Lock #4, Woodbury, Butler County, Hi-way 686; Morgantown, Butler County, Hi-way 231; Rochester, Butler County, Hi-way 369; Paradise, Muhlenberg County, Hi-way 176; South Carrollton, Muhlenberg County, Hi-way 431; Livermore, McLean County, Hi-way 431; Calhoun, McLean County, Hi-way 81; Jewell City, McLean County, Hi-way 147; Sebree, Webster County, Hi-way 136; Rangers Landing to Hamilton Ferry, Hi-way 54; to Spottsville, Henderson County, Lock #1.

Red River (early spring, late summer, and fall): Many riffles in upper part, boat carried in some. Small- and largemouth bass and good musky.

Powell County, Hi-way 15 to Nada, turn left on Hi-way 77 to Red River. Take out places Bowen, Rosslyn, Stanton, or Clay City on Hi-way 15. From Clay City to Hi-way 82 on Clark and Estill County line. Total trip 60 miles.

Licking River (early spring to late fall): Upper portion many swift riffles, less on lower section. Upper part musky, black bass, redeye; lower section void of musky. Black Water Bridge to Rowan and Menifee County line, to Scott Creek, to Farmer, to Isle Mill, to Moors Ford, to Wyoming, to Shurbon, to Mill Creek, to Myres, to Blue Lick, to Painters Creek, Harrison County, Clayville, Hi-way 62; McKenneyburg, Hi-way 339; Falmouth, Hi-way 27; Butled, to Newport. Some 303 miles of fishing waters.

For those who want to try their hand at musky fishing try the following; Tygart Creek, Carter and Greenup counties; Triplett Creek, Rowan County; Kenniconick Creek, Lewis County.

North Carolina

The over-all fine fishing of North Carolina's

coastal region is enhanced by the fresh-water streams, lakes, and sounds nearby. Spring and autumn offer the best bass fishing.

One of the top fishing grounds anywhere is fresh-water Currituck Sound, dividing the mainland from the Outer Banks. Largemouth bass are taken with plugs, bugs, flies—on anything. Information regarding boats and guide service is available at Currituck village, on N. C. Highway 34; Coinjock, on U. S. Route 158 and the Inland Waterway, and nearby Waterlily; Poplar Branch, just off U. S. Route 158; and Point Harbor on the southern tip of the Currituck Peninsula.

Just across the Wright Memorial Bridge from Point Harbor in the Kitty Hawk-Nags Head area are many fresh-water ponds, within sight of the Wright Memorial, which yield good catches of largemouth bass. This section also may be reached by U. S. Route 64 (free ferry at Alligator River) which crosses Croatan Sound to Roanoke Island and Manteo by the Umstead Memorial Bridge.

Along U. S. Route 264 is Lake Mattamuskeet, largest natural fresh-water lake in North Carolina, where largemouth bass fishing is unexcelled (special permit, obtainable from Refuge Headquarters, New Holland, required). Information: Refuge Manager, New Holland, N.C.

Largemouth bass also abound in such favorite spots as Town Creek, Northeast River, and Black River, near Wilmington. Information: Greater Wilmington Chamber of Commerce, Wilmington, N.C.

In the Sandhills area, on Sandhills Wildlife Management Area near Hoffman on U. S. Route 1, is Broadacres Lake. It's a great producer. Bass here like the plastic worms, etc.

Largemouth, smallmouth, and spotted bass are present in all of the larger power reservoirs of the mountain area. The better largemouth lakes are Fontana, Santeetlah, Chatuge, and James. Others are lakes Summit, Thorpe (Glenville), Adger, and Lure. The heaviest largemouths in the area come from Fontana and Chatuge.

The better smallmouth lakes include Hiwassee, Nanthala (Aquone), Santeetlah, and Fontana. Spotted bass are present in most of these lakes, with the larger ones being taken from Hiwassee.

Many rivers, creeks, and lakes between the seacoast and mountains are easily accessible and then usually provide good sport for bass anglers. Again fishing usually is best in spring and autumn.

Among the lakes is Kerr Reservoir (Buggs Island Lake) a power lake north of Henderson and accessible by U. S. Routes 1-15-158 and N. C. 39. The lake, lying athwart the North Carolina-Virginia line, covers about 49,000 acres and has an 800-mile shore line. Resident and nonresident fishing licenses obtained from either North Carolina or Virginia are recognized by both states, through reciprocal agreement. There are good facilities all around the lake for fishing parties.

In southeastern North Carolina, Lake Waccamaw, just off U. S. Routes 74-76 near Whiteville, is one of the largest natural lakes on the eastern seaboard, covering 22,400 acres, 7 miles long and 5 miles wide.

In the Piedmont are numerous power lakes where fishing is good. These include Lookout Shoals, on U. S. Routes 64-70 west of Statesville, and Oxford off U. S. Routes 70-64 near Hickory. High Rock is a power lake between Lexington and Salisbury on U. S. Routes 52-29-70. Access areas for anglers and boat operators are maintained at many places by the North Carolina Wildlife Resources Commission. A directory of these and other public outdoor facilities may be obtained on request to the State Advertising Division, Raleigh, N.C.

A county-by-county list of bass waters follows:

Alamance County

City Lake and Saxapahaw Pond. Best for fishing early spring, late fall.

Alexander County

Oxford Lake. Best in March, April. Hotels in Hickory (6 miles) or Taylorsville (8 miles).

Alleghany County

Little River, Piney Creek. Best months May, June. Hotels in Roaring Gap, Sparta.

Anson County

Wadesboro City Lake. Good fishing except after rains when lake muddies for week or two.

Ashe County

North and South forks of New River. Smallmouth bass, August and September.

Avery County

Toe River. Bass fishing only on upper end recommended.

Beaufort County

Pantego Creek—June and October. Pungo River, Painter Creek, Grindle Creek, Tanters Creek.

Bertie County

Cashie, Chowan, Roanoke rivers—March, May. Plenty of fresh-water creeks fishable.

Bladen County

Black River, South River—March, April, May, September, October. White Lake, Singletary Lake, Jones Lake. Only fair to indifferent fishing. Jones Lake is reserved for Negroes only.

Brunswick County

McKenzie Pond. Good bass fishing. Fishing in some portions of Waccamaw and Brunswick rivers. Accommodations Southport, Wilmington.

Buncombe County

French Broad River, smallmouth bass, not recommended north of Asheville. Lake Craig, Lake Louise, Swannanoa River—smallmouth bass from Asheville to Grovestone. No fishing on Asheville watershed.

Burke County

Lake Rhodhiss—March, April, May. Hotels at Morganton. Lake James—April, May, June.

Caldwell County

Oxford Lake—March, April. Hotels at Lenoir, Hickory (6 miles), or Taylorsville (8 miles).

Camden County

Pasquotank River and tributaries. North River—spring and fall. Several good creeks—South, Broad, Little, etc.

Carteret County

South River and Upper Newport River.

Catawba County

Lake Hickory—March, April. Usually good bass fishing.

Chatham County

Buckhom Lake (this is out-of-the-way place but has good fishing).

Cherokee County

Hiwassee Lake. One of best bass lakes. Some fishing in Upper Valley River and Hanging Dog Creek.

Chowan County

Chowan River and Yeopim, Pembroke, Bethel creeks, Dillards and Bennetts ponds.

Clay County

Lake Chatuge—April and May.

Columbus County

Lake Waccamaw—April, May. Hotels, furnished cottages on lake. Waccamaw and Lumber rivers—April and September. Hotels Whiteville and Chadbourn.

Craven County

Trent River, considered a good stream. Tributaries of the Neuse below New Bern. Hotels, etc. New Bern and cabins at Minnesott Beach. Catfish and other lakes. Good bass on lake or at Croatan.

Cumberland County

Rockfish Creek, Sunset Creek.

Currituck County

Currituck Sound, North and Northwest rivers, Tulls Bay. All species caught in fresh coastal waters are found here, one of the best fishing spots in the state. Especially noted for black bass—April, May, June, September. Guides, lodging every section.

Dare County

South Lake, East Lake, Alligator River, Mhoying Creek Lake—April and July. Marton Point Creek—May and June. Hotels Nags Head. Kitty Hawk Bay and Collington—March through November. Hotels, etc. Nags Head. Fresh-water ponds nearby.

Duplin County

Northeast Cape Fear, Goshen rivers. Accommodations Warsaw and Kenansville.

Durham County

Lake Michie. This lake offers fair fishing. Accommodations Durham.

Edgecombe County

Noble's Mill Pond—spring and fall. Tar River near Rocky Mount, smallmouth bass—March 15–April 1. Belloney's Mill, Whitakers.

Franklin County

Cypress Creek—May, June. Accommodations at Louisburg. Lots of fishing here. Clifton's Pond, Perry's Pond. Last is one mile from Pearces.

Gates County

Williams Pond—March 20 through November. No nearby accommodations.

Graham County

Lake Santeetlah. Cabins on lake, lodges near Robbinsville and at Tapoca. There is excellent fishing in the lake and unusually good fishing in streams feeding it, especially Santeetlah Creek, Lake Cheoah. Accommodations Tapoca, Robbinsville.

Greene County

Contentnea Creek—June through September.

Guilford County

Brandt Lake—early spring, late fall. Hotels, etc., at Greensboro.

Harnett County

Upper and Lower Little rivers; Cape Fear River.

Haywood County

Pigeon River. Bass near Waterville and from Canton to Lake Logan.

Henderson County

Lake Henderson—March, June, September, October. Hotels, etc., at Hendersonville; French Broad River, hotels, etc. Hendersonville and nearby; Green River, heads west off Highway 25, 5 miles from Hendersonville and runs into Lake Summit and on into Lake Adger. Fishing in headwaters and between lakes.

Hertford County

Wiccacon Creek. Local enthusiasts call this "the best fresh-water fishing in North Carolina." Potecasi Creek (and guts off it). Chowan and Meherrin rivers and tributaries.

Hoke County

Lumber River—June. Accommodations at Raeford, Laurinburg. McNeill Pond—May and June, hotel at Raeford.

Hyde County

Mattamuskeet Lake. Bass fishing best in March, April, May. Lodge at New Holland, cabins New Holland and Swanquarter, Fairfield. Boats New Holland, Hodges Fork, Swindell's Fork. Mattamuskeet is a federal wildfowl refuge. Open year round (small fee) except during waterfowl-shooting season (also many creeks).

Iredell County

Lookout Lake—April, May, June, September, and October. Accommodations in nearby towns.

Jackson County

Glenville Reservoir; Tukaseigee River, good bass stream.

Johnston County

Black Creek—March, May, June. Holt's Lake, cabins on Lake. Hotel at Smithfield.

Jones County

White Oak and Trent River, accommodations at Trenton and Maysville.

Lee County

Morris Pond—March. Hotels at Sanford (5 miles), fishing usually good; Cape Fear River near Bucham—mostly in tributaries—March, April. Hotels, etc., in Sanford (10 miles).

Lenoir County

Contentnea Creek—June to October, hotels, etc., Kinston. South Creek—June and October. Nobles Mill Pond—June to November. Devis Mill Pond—June through September. Falling Creek—June, July, and August. Kelly's Mill Pond—June to October. Several other fishing ponds handy.

Macon County

Nantahala Lake. Excellent bass fishing. Accommodations Franklin, Andrews, Bryson City. Highland Lake, hotels at Highlands. Lake Emory, near Franklin. Little Tennessee River, accommodations at Franklin.

Madison County

Laurel River and many tributaries. Ten miles from Marshall on Highways 25 and 70. Accommodations at Marshall, Mars Hill, Hot Springs.

Martin County

Sweetwater Creek, Conoho Creek, accommodations at Williamston.

McDowell County

Lake James—April, May, and June, hotels Marion, cabins on lake. Catawba and North Catawba rivers. Buck Creek and Armstrong Creek. Smallmouth bass below Lake Tahoma on Buck Creek.

Montgomery County

Lake Tillery, Badin Lake, and Little River—March and April. Accommodations at Troy, Albemarle, Badin.

Moore County

Thaggard's Pond, good bass, hotel at Lakeview.

Nash County

Boddies Pond—April, May. Tar River near Rocky Mount, March 15–April 1, hotels at Rocky Mount.

Northampton County

Jordan's Pond, located near Seaboard. The national champion smallmouth was taken from here in 1940.

Onslow County

Northeast River—August, hotels at Jacksonville. White Oak River—August, September. Catherine Lake.

Orange County

University Lake at Chapel Hill—boats.

Pamlico County

Neuse and Bay rivers. Vandemere and Goose creeks. May get commercial fishermen to furnish guide services.

Pender County

Northeast Cape Fear River—early spring, October, and November. Black River—May to July, October, and November, fishing camp near Currie. Long Creek and Fishing Creek—March to July, October, and November, good camping at Northeast Cape Fear River Bridge.

Perquimans County

Tributaries of Perquimans River.

Person County

Chub Lake—June, hotel at Roxboro, fishing good at times.

Pitt County

Trantor's Creek, Grindle Creek—fall and spring, cabins near Grimesland Bridge. Chicord Creek and Bear Creek—fall and spring. Contentnea Creek—fall and spring.

Polk County

Lake Adger—June, July.

Randolph County

Asheboro City Lake—June, hotels in Asheboro.

Richmond County

Old Pate Pond—February, March, April, September. Old CCC Lake. Roberdell Pond—February, March. Peedee River and Blewett Lake.

Robeson County

Lumber River, accommodations at Lumberton, Maxton. Good fly-fishing waters. Keith Millpond—June, September, October. Warwick Millpond—March, latter part of May and June. Pope's Pond—March, May, June.

Rutherford County

Lake Lure—April, June, July, hotels and cabins Lake Lure, Chimney Rock. Hard-fished lake.

Sampson County

Black River—May, June, October, no accommodations. South River. Also good fishing on Big Coharic, Little Coharic, and Six Runs. Good fly and plug waters.

Scotland County

Richmond Mill Pond, Laurel Hill. Sandhills Wildlife Management Area, several good millponds in county.

Swain County

Fontana Lake, accommodations at Robinsville, Bryson City, Tapoca, and nearby; boats. Tuckaseigee River and tributaries, reached via U. S. Route 19, Sylva to Bryson City. Little Tennessee, hotels at Bryson City.

Transylvania County

French Broad River. Cascade Lake and Little River, reached via U. S. Route 64 to Penrose, thence via Little River Road. Frozen Lake, 16 miles from Brevard, 3 miles off U. S. Route 64, boats.

Tyrrell County

Alligator River, Scuppernong River, also Frying Pan (arm of Alligator, highly recommended). Lots of fishable water in this area.

Union County

Lake Lee—June through September.

Wake County

Lake Myre—March, April, May, June, September, October (lake 10 miles from Raleigh on Pool Road near Wendell). Robertson's Pond—March, April, May, June, September, October. No accommodations at pond (4 miles east of Rolesville). Sunset Lake—March, April, May, June, September, October (18 miles south of Raleigh near Holly Springs).

Watauga County

Upper part Watauga River—April 15 to May 15.

Wayne County

Mill Creek—spring and fall, accommodations at Smithfield or Goldsboro. Good for bass.

Washington County

Phelps Lake with accommodations at Columbia, Plymouth, one of best bass waters. Scuppernong River—November, accommodations at Plymouth, Columbia. Many creeks and Albemarle Sound offer sport.

Wilkes County

Elk Creek, about 10 fishable miles, hotels, etc., North Wilkesboro or camp out.

Wilson County

Wiggins Mill—June through September, hotels, etc., at Wilson (4 miles south of Wilson on U. S. Route 301). Farmers Mill (Silver Lake)—June through September (5 miles west of Wilson, Highway 58). Contentnea Creek—June through September, hotels etc. at Wilson. Note: Contentnea Creek runs through Wilson County, about 25 miles of which 15 are considered fishable. Nearest point to Wilson is 4 miles on U. S. Route 301.

Yancey County

South Toe River, fishable from mouth of river to

Carolina Hemlock camping ground. Cane River, bass in lower section to Burnsville.

Yadkin County

Dobbins Lake—last of May and June.

Florida

Florida is so choked, literally, with good bass waters, that even cataloguing them is next to impossible. An angler just can't go wrong in this state; besides the good fishing everywhere, there are adequate accommodations in every community and on every bit of choice fishing water.

For a list of the most consistent bass producers in Florida, we'll rely on Robert A. Dahne, information chief of the state's Game and Fresh Water Fish Commission. His breakdown is as follows:

South Florida

Some of the state's best bass fishing will be the northwest corner of Lake Okeechobee, out of Glades County, on weedless spoons, popping bugs, and other top-water lures. Tamiami Canal region, between Miami and Tampa, will hold good for all fishing. For other sections of Okeechobee, small bass hit well on natural baits or fly-rod lures. Big bass do better on live shiners. All canals and Lake Trafford will produce bass.

Central Florida

Bass will take live, dark minnows at night in Lake Weir, and standard shiners do well in the Withlacoochee River between the Rutland Bridge, near Bushnell, and Ross Bridge, between Ocala and Hernando. Bass in Lake Kissimmee and Kissimmee River will be hitting hard on spoons and live shiners. Lake Pierce bass seem to go for live bait at any time, with deep-running lures in the early morning. Don't overlook Fisheating Creek and the phosphate pits around Mulberry, south of Lakeland. Tiny canals around Lake Wilmington in Indian River County will produce small- to medium-size bass. Try Lake Istokpoga in Highlands County between Lakeland and Lake Okeechobee. Medium bass will take any artificial that resembles a live shiner, as well as small popping bugs and shallow-running spoons.

Northeast Florida

Bass will be hitting spoons in Doctors Lake, near Green Cove Springs, and largemouths in Crescent Lake, near Crescent City, should be walloping shiners and artificials which resemble them. Fly fishing good in Suwannee River, especially around river mouth. Santa Fe Lake and River, will produce big bass, the lunkers preferring live shiners. St. Johns River near Orange Park will turn up fine catches in early morning hours on small artificials. If you like to fish new wilderness area, find the limestone sink known as California Lake in South Dixie County, which is seldom fished and productive of good bass and bluegills in June.

A good Florida largemouth.

Northwest Florida

Major hot spot is Apalachicola River below Jim Woodruff Dam, near Chattahoochee. The Ochlockonee River and Lake Talquin turn up some excellent bass in June. Try noisy top-water plugs, underwater weedless, and live shiners.

A list of other good bass waters, by counties, follows herewith:

Alachua County

Lochloosa Springs, Santa Fe Lake, Newman's Lake, Pinkerson Prairie, Lochloosa and Orange

Lake, Tuscawilla Lake, Waubug Lake, Lochloosa Lake, Newnan's Lake.

Bay County

Bear Creek; Bay and Washington River ponds; Pine Log Creek.

Bradford County

Hampton Lake.

Brevard County

Lake Washington, St. Johns River, Sawgrass Lake.

Broward County

South New River, Miami River Canal, South Miami River Canal.

Calhoun County

Chipola River, Dead Lakes.

Citrus County

Lake Tsala Apopka, Withlacoochee River, Homasassa River, Chassahowitzka River, Moccasin Slough, Crystal River, Floral City Lake.

Clay County

Black Creek, Kingsley Lake, Kingsley Beach, St. Johns River, Doctors Lake, Peters Creek, Smith Lake, Lake Geneva, Black Creek.

Collier County

Lake Trafford.

Columbia County

Lake Lona and Long Pond.

Dixie County

Suwannee River.

Duval County

Goodby Lake, St. Johns River, Julington Creek, Ribault, 9 Mile Creek, Dunn's Creek, Thomas Creek.

Escambia County

Escambia River, Perdido River.

Flagler County

Lake Deston.

Franklin County

Apalachicola River, East River, Graham Creek, Grim Creek.

Gadsden County

Lake Talquin.

Gilchrist County

Suwannee River.

Glades County

Lake Okeechobee, Hicpochee Lake.

Gulf County

Dead Lakes, Chipola River, Lake Minoco, Werappo Creek, Apalachicola River and Canal, Brothers River.

Hamilton County

Withlacoochee River.

Hendry County

Lake Okeechobee.

Hernando County

Neff Lake, Withlacoochee River, Hammock Creek.

Highlands County

Lake Istokpoga, Lake Placid, Kissimmee River, Arbuckle Lake, Lake Verona, Bonnett Lake, Istokpoga Canal.

Hillsborough County

Hillsborough River, Keystone Lake, Miley Landing.

Holmes County

Wrights Creek, Choctawhatchee, Hammock Pond.

Jackson County

Bozek Pond, Ocheesee Pond, Merritts Mill Pond, Ocheesee Lake, Compass Lake, Blue Springs, Waddell Mill Pond, Merritts Lake.

Jefferson County

Aucilla River.

Lafayette County

Koon's Lake.

Lake County

Lake Dora, Lake Harris, Lake Susan, Lake Morris, Lake Jem, Lake Griffin, Lake Apopka, Dora Canal, Lake Eustis, Apopka Canal, Lake Gale, Dead Lakes, Haynes Creek, Dead River, St. Johns River, Helleans River.

Lee County

Telegraph Creek.

Leon County

Ochlockonee, Miccosukee Lake, Lake Talquin, Lake Jackson, Lake Iamonia, Lake Munson.

Levy County

Wacasassa River, Withlacoochee River, Black Water, Long Pond, Suwannee River, Withlacoochee Backwater.

Liberty County

Lake Mystic, Kennedy Creek, Owl Creek, River Styx, Florida River, Ochlockonee River, Whitehead Lake, Equlusee Creek, Michew Lake.

Madison County

Cherry Lake.

Manatee County

Braden River, Ward Lake.

Marion County

Lake Weir, Oklawaha River, Orange Lake, Withlacoochee River, Halfmoon Lake, Lake Bryant, Lake George, Lake Delaney, Lake Kerr, Salt Springs, Lake Warner, Lake Jumper.

Martin County

Jensen Savannah, St. Lucie Canal.

Nassau County

Mills Creek, Little St. Mary's River, Plummer Creek.

Okaloosa County

Yellow River, Shoal River, Log Lake, Garners River.

Okeechobee County

Lake Okeechobee, Kissimmee River.

Orange County

Lake Carlton, Lake Apopka, Johns Lake, Lake Carlton, St. Johns River.

Osceola County

Lake Marion, Lake Hutchineka, Hart Lake, Kissimmee River, Lake Kissimmee, Lake Hatchurch.

Palm Beach County

Everglades, Lake Osborne, Mangola Lake, Lake Okeechobee, Suwannee River.

Pasco County

Hunter's Lake.

Pinellas County

Lake Tarpon, Salt Lake.

Polk County

Lake Pierce, Crooked Lake, Lake Placid, Blue Lake, Lake Easy, Lake Reddy, Lake Marion, Marion Creek, Lake Juliana, Lake Ariana, Lake

Howard, Chain of Lakes, Lake Shipp, Lake Sanitary, Lake Lena, Chamber of Commerce Docks, Lake Parker.

Putnam County

Levy Prairie Lake, St. Johns River, Dunn's Creek, Oklawaha, Swan Lake, Lake George.

Santa Rosa County

Yellow River, Escambia River, East River, Gamers River, Palmer Lake.

Seminole County

St. Johns River, Lake Jessup, Wekeva River, Lake Henry, Lake Monroe.

St. Johns County

Pellican Creek, McCullah Creek, Ponte Vedra Lagoon, St. Johns River, Trout Creek, River Dale.

St. Lucie County

St. Lucie River.

Sumter County

Lake Panasoffkee, Withlacoochee River.

Taylor County

Aucilla River, Steinhatchee River.

Volusia County

St. Johns River, Tomoka River, Lake George, Spring Garden Run, Dead River.

Wakulla County

Ochlockonee River, Wakulla River.

Walton County

Choctawhatchee River, Black Creek, Mitchell River.

Washington County

Choctawhatchee River, Pate Pond, Crew Lake, Pine Log Creek, Holmes Creek, Crystal Lake, Wagners Pond, River Pond.

Louisiana

The state has approximately 8000 miles of freshwater rivers, all of which contain bass but many of which are seldom fished. Since many of the main river systems—the Mississippi, Red, Atchafalaya, Ouachita, Sabine, and Pearl—flow at a higher level (inside dikes and levees) than their drainage plains, they form numerous bayous, lagoons, and oxbows that also are full of bass.

There is actually more bass-fishing water in Louisiana than any one person could possibly explore. Much of it exists so deep in remote swampy sections of the state that it's practically virgin. Several years ago the author fished several such ponds in Tensas Parish simply by hiking across the spongy countryside. Because of too many impossible governmental administrations such as that of Earl Long, not even the state's conservation bureau has been able to tabulate the bass-fishing waters in the state.

Many southern states have waters similar to those in Louisiana. Florida has large natural lakes, and many of them; Mississippi, Arkansas, Tennessee, and others have oxbows in flood plains of large rivers; all states from Virginia to Texas have blackwater streams and ponds; Arkansas, Texas, and Mississippi have bayous. But Louisiana has them all, in bewildering distribution. In discussing inland waters we take up first the basin of Red River, follow with the Mississippi, pick up choice spots in the Southwest, and then move eastward from Sabine to Pearl River.

Caddo Lake (northwest of Shreveport), which lies partly in Texas, has been noted for years for its bass. The states have kept a watchful eye on oil development in the area, to prevent destruction of fish by oil or salt water released from subsurface pools. So far, this is a negligible factor, although derricks stand in the lake itself.

Nearer Shreveport lies Cross Lake, and Bodcau Lake is on Bodcau Bayou northeast of town. Other large lakes down the valley of the Red are Cannisnia, Bayou Pierre, Bistineau, Black, and nearby Saline. The latter two are connected by lakes Clear and Prairie, and by Black and Saline bayous.

Trees, shrubbery, and vines close in on these dark waters and lend an air of what writers might call brooding mystery. Cypress trees, trailing moss stand in the shallows. Their roots spread, forming underwater hiding places and obstacles, and grotesque "knees" thrust their rounded tops above the surface. Tupelo gums, pines, palmettos, and other growths crowd the water's edge.

Another better-than-average body of water of this region is Cane River Lake south of Natchitoches. It lies in a former bed of Red River. Many waters lie hidden in or flow through the timbered depths of Kitsatchie forest near Alexandria. Numerous oxbow lakes are in the valley of the Red between Alexandria and the Mississippi. There's much swampy ground in the combined flood plain north and east of Marksville, and all backwaters of any size and depth carry bass. Accommodations, boats, and other services are not plentiful, though.

Best fishing of the Mississippi flood plain is that of oxbows and bayous. Among the more productive oxbows are Lake Providence, north of Lake Providence. Lake Bruin, between Tallulah and St. Joseph, is circled by roads that make it easy to reach. Lake St. John, a dozen miles south of Bruin and near Ferriday, is good for bass. False River, at New Roads, is one of the largest oxbows in the United States.

Some of the preferred fishing of northern Louisiana is in backwaters of the Ouachita River from Bastrop to below Harrisonburg. Ouachita feeders include Bayou Boeuf and the northern Bayou Lafourche. Boeuf is fished from Arkansas past Rayville; it merges with Ouachita near Wildsville. Lafourche is fished from between Rayville and Monroe to Columbia. It is somewhat overshadowed by Bayou Boeuf. Castor Creek, tributary of Red River, can be fished from south of Ruston to Tullos.

The state likes to brag about the waters of the Southwest. Leesville, Oakdale, Oberlin, Kinder, and Lake Charles are all close to bayous and rivers. Bayou L'Anacoco is one. It flows past Leesville and into the Sabine west of De Ridder. Calcasieu River is fine bass water, from its headwaters south of Natchitoches to Calcasieu Lake. Its tributary, Bundick Creek, which runs past De Ridder, is productive. So is Bayou Nezpique, which dawdles past Jennings and Lake Arthur and joins Grand Lake. Bayou Cannes, reached from Jennings, Eunice, or Ville Platte, and Bayou Cocodrie near Bunkie, Washington, and Opelousas, are worth trying.

The virtually unified flood plains of the Mississippi and Atchafalaya from the neighborhood of Opelousas, Melville, and Baton Rouge to the range of tidal influence, are rich in possibilities. Atchafalaya splits off from the Lower Red and carries part of its burden to the Gulf via Grand Lake (there are two of the same name), which is long and sprawling, with numerous bays and feeder bayous. Many parts of this Grand Lake layout yield bass. Bayou Eugene and Big and Little Pigeon bayous are locally well known. Bayou Teche parallels Grand Lake on the southwest.

Lake Verret, between Grand Lake and Napoleonville, is fished for bass. Grand Bayou is a tributary of Lake Verret. Many fishermen like Lake Boeuf east of Thibodaux and Little Lake des Allemands. Big Lake des Allemands is shallow and not so productive.

We might as well say again—for no matter how often a fisherman goes there he is amazed by it— that southern Louisiana is threaded by uncounted large and small waterways, many fresh, many brackish, but all furnishing sport. The visitor has an extraordinary selection of places to fish.

A number of choice fresh waters are in the corner of Louisiana east of the Mississippi and north of the New Orleans-Lake Ponchartrain area. Amite River flows near Clinton and Baton Rouge to enter Lake Maurepas. And don't pass up the Amite tributaries. Tickfaw River, flowing past Greensburg and Springville into Maurepas, is of the same quality. Tangipahoa River is popular, from above Amite to Ponchartrain. Another favorite is Chefuncte River and its tributary Bogue Falia upstream from Madisonville and Covington. Bogue Chilto, a Pearl River feeder, can be reached between Franklinton and the confluence below Bogalusa. The latter town is a good place from which to set out to fish Pearl River. The Pearl flows through wild swamp country, and the stranger should not go in unescorted. The Honey Island region of the Pearl River bottoms northeast of Slidell has fertile waters.

South Carolina

This state, with a foothold in the mountains and a beachhead on the Atlantic, contains more bass fishing than anyone knows about—and far more than native anglers are able to use in a year's time. Much good bass-fishing water lies untried and untested from year to year. A good example is the maze of moss-hung waterways and tributary streams in the lowlands from Charleston to Georgetown. An angler with a car-top boat and small outboard could spend season after season exploring these places deep in the boondocks—and seldom see another fisherman. He'd catch plenty of largemouths while doing so too. What's more, his chances of catching a real trophy fish would be excellent. A bit of good advice to any visiting fisherman would be to contact the local game wardens here. All are friendly, helpful, and know the region well.

Most local fishermen concentrate on the larger reservoirs of the state. Largest and most productive of these is the Santee-Cooper Reservoir which

Bass fishing in the Santee-Cooper Reservoir near Moncks Corner, South Carolina. This body of water has great potential for big bass.

flooded 170,000 acres of Santee River swamps to form two giant lakes—Moultrie and Marion. Bass fishing is great in both, but especially in stump- and tree-filled Marion. Plenty of accommodations around Moncks Corners and Manning.

Other South Carolina reservoirs include Catawba-Wateree, 26,160 acres near Camden; Lake Murray, 50,800 acres near Columbia; Clarks Hill Lake, 78,500 acres near Aiken; Lake Greenwood, 11,800 acres near Greenwood.

South Carolina's rivers are greatly neglected by fishermen—which is most unfortunate, because all have plenty of bass. Also, most are fine for lazy and leisurely float tripping. Here are some excellent rivers to try: Edisto, Combahee, Santee, Wateree, Witheree, Salkehatchie, Ashepoo, Cooper, Black, Waccamaw, Pee Dee, Little Pee Dee, Congaree. To these add the thousands of farm ponds where many bragging-size largemouths are taken every year.

Virginia

Virginia has more than 100,000 acres of impounded bass water, plus dozens of excellent rivers which harbor the black bass.

The best largemouth bass water is found in tide-water and coastal areas where millponds, reservoirs, and brackish estuaries provide an ideal habitat for the species. Some western waters like Carvins Cove, Holston Reservoir, Claytor Lake provide some excellent bass fishing to be sure, but generally speaking the east-coast waters are more productive, and productive over longer periods.

In a thumbnail sketch of this kind only the more prominent waters can be mentioned—but this does not mean other waters, equally as good, do not exist. They do.

Back Bay, in Princess Anne County near Virginia Beach, is Virginia's big ace in the hole when it comes to bass. Here 25,000 acres of locked-up, fresh water provide unique largemouth fishing. Spring and fall months are best. Those interested in fishing in this famous water should first make local arrangements at Back Bay itself or through local guides or the county game warden.

The huge 51,000-acre impoundment called Buggs Island Reservoir near Clarksville is getting more and more popular every year as a bass lake. This is a typical TVA-type of lake, which has many beautiful coves, recesses, and sheltered spots for fishing. Because of its tremendous size and capabilities, it can absorb a great deal of fishing pressure. Accommodations are abundant and handy.

Bass fishermen will find Claytor Lake, near Pulaski, a splendid big fishing lake. All three Virginia bass—largemouth, smallmouth, and the spotted—are found in this 4500-acre reservoir. What's more, the 100-mile shore-line lake offers some excellent walleye fishing. Facilities for boating and fishing are available to the public through Claytor State Park.

Good bass fishing is to be had in other impounded reservoirs in the state. Among some of the prominent ones are Chickahominy in New Kent County, Carvins Cove in Roanoke County, South Holston Reservoir in Washington County, Philpott Reservoir in Patrick (3370 acres), Lake Jackson in Prince William County, and Lake Cahoon and Lake Prince in Nansemond County. Chickahominy, which is 25 miles southeast of Richmond, is particularly hot in June or at night later on.

Smallmouths are found in all of the larger rivers in the Piedmont and mountain sections. The best smallmouth waters are the James, Shenandoah (both forks), Holston, Rappahannock, Jackson, Back Creek, Cowpasture River, Maury River, and Little River.

Largemouths are common in many brackish rivers at tidewater. Among these are Chickahominy River, James River, Appomattox Creek, Mattaponi Creek, Piscataway Creek, Piankatank and Pamunkey rivers.

Georgia

Here is another of those states with so much excellent bass fishing that it's hard to classify. Although the middle section of the state is in such a state of erosion that most streams continually run red with silt, there are fine bass waters both to the north and south. The world's record largemouth, a 22-pounder, came from a black-water pond near Valdosta in the southern portion.

Although it has known poor years during periods of drought, there's no doubt but that vast, strange, 600-square-mile Okefenokee Swamp is the state's most interesting fishing hole. A lonely and soggy region where the earth "trembles," nearly all of Okefenokee's open-water areas contain bass. This isn't a place to fish or to explore alone, but with a guide it's possible to cast the canals and lakes, the winding waterways and alligator holes in safety. If fishing is slow, the scenery and the abundance of

Bass fishing in Okefenokee Swamp, Georgia.

wildlife are far more than enough to make up for it. There is also excellent bass fishing in the St. Marys and the more celebrated Suwannee rivers which drain the swamp. Guides for both swamp and river fishing can be contacted at Folkston, Fargo, or Waycross.

There is good reservoir fishing in Georgia too. Clark Hill Lake above Augusta is a hot spot. Other reservoirs are Burton, Nacoochee, and Rabun on Tallulah River, and Tugaloo and Yonah on the Chattooga-Tugaloo rivers where they form the boundary with South Carolina. Clayton is the better-known resort and entry point. Burton and Rabun are very good.

A Tennessee Valley Authority dam across the Hiwassee River just below the confluence of the Hiwassee and Shooting Creek in North Carolina has backed the water up both valleys across the line into north Georgia near Hiwassee. Now called Lake Chatuge, the reservoir has developed into a popular bass-fishing spot.

Near Blairsville, Nottely River has bass. Blue Ridge Lake on Toccoa River at Blue Ridge also supports bass. The river is mostly good bass water.

Coosawattee and Oostanaula rivers, which join above Calhoun, have bass, but the Etowah River flows through mining and industrial areas at and above Cartersville and has suffered. The Chattahoochee has spotty bass fishing to the vicinity of Atlanta. It roils easily and often is red from the washed clay of the orchard-dotted hills around Cornelia.

There are few prettier sights in Georgia than the peach orchards around Macon and Fort Valley in full April bloom, unless of course, you pause to consider the beauty of ripe Elbertas in July. It's too bad that the streams of this Georgia mid-section can't be as pretty as the trees and their blushing fruit.

We don't want to be too hard on middle Georgia, however. Some rather decent fishing can be found if the visiting angler has time to shop around, and hits it at the right time. Trouble is that, sure as shootin', he'll get to the right spot just after a shower of rain and find the stream or lake r'iled up and unfishable.

Above Macon, on either side of Jackson, are Lloyd Shoals Dam on the Ocmulgee, which backs up the waters of South and Yellow rivers, and High Falls Dam, also on the Ocmulgee. Off to the southeast, below Milledgeville, is Black Lake on Oconee River. Oconee often is clearer than Ocmulgee. Near Crawfordville, Alexander H. Stephens State Park has a bass lake.

Two large reservoirs have been formed on the Chattahoochee between Columbus and West Point, and there's bass fishing when the river is clear enough.

There are power reservoirs along Flint River at Cordele and Albany. Lake Blackshear, at Cordele, yields nice bass. Kinchafoonee and Muckalee creeks enter the Flint at Albany. Both have bass. The Flint is yellowish from silt much of the time but does clear enough to be fishable on occasion. Probably the best fishing near Albany, however, is found in the lime sinks, ponds, and smaller streams. Lake Sinclair near Milledgeville is very good.

Practically all the streams and ponds of south Georgia contain fish. Highways through Savannah, Jesup, Waycross, Valdosta, Thomasville, and Bainbridge cross dozens of interesting black-waters. The Ogeechee and Canoochee, entered from Ways Station near Clyde, the Little and Big Satilla and the smaller Alapaha, all in the vicinity of Blackshear, the Alapaha, Little, and Withlacoochee rivers near Valdosta, the Ochlocknee near Thomasville, the tributaries of the Flint near Bainbridge—all are fertile black-waters. Lake Donaldson near Decatur has many good bass.

Alabama

As with all states in the cotton belt, there's no shortage of bass fishing in Alabama—and most of it is good. The line-up of best fishing holes would run something like this:

Shoal Creek, Elk River, and Waterloo are the most noted largemouth areas, as are the tail-waters of Wilson and Wheeler dams. June anglers get their best results with top-water plugs, bugs, and streamer flies. Live-bait fishermen score with small shad minnows, shiners, and creek chubs.

At Guntersville and Scottsboro, popping bugs, top-water casting lures, and weedless underwater artificials pay off around the weed beds.

Good bass fishing is found around Lock No. 4 on the Coosa in St. Clair County, as well as on Inland Lake in Blount County. Top-water, black eels, and underwater jointed baits are good.

Jefferson and Tuscaloosa County sections of the Black Warrior River hold good bass, and so does Lake Purdy near Birmingham.

One of the newest and best largemouth fishing spots in Alabama is Demopolis Lake, near Demopolis. Inquire at local tackle shops what they're hitting and where.

Try the Pea and Choctawhatchee rivers with top-water baits. In the central section, fish Jordan, Martin, Mitchell, and Lay lakes. Here, the recommended rivers are Coosa, Tallapoosa, Cahaba, and Alabama. With the introduction of threadfin shad last year, Lake Martin should reach its peak this season.

Tensaw and Stiggins Lake in Baldwin County are known for their largemouths, and June is considered a top month. There's also good bass in Mobile County, where rivers and creeks empty into Mobile Bay. Use top-water lures and live minnows.

An extra word about the Tensaw and Mobile River deltas. An angler with boat and trailer can do no better than drive east across the causeway from Mobile, float his boat at any of the public launching sites along the way, and then explore the endless bends and pools upstream. At times phenomenal catches of largemouths are made hereabout.

A list of Alabama's impounded waters which contain bass follows. Boats and accommodations are available on or near all these lakes.

Guntersville Lake, Pickwick Lake, Wheeler Lake, Wilson Lake, Jordan Lake, Lay Lake, Mitchell Lake, Martin Lake, Mobile Delta, Barbour County Lake, Butler County Lake, Clay County Lake, Coffee County Lake, Crenshaw County Lake, Cullman County Lake, Fayette County Lake, Lamar County Lake, Marengo County Lake, Marion County Lake, Pike County Lake.

Mississippi

Mississippi is very similar to Georgia and Alabama both in the quality and quantity of fishing waters. There's more than enough to go around. Also, no one has ever taken the time to list or tabulate all of the waters which contain bass. This much is certain: there's many a back country, black-water brook or pond that has seldom if ever been fished. An enterprising angler can find these places and have the bass-fishing time of his life.

From the incomplete creel census data available, the state's Game and Fish Commission considers the following areas as tops for bass—year in and year out:

Lake Bogue Homa (Jones County), Eagle (Warren), Bee (Holmes), Beulah (Bolivar), Moon (Coahoma), Tunica Cutoff (Tunica), Mossy (Holmes), Grenada Reservoir (Grenada), Enid Reservoir (Yalobusha), Sardis Reservoir (Panola), Washington (Washington), Ferguson (Washington), Pickwick (Tishomingo), Pascagoula and Biloxi rivers. The last named are splendid float-trip possibilities—especially if an angler pauses long enough to explore their tributaries.

A list of the state's major impounded waters follows:

Pickwick Reservoir near Iuka, partly in Tennessee, Sardis Reservoir, Enid Reservoir, Grenada Reservoir, Arkabutla Reservoir, Bogue Homa Lake, Bluff Lake, Moon Lake, Lake Ferguson, Lake Lee, Lake Washington, Chotard Lake, Eagle Lake, Pascagoula River, Biloxi River, Wolf River, Jordon River, Clarke State Park, Percy Quin State Park, Shelby State Park.

West Virginia

There's splendid bass fishing in West Virginia. Flowing northeast through the eastern panhandle are the Cacapon River and South Branch of the Potomac, two of America's finest smallmouth bass streams. Once the Shenandoah and the North Branch of the Potomac were in this category, but now both suffer somewhat from pollution.

Through Clay and Braxton counties of central West Virginia winds the Elk River, another topnotch bass producer.

Another grand smallmouth river is the New, which begins high up in Virginia and rushes northward across the state to meet the Kanawha. Long stretches of this river are far from highways and deep in rocky gorges—word to the adventurous angler should be sufficient.

Perhaps the loveliest of all West Virginia rivers is the Greenbrier, a natural for floating in a canoe as well as for wading. In the upper reaches and in its branches are trout. Downstream from Marlinton it's good bass water. The river flows alternately through lush bluegrass valleys, through rhododendron jungles, and through rocky hemlock canyons. The entire setting of Greenbrier County is one of America's most beautiful. For anglers who like background and atmosphere with their sport, this region is hard to beat.

There isn't too much lake fishing for warm-water species in West Virginia. Mountain Staters had high hopes for Tygart Reservoir near Grafton, but outside of fair crappie fishing each spring, there's not too much action there. Pollution is probably a factor. Today, the best producer is 1000-acre Bluestone Lake near Hinton.

Bluestone is primarily a flood-control reservoir formed by a U. S. Engineers dam on the New River. It lies mostly in Summers County and is accessible to U. S. Routes 60, 19, 21, and 219. Fishing for bass has been good since the lake filled several years ago.

An aerial view of Lake Hamilton, a good bass lake near Hot Springs, Arkansas.

Arkansas

This is one of the greatest of all bass-fishing states. Float tripping such beautiful rivers as the White and North Fork has always been well known among bass fans, but in recent year fishing has also been phenomenal in the new large reservoirs. Norfork Lake near Mountain Home has been a hot spot. At times Bull Shoals, up on the Missouri border, has been even better for trophy fishing. Lakes Hamilton and Catherine near Hot Springs have always been reliable, and now nearby Ouachita has surpassed them with near-record strings. The truth is that it's hard to go wrong in finding a good place to catch bass in Arkansas.

A list of outstanding Arkansas bass waters follows. Accommodations, bait, boats, motors, and even guides are available on or near all of these waters. On most of the streams outfitters are ready to push off on float trips on a moment's notice.

Lower White River, Lake Enterprise, Lakes Bull Shoals and Norfork, Lake Atlanta, Lower Saline River, Lake Chicot, Corning Lake, Lake Bailey, Lake Ft. Smith, Horseshoe Lake, Lake Wallace, Conway Lake, Spring River, Lake Catherine and Lake Hamilton, Horsehead Lake, Bearcreek Lake, Blue Mountain Lake, First Old River, Big Lake, Lake Ouachita, Buffalo River, Narrows Reservoir, Upper Ouachita River, Eleven Point River, Lake Winona, Rolling Fork River, Grand Marie Lake, Upper White River, Taylor Bay, Nimrod Lake.

Photo by Phelps

A fine catch of largemouths from Lake Catherine, Arkansas. This lake near Hot Springs has been a good producer for many years.

Puerto Rico

Largemouth bass grow big and plentiful in nearly all of the reservoirs of Puerto Rico. In Lake Guajataca especially there are some big lunkers. Sometimes it's hard to find accommodations or even to rent boats around some of the lakes. The fishing is usually good enough, though, to make many discomforts worth-while.

A list of Puerto Rico bass waters follows:
Lake Guajataca, Lake Loíza, Lake Dos Bocas, Lake Caonillas, Lake Cidra, Lake Guayabal, Lake Patillas, Lake Luchetti, Lake Curias, Lake Guineo, Lake Matrullas, Lake Melania, Grande River, Espíritu Santo River, Lake Garzas, Lake Carlta, Manatí River, Cibuco River.

Cuba

Bass exist in several waters in Cuba, but those bass fishermen who have invaded the Zapata Swamps in Cuba have invariably found the best bass fishing of all their fishing experiences. Treasure Lake in the middle of the Zapata Swamp is about three miles by five in size. In addition to largemouth bass it has a large population of big tarpon. A bass fisherman can easily take 150 or more bass a day from this lake. They've been weighed up to 16 pounds with reports of much larger ones. Practically any bait takes bass here. You can concentrate on surface plugging and be busy with bass most of the time.

Getting to this lake is not simple. There is one fishing camp on it, operated by the Instituto Nacional de la Industria Turistica. Dyer's camp accommodates only 8 fishermen at a time. Trips here are arranged through Outdoor Vacations, 103 Guitar Bldg., Columbia, Missouri. The complete cost for a week is about $350, and this covers practically everything, including air travel to and from Miami. You go from Havana by taxi the 100 miles to Jagüey Grande. From there you go by primitive train across 15 miles of swamp and farmland. You transfer in

Casting with a cane pole in a typical Southwest lake

the middle of the swamp for a 6-mile ride to camp. The camp life here is good.

Bass were released here, according to the story, as a mosquito-control measure several decades ago. Conditions were ideal, and they've prospered in Treasure Lake as in few other places. There are a few other lakes in the swamp that also provide bass fishing but none known to be better than Treasure Lake (El Tesoro). Of all bass-fishing waters anywhere, this is probably the best bet to hook a new world-record largemouth.

Chapter 16

THE SOUTHWEST

Traditionally an arid country, it isn't possible to drive very far through the Southwest any more without encountering an abundance of boats and trailers. There are two reasons for this: dozens of giant reservoirs built in the last quarter century and good fishing in all of them. And although nothing like these lakes ever existed in original bass range, largemouths are thriving in nearly all these lakes. It's a happy situation for bass fishermen everywhere.

Oklahoma

Once one of the most bone-dry states of all, Oklahoma is a bass fisherman's paradise because today the state contains almost 300,000 acres of impounded waters with almost that much more in prospect for the future. Bass fishing here is practically a year-round proposition—and it has become big business too.

Just after World War II a visiting sportsman would have had trouble finding suitable accommodations in Oklahoma, but that's all changed. Nowadays there are excellent resorts and cottages, boat docks and bait shops around every major lake. In addition, the state park bureau has installed a system of inns and resorts designed for outdoor families. Result: smooth sailing for bass fishermen.

Oklahoma's largest body of water is Texoma Lake, which is shared with Texas and which is located midway between Oklahoma City and Dallas. Here alone is a reservoir of 100,000 acres where the largemouths grow to prodigious size. Except for seasonal high winds which often keep fishermen off the lake, this is one of America's great bass fishing holes.

Located in the picturesque Cookson Hills northeast of Tulsa, Tenkiller Lake is little more than one tenth the size of Texoma—but the growth rates of its bass rank with the fastest anywhere. Tenkiller is an extraordinary place to prospect for big bass. As around other Oklahoma lakes, accommodations are available. The Cookson Bend resort is a good place to start.

Although the big reservoirs absorb about 95 per cent of the bass-fishing pressure, there are other possibilities—such as the beautiful Illinois (below Tenkiller) and Kiamichi rivers, where float trips are highly recommended. Long stretches of these rivers are seldom disturbed, and the bass are unsophisticated. Oklahoma also can brag of over 100,000 farm and ranch ponds; nearly all contain bass.

Following are listed Oklahoma's "Great Lakes" in order of their size.

Lake Texoma, Grand Lake (Lake of the Cherokees), Fort Gibson Lake, Tenkiller Lake, Great Salt Plains Lake, Altus-Lugert Lake, Canton Lake, Lake Murray, Wister Lake, Hulah Lake, Lake Spavinaw No. 2, Carl Blackwell Lake, Lake Hefner, McAlester Lake, Lake Lawtonka, Lake Overholser, Lake Spavinaw No. 1, Fort Supply Lake, Shawnee Lake, Heyburn Lake, Clear Creek Lake, Greenleaf Lake, Duncan Lake.

In addition, here is a list of fishable (for bass) municipal lakes in the Osage region.

Barnsdall Lake, Blackwell City Lake, Fairfax City Lake, Hudson Lake, Newkirk City Lake, Pawnee City Lake, Pawhuska City Lake, Perry City Lake, Ponca City Lake, Shidler City Lake.

Texas

Texans are likely to brag about their great bass fishing, but they aren't likely to agree on just which places are best. And although this also was a waterless state originally, large reservoirs are fairly well scattered from border to border. Just for example, Ken Foree, outdoors editor of the Dallas *News*, lists his favorites like this: 1, Falcon Lake on the Rio Grande near Laredo; 2, Dow Lake or Harris Reservoir near Freeport; 3, Lake Texoma on the Oklahoma border; 4, Lake Belton; 5, Mathis Lake near Corpus Christi; 6, Whitney Lake below Dallas.

There is some river bass fishing in Texas, but the best of it is centered in the eastern portion of the state. Bass are available in the oxbows of the Red

River, for example, and in the Sulphur River west of Texarkana. Add also Blue and Long lakes northeast of Point Pleasant.

About half of big Caddo Lake lies on the Texas side northeast of Marshall. This is bass water. Fully as good is Black Cypress Bayou, which meanders into the lake from the direction of Jefferson.

From Center and the neighborhood of Nacogdoches south through Lufkin, Jasper, and smaller points to the coast, much fishing is found in waters of the Davy Crockett, Angelina, and Sam Houston forests. Lufkin is just north of the Big Thicket, a region of dense vegetation, of lazy, interwoven bayous and sloughs. It is good sense to go in with somebody who knows it well. Largemouth bass there run to good size. Attoyac Bayou and Angelina and Neches rivers furnish sport.

Lake Dallas, the Dallas water supply is on Elm Creek. A series of dams has been built on Trinity River upstream from Fort Worth. Lake Worth is the older; others are Eagle Mountain Lake and Lake Bridgeport. The former is south, the latter west of Decatur.

Three reservoirs are in the Wichita Falls area. Lake Kemp on Wichita River north of Seymour is by far the largest; it has a 100-mile shore line. Diversion Lake is downstream to the east, and Lake Wichita is on a tributary at the edge of town. All are bass lakes.

Texans extol the virtues of picturesquely named 'Possum Kingdom Reservoir on the Brazos near Mineral Wells, Breckenridge, and Graham.

Below Mineral Wells there's fishing for bass in creeks and sloughs of the Brazos.

Cleburne fishermen visit Cleburne State Park, where there is a public lake. There's some fishing along Paluxy River near Glen Rose, southwest of Cleburne.

In the Waco area, fishermen have Lake Waco, on a Brazos feeder. There are bass in Leon River, which skirts the hills around Gatesville, and at the falls of the Brazos below Marlin.

From the neighborhood of Austin for 200 miles west, southwest, and south, the questing angler can find much of interest. For the most part this is hill country, well wooded, and is threaded by clear streams and dotted with sparkling artificial lakes. Texans grow lyrical singing the praises of Medina Lake northwest of San Antonio. It has almost 100 miles of shore line broken by many fingers probing the adjacent hills. Medina River is fished above and below the lake. Numerous state parks have been created: There's Bastrop-Blueseher near Bastrop, Lockhart near Lockhart, Palmetto near Luling,

Longhorn near Burnet, Blanco near Blanco, Kerrville near Kerrville, Garner north of Uvalde, and others. These either have fishing water within their boundaries or close by. Much of the countryside has a limestone base, and springs gush from hillsides; the waters reflect the purity of their source, and the quality of the fishing is also affected favorably.

Colorado River is good for bass fishing. Several dams have stored reservoirs near Austin. Tom Miller Dam forms Lake Austin, Mansfield Dam Lake Travis, both near Austin. Inks and Buchanan dams and one at Marble Falls are upstream. The river is broad, and shoals alternate with deep pools.

San Gabriel Lake near Georgetown is fed by limestone springs. San Marcos is a resort partly because of San Marcos River and its large springs. There are several dams along Guadalupe River near New Braunfels. Pedernales River supplies fishing in the neighborhood of Johnson City. Guadalupe also is fished from Kerrsville.

Fishing is permitted in Chicon Lake near Natalia, southwest of San Antonio, and there's fair fishing in Lake McQueeney, to the east near Seguin. South of San Antonio at Three Rivers, Frio, Nueces, and Atascosa rivers join.

Devil's River has been dammed northwest of Del Rio to form two irrigation reservoirs known as Lake Walk and Devil's Lake. Fishing is permitted, for a fee.

Junction, Menard, Cleo, and other towns in the area are entry points to bass waters in the upper Llano and San Saba rivers.

San Angelo and Brownwood are headquarters for fair fishing. South and Middle Concho rivers join at Lake Natsworthy south of San Angelo. Best South Concho fishing likely is that between Eldorado and San Angelo. Middle Concho above the lake also is popular. Principal Brownwood sport is at Lake Brownwood, a few miles north of town.

The Abilene area has some fishing. Lakes Abilene and Kirby lie to the south; Phantom Lake, a suburban angling mecca, is nearer. There's a lake near Cisco, where fishing is permitted for a fee.

There's little water sport in the Texas panhandle because of the alkali. Twin Draw Lake near Post, southeast of Lubbock, is stocked with bass. There's fishing, too, at Buffalo Springs and in Yellow House canyon near Slaton.

In the neighborhood of Childress, good water has been created through construction of Lake Childress 8 miles west of town, and Lake Pauline southeast of Quanah. Amarillo's fishing is in Lake Amarillo on Paloduro Creek southwest of town, and in the uncertain waters of Tierra Blanca Creek.

In far west Texas beyond Fort Stockton, fishing is in Toyah River basin. This is the trans-Pecos country north of the Davis Mountains. Phantom and Balmorhea lakes near Balmorhea are heavily fished. So are Toyah River and Toyah Lake. The latter is near Pecos. Northwest of that town, Red Bluff Lake has been impounded by damming Pecos River, and this water, too, carries a heavy fishing load.

Arizona

Arizona's bass fishing can be grouped into two major areas, the Salt and Colorado River lakes and four individual lakes: Carl Pleasant, San Carlos, Bartlett, and Horseshoe. The Salt River chain of lakes in east-central Arizona is formed by a series of dams on the Salt River, which cuts across the state from its headwaters in eastern Arizona to its junction with the Gila River south of Buckeye. That is, it did reach the Gila until the series of dams, beginning with Roosevelt, were built and formed the present chain of lakes. Starting at Phoenix and going east, the lakes are: Saguaro, Canyon, Apache, and Roosevelt. Boats and camping facilities are available at all of them. Of the four, Roosevelt is generally considered to be the best producer of bass, with Apache running second. Canyon and Saguaro have become playgrounds for water-sports enthusiasts, but still manage to produce some fine fishing.

The Colorado River lakes begin at the lower end of the Grand Canyon where the largest and most famous, Lake Mead, is formed by Hoover (Boulder) Dam at Boulder City. The bass fishing at Lake Mead is world-famous and is thought by many to be the best in the country. Whether or not it is the best is not important, but it can be safely said that it is second to very few.

The next lake in the chain is Lake Mohave, and it has the distinction of being an excellent fishing spot for both black bass and rainbow trout. Toward the lower end of the lake the water is not so cold, and boasts very good fishing for bass and other warm-water species.

Between lakes Mohave and Havasu, the next actual lake in the chain, is an area sometimes called a lake, but which is actually a sort of swamp where the river meanders and forms a large area of fishing water. The Topock Swamp, as this area is called, produces some very good fishing, although the supply of water into it is somewhat uncertain.

Lake Havasu itself is a good producer of most warm-water species, and moves into the limelight where large bass are concerned.

Between Lake Havasu and Imperial Dam near Yuma are a number of small lakes not often heard of except locally, but nevertheless worthy of mention since they do furnish some good fishing. Among these are Cibola, Ferguson, and Martinez lakes. The final lake on the river is Mittry Lake, just outside Yuma.

With bass as the chief target in all of these lakes and in the river itself, numerous boat landings are scattered along the river and the lakes, and fishermen can usually find a boat to rent and a place to camp at most of the more popular spots. Some cabins are also available at the areas where there is a greater concentration of activity.

The Colorado River itself should also be mentioned, since it, too, produces some good fishing along its entire length from Lake Mead south. In the upper reaches near Lake Mohave trout are found in the river, but over the major portion of its length bass are the big attraction.

The Verde River, which flows southward through central Arizona, also boasts two lakes. They are Horseshoe Lake to the north, and below it, Bartlett Lake. While these two lakes are chiefly for purposes of flood control and are not used primarily for irrigation purposes, they do furnish some fair to good fishing. The Verde River furnishes smallmouth bass fishing. The Verde joins the Salt below the dams, and their combined flow furnishes several miles of fishing and recreation area.

North and slightly west of Phoenix is Lake Carl Pleasant and its little brother Frog Tanks. Lake Pleasant produces some good bass fishing from time to time, but it is not so dependable as the other lakes mentioned.

On the Gila River southeast of Globe is San Carlos Lake, formed by Coolidge Dam. The Gila River has not been able to keep the lake supplied with water in recent years, however, and San Carlos does not produce much in the way of bass fishing.

New Mexico

Bass fishing both for largemouth and smallmouth may be enjoyed in New Mexico the year round.

Conchas Lake, one of our biggest waters, is stocked with bass, and so is Alamogordo Lake and Elephant Butte Lake. Bear Canyon Lake has trout as well as bass. There are bass in the small deep lakes near Santa Rosa, and in Red Bluff Lake. Other lakes for good warm-water fishing are Avalon, Bitter, Bottomless, Caballo, Jackson, Municipal, and Six-Mile lakes.

The Pecos River contains bass from McMillan Dam south. The lower Pecos River is generally good for the warm-water game species. Berrendo and Hondo creeks and Felix River, all in the Pecos Valley, are good waters.

The lower Rio Grande and the drainage canals near Las Cruces and Socorro and south of Belen all afford fine fishing, and there are less important but good fishing waters here and there throughout the state.

Boats are available at Elephant Butte, Caballo, and Conchas lakes and at several of the other large lakes.

Alamagordo Lake, Anaconda Lake, Avalon Lake, Bass Lake, Bitter Lake, Bottomless Lake, Caballo Lake, Calley Lake, Chain Lakes, Conchas Lake, Dosher Lake, Elephant Butte Lake, El Paso Lakes, Fin and Feather Lake, Harroun Lake, Harroun Dam, Hidden Lake, Mossman Reservoir, Municipal Lake, Pasamonte Lake, Power Dam Lake, Railroad Reservoirs, Red Lake (Navajo Res.), Red Bluff Lake, Rio Grande Beach Lake, Riner Lake, Zuni Reservoir, Ojo Caliente Lake, Belen-Riverside Drain (Los Lunas South), Belen-Riverside Drain (Los Lunas North), Berrendo Creek (Trib. to Lower Pecos), Black River (L) (Trib. to Lower Pecos), Black River (U) (Trib. to Lower Pecos), Bosque del Apache Drains (Trib. to Rio Grande), Conejo Creek (Trib. to Pecos River), Cottonwood Creek (Trib. to Pecos River), Del Rio Drain (Trib. to Rio Grande), East Drain (Trib. to Rio Grande), Felix River (Trib. to Pecos River), Gila River (L) (Trib. to Little Colorado), Isleta Drain (Trib. to Rio Grande), La Mesa Drain (Trib. to Chamberino Drain), La Mora Creek (Trib. Pecos River), Mora River (Trib. to Canadian River), Nemexas Drain (Trib. to Rio Grande), Pecos River, Penasco River (Trib. to Pecos River).

Utah

Bass-fishing waters are scarce in Utah—extremely scarce, in fact. Some bass live in the Logan River north of Brigham in the northern part of the state. The Provo River and Deer Creek, both below Salt Lake City, furnish some bass fishing. But probably an angler's best bet is Utah Lake just west of Provo.

Many farm and ranch ponds in the state contain bass, but to find them is a matter of inquiring locally.

Colorado

This is strictly a trout state, and a bass fisherman must look far to find sport of any quality. Virtually all the bass in the state are confined to farm and ranch ponds or irrigation ditches in the southeastern quarter of the state. Local inquiry is the only way to find these places.

Nevada

Nevada's bass fishing consists mostly of Lake Mead on the Arizona border. This happens to be one of America's best fishing holes, because the largemouths are both big and numerous. The lake is big enough to distribute fishing pressure. Good camp sites here for a traveling angler.

Bass also exist in Lake Walker (30 miles long by 8 miles wide), between Yerington and Hawthorne.

Mexico

There is much good bass fishing in Mexico, largely in the watersheds which drain into the Gulf of Mexico rather than to the Pacific. Some good waters are close to the United States border. One example is Angostura Reservoir just south of Douglas, Arizona. It's possible to charter a small plane in Douglas and then to be fishing in Angostura an hour after take-off.

A complete list of all Mexican bass-fishing waters has never been compiled, but the Mexican Tourist Director reports that the following waters have excellent bass fishing:

Don Martín Dam, Ojo Caliente, Yuriria Lagoon, Tuxpan Lagoon, Atezca Lagoon, El Estribon Dam, Valle de Bravo Dam, Pátzcuaro Lake, Tacámbaro Lagoon, Duero River, Tepuxtepec Dam, Zacapu Lagoon, Tequesquetengo Lake, Las Estacas, El Rodeo Lagoon, Cuatetelco Lagoon, Necaxa Dam, Valsequillo Dam, Vicencio Lagoon, El Centenario Dam, La Llave Dam, El Azucar Dam, Mante River.

Chapter 17

THE WEST

Much of bass-fishing waters in the West are made to order for campers. These people are setting up comfortable camp right on the edge of good bass water.

Except for the Sacramento perch which inhabited the Sacramento River Drainage in moderate numbers, no members of the bass (or sunfish) family lived on the West Coast until half a century ago. Today the largemouth bass, at least, is an important game fish in every Pacific Coast state because he has been introduced into nearly every new reservoir that has been built in the last few decades. What's more, as new reservoirs continue to be built to serve an exploding human population, bass will be released in still other waters.

Largemouths have adapted especially well to their new West Coast homes because at times and in places the fishing for them has been the equal of that anywhere. And the bass are attaining a size similar to those in the Southeast.

California

There are now 39 large warm-water reservoirs of 500 acres or more in California. These add up to more than 160,000 acres of impounded, public fishing waters. State and federal agencies figure to build about 20 more before 1970, and these will add another 80,000 acres of water—practically all suitable for bass. Considering that the California Department of Fish and Game does an excellent job of managing the state's fishing waters, the prospects for the future are very bright.

One excellent example of the department's work at Havasu Lake on the Colorado River is worth describing. Once the bass fishing here was great, but in recent years it deteriorated badly. Biologists found that bass simply didn't have enough smaller fishes for food. So the state introduced a new species —threadfin shad—and the return to good bass fishing has been almost dramatic.

Probably California's best bet for bass is Shasta Lake, formed by damming the Sacramento, McCloud, and Pit rivers about 10 miles north of Redding. Five- and six-pounders aren't rare.

Clear Lake, north of San Francisco and the largest natural lake in the state, rates high. So do Havasu Lake, the Imperial Reservoir on the Colorado River near the Mexican border, Isabella Lake formed by a dam on the Kern River, and Santa Margarita Lake on the upper Salinas River. Although Sacramento Delta waters are best known for stripers, there's excellent largemouth fishing here too. Local inquiry is necessary to find out exactly when and where.

An example of how productive California waters can be is Irvin Lake a few miles from Santa Ana. Although it's little more than a pothole, it has produced several *Field and Stream* contest winners in recent years.

Cachuma Reservoir, East Park Reservoir, Folsom Reservoir, Millerton Reservoir, Imperial Reservoir, Berryessa Reservoir, Lake Havasu Reservoir, Stony Gorge Reservoir, Burns Reservoir, Farmington Reservoir, Hansen Reservoir, Mariposa Reservoir, Pine Flat Reservoir, Salinas Reservoir, Pardee

Reservoir, Hogan Reservoir, Melones Reservoir, Tullock Reservoir, Tinemaha Reservoir, Exchequer Reservoir, Railroad Canyon Reservoir, Vali Reservoir, Barrett Reservoir, Lower Otay Reservoir, Hodges Reservoir, El Capitan Reservoir, San Vicente Reservoir, Henshaw Reservoir, Nacimiento Reservoir, Anderson Reservoir, Coyote Reservoir, Shasta Reservoir, Dallas-Warner Reservoir, Woodward Reservoir, Turlock Reservoir, Don Pedro Reservoir, Piru Reservoir, Bullard's Bar Reservoir, Salt Springs Valley Reservoir.

Oregon

This is primarily a trout-fishing state, but a few good bass waters do exist. Best of all, by concensus of the state's sportsmen, is Owyhee Reservoir in Malheur County in the southeast corner of the state. It is not an easy lake to reach, relatively, and even launching a boat there can be a chore, but the bass fishing is worth any trouble.

Klamath and Lake counties contain several lakes, including Lake of the Woods, and have fair bass fishing.

Warm-water game fish such as bass are found in many of the coastal lakes. On the north coast are Sunset and Cullaby lakes in Clatsop County and Devils Lake in Lincoln County. Further south on the coast are Sutton, Mercer, Cleawox, Siltcoos, and Tahkenitch lakes. Still further south are the Tenmile Lakes in Coos County and Garrison Lake in Curry County. Fishing for warm-water species is done the year round with the most productive period being from May to October.

The following waters of the Columbia River Flood Plain and north coast contain bass. This list was compiled by the Oregon Game Commission.

Multnomah County

Three State Highway Ponds, immediately adjacent to Sandy River at U. S. Route 30 highway crossing. 8 acres.

Marsh Pond, south of Reynolds Aluminum Plant and 1 mile north of Troutdale. 45 acres.

Unnamed lake behind Sundial Beach, 1/4 mile downstream from mouth of Sandy River at its junction with the Columbia River. 60 acres.

Blue Lake, 3 miles northwest of Troutdale and 1 mile south of the Columbia River, east of Portland. 125 acres.

Fairview Lake, immediately adjoining Blue Lake on the south and 3 miles northwest of Troutdale near the Columbia River. 110 acres.

Columbia Slough. This slough runs approximately 7 miles east and 9 miles west of the Peninsula Drainage Canal with a natural outlet into the Willamette River.

Columbia Slough Pond No. 5, immediately to the east of N.E. 48th Street off Northeast Columbia Boulevard in city of Portland. 6 acres.

Columbia Slough Pond No. 6, immediately to the east of N.E. 33rd Street off of Northeast Columbia Boulevard in the city of Portland. 10 acres.

Smith Lake, bordered on east by North Portland Road and on south by Columbia Slough. 400 acres.

Bybee Lake, 2 miles southeast of the Willamette River junction with the Columbia River. 200 acres.

Ramsey Lake, immediately east of the junction of the Willamette River and the Columbia River. 150 acres.

Sturgeon Lake, between the Columbia River proper and Multnomah Channel outside of the main dike in the central part of Sauvie Island. 3000 acres.

The lake may be entered via the road to Oak Island or the county road on the east side reaching the lake at the north end. A boat can enter the lake from the Multnomah Channel via the Gilbert River.

Columbia County

McNary Lake, between the Columbia River and Multnomah Channel at the narrow part of Sauvie Island. 67 acres.

Grassy Lake, between Columbia River and Multnomah Channel near narrow part of Sauvie Island and north of Sturgeon Lake. 118 acres.

Cunningham Lake, in the section of Sauvie Island downstream and nearly opposite the town of St. Helens between Multnomah Channel and the Columbia River. 181 acres.

Pope Lake, within the secondary dike on Sauvie Island near the Columbia County line on the east edge of the island. 8–10 acres.

Gilbert River, this river connects Sturgeon Lake with the Multnomah Channel supplying the water source and tidal action for the lakes. 5 miles in length and 50–100 yards wide. Boats may be used to enter the river either from Sturgeon Lake or Multnomah Channel.

Clatsop County

Coffenbury Lake, 2 miles west of the town of Warrenton in the coastal sand area 1/2 mile inland from the ocean. 50 acres.

Crabapple Lake, 1/4 mile east of Coffenbury Lake but 1 1/2 miles west of the town of Warrenton. 14 acres.

Cullaby Lake, 1/2 mile east of Coast Highway 101 and 5 miles north of Seaside. 200 acres.

Smith Lake, about 200 yards west of Coast Highway 101 and 2 miles south of the town of Warrenton. 35 acres.

Sunset Lake, 1/2 mile west of Coast Highway 101 in the sand area and 5 miles north of Seaside. 175 acres.

West Lake, the main coastal Highway 101 passes the north end of the lake 5 miles north of the town of Seaside. 332 acres.

Washington

Washington has pretty good bass fishing in widely scattered waters, although the fish seldom ever approach trophy size. No doubt the best bet is Equalizing Reservoir below Grand Coulee; fishing is fast here. Another good bet is Moses Lake in Central Washington.

An angling group known as the Western Bass Club was recently organized in Seattle (Edgar Burkbile, Secy., 5232 Columbia Dr.), and they have compiled the following list by counties of almost 150 bass waters in western Washington.

Cowlitz County

Coal Creek Slough, Mt. Solo Slough, Owl Creek Slough, Silver Lake, Wallace Slough, Wall Boom Slough.

Grays Harbor County

Horseshoe Lake, Kinnamon Lake, Moore's Lake, Oyehut Lake, Saruinski Lake, Sylvia Lake.

Island County

Lone Lake, Pondilla Lake, Whidby Lake.

Jefferson County

Crocker Lake, Leland Lake, Lord's Lake, Rice Lake.

King County

Bass Lake, Bitter Lake, Black Diamond Lake, Bow Lake, Cottage Lake, Doloff Lake, Echo Lake, Francis Lake, French Lake, Holm Lake, Jones Lake, Juanita Lake, Killarney Lake, Klaus Lake, McLeod Lake, Morton Lake, Panther Lake, Phantom Lake, Sammamish Lake, Sawyer Lake, Sikes Lake, Tradition Lake, Trout Lake, Washington Lake.

Kitsap County

Bear Lake, Fairview Lake, Flora Lake, Island Lake, Long Lake, Matthew Lake, Square Lake, Wicks Lake, Wye Lake.

Mason County

Greenwood Lake, Hanks Lake, Isabella Lake, Island Lake, Jiggs Lake, Lost Lake, Mason Lake, Trout Lake.

Pacific County

Briscoe Lake, Clam Lake, Cranberry Lake, Echo Lake, Goose Lake, Island Lake.

Pierce County

American Lake, Florence Lake, Gravelly Lake, Hart's Lake, Jackson's Lake, Josephine Lake, Kapowsin Lake, Kregar Lake, Lower Twin Lake, Ohop Lake, Rapjohn Lake, Shaver Lake, Silver Lake, Steilacoom Lake, Surprise Lake, Tapps Lake, Upper Twin Lake.

San Juan County

Blakelee Island: Horseshoe Lake, San Juan Island: Egg Lake, Sportsman's Lake.

Skagit County

Big Lake, Campbell Lake, Erie Lake, McMurray Lake, Minkler Lake.

Snohomish County

Armstrong Lake, Ballinger Lake, Beecher Lake, Bevis Lake, Blackman's Lake, Bryant Lake, Cassidy Lake, Hall's Lake, Hazel Mill Pond, King Lake, Kirk Lake (Baker), Panther Lake, Stevens Lake, Sunday Lake.

Thurston County

Bald Hill Lake, Bigelow Lake, Black Lake, Chambers Lake, Hewitt Lake, Long Lake, Paterson Lake, Scott's Lake, St. Clair Lake.

Wahkiakum County

Brooks Slough, Skamokawa Slough, Elochoman Slough, Welcome Slough, Grove Slough, Birnie Slough, Skamokawa Creek.

Whatcom County

Samish, Weizer, Whatcom lakes.

Montana, Idaho, Wyoming

Some bass fishing does exist in farm and ranch ponds of these three states, but actually it is of little consequence. A bass fisherman should either concentrate on trout fishing, which is excellent here, or travel elsewhere.

Hawaii

Bass, of course, are not native to any of the Hawaiian Islands, but today they're well established in many waters. Fishing is good on such Public Fishing areas as Wahiawa on Oahu Island, Kohala on Hawaii, Wailua on Kauai.

Besides the public areas, there are many streams, reservoirs, and rivers throughout the state which contain fishable stocks of bass. Many are privately controlled, predominantly by sugar-cane cultivating companies, and permission must be obtained to fish them. On the whole, permits are very liberally granted. The best and most fresh-water fishing is on the island of Kauai.

Chapter 18

CANADA

The author playing a smallmouth at Trout Lake, near North Bay, Ontario.

In all the world, no other country contains such a high ratio of clear, cool, sweet waters as compared to its dry land. And this is fine for the bass fisherman of North America because much of this water in the southern parts of the eastern provinces is excellent bass water. Many lakes contain either largemouths, smallmouths, or both.

Canada isn't a promised land for an angler with a record bass on his mind because the short growing season in the North precludes their reaching great size. But just the same, bass fishing in Canada has a charm all its own. Usually it's a case of casting in an evergreen setting scented and air-conditioned by nature. And the bass, particularly the smallmouths, are terrific performers in waters which are chilled the year round.

No fisherman will have any trouble finding accommodations or facilities to fit his budget, no matter what it is, in any corner of Canada where bass fishing exists. He can enjoy his fishing from a plush American-plan resort or he can camp for a dollar, for example, in a neatly manicured national or provincial park. There are cottages and cabins of every description, with the rent depending largely on the plumbing, and for the most adventuresome fishermen of all, it's hard to match a canoe trip deep into a wilderness area.

No bass addict has really been "around" until he has sampled the fishing in the wonderfully hospitable country to the north.

Ontario

Ontario has an honest claim to being a whole continent's favorite fishing ground with a lake- and river-surface area estimated as 80,000 square miles —one fifth the total extent of the province. In addition to the Great Lakes, all but one of which touch Ontario, there are numerous large bodies of water such as the Lake of the Woods and Rainy Lake on the international border; and Nipissing, Nipigon, and Simcoe, completely contained within the province. Many other well-known waters average near 100 square miles—for instance, the Rideaus, Muskokas, and the Timagami chain of lakes. To these add the many comparatively smaller, but nevertheless quite extensive lakes that lie in an endless chain across the Precambrian Shield of northern Ontario, and the count will be well over 100,000. According to expert geographers, only 40,000—less than half the total—are named. Many of these waters are great for bass. And no Canadian province has more parks, campgrounds, or public facilities for visiting fishermen than Ontario.

There are five major fishing "regions" in Ontario where you can fish from canoe, rowboat, motor launch, or cruiser—or you can even stand on the shore. Of course, most anglers know that the farther you go from the beaten track, the better are your chances of getting fish. And yet—the exception that proves the rule—some of the world's best bass fishing is right off Long Point, on the north shore of

*Bass fishing by canoe on the Basswood River, Ontario. The angler is
George Laycock with his guide, Jeep Latteral.*

Lake Erie—an hour's drive from Buffalo, two hours
from Detroit.

Southeastern Ontario

This area includes such famous fishing waters as
the St. Lawrence River, Lake St. Francis, the Rideau
Lakes, Lake Ontario around the Isle of Quinte, and
all those hundreds of streams and pools lying north
of the St. Lawrence, from Belleville to Pembroke.

Lake St. Francis and the St. Lawrence provide the
best of trolling or casting for bass. Boats can be
rented along the shores of the river. Such towns as
Prescott, Cornwall, Brockville, Gananoque, and
Kingston specialize in outfitting sportsmen, and
good guides are available. Combined with the excellent fishing opportunity of this great river is the
beauty of the Thousand Islands. Farther west, in
Lake Ontario, is the Isle of Quinte, or Prince Edward
County. There is smallmouth bass in the adjoining
Lake Ontario waters, and on the island itself are

dozens of small lakes where good accommodations
are available.

Beginning less than 50 miles north of Belleville
and Kingston and extending through what is known
as the "Land O'Lakes" district, through Frontenac
and Hastings counties and north to the very out-
skirts of Ottawa is land of lakes and streams which
contain bass. There are numerous fishing camps and
resorts here. Main outfitting points are Napanee,
Tweed, Madoc, Kaladar, Carleton Place, and
Renfrew.

Just east of this area, are the Rideau Lakes, readily
accessible from Kingston, and offering fair fishing
for large- and smallmouth bass early in the season.
There are many resort hotels as well as fishing camps
throughout the Rideau District.

Central Ontario

Central Ontario covers the populated and industrial areas around Toronto and such vacation

These fishermen are starting out on a bass trip at Camp Champlain dock on Trout Lake, Ontario.

districts as Muskoka, Georgian Bay, and the Kawartha Lakes. Within its bounds lie the Bruce Peninsula on the west and the Haliburton Highlands on the east. Considering Toronto as the hub, a 57-mile drive will take an angler to Barrie, and bass fishing in Lake Simcoe. In spite of the fact that thousands of people live in the area, this is still one of the province's best bets for the fisherman who doesn't want to go too far or work too hard for his fish.

North and west of Lake Simcoe lies the Georgian Bay-Bruce Peninsula area with its good bass fishing. Meaford is a favorite outfitting point. Farther east around the point of Nottawasaga Bay toward Collingwood there is again good bass fishing, and the 7-mile sandy beach at Wasaga, with its resorts, makes this an ideal spot for fishermen to take their families. From Collingwood northward along the shores of Georgian Bay, bass fishing is what you make it. Midland, Penetanguishene, Honey Harbour, Go Home Bay, and the whole rocky shore up

to Parry Sound are good. This whole area, westward from Orillia and covering the length of Georgian Bay, is good fishing territory, ranging from the open waters of the bay, where motor launches are used, to the more sheltered sections behind the islands, and on inland lakes and streams. From Orillia, looking eastward, there's bass fishing at Coboconk, Miner's Bay, and Minden, and on northward to Algonquin Park. Immediately north of Orillia one hits the most highly developed resort area in Ontario—the Muskoka Lakes. Well-populated with resorts as they are, lakes Muskoka, Rosseau, and Joseph still provide some bass fishing in early summer.

Huntsville marks the entrance to the Algonquin Park area, which contains numerous bass lakes. In this natural park the canoe is the ideal means of transportation. Any of the resorts or camps in the park, or around Dwight, will outfit and provide guides. This is fairly primitive country.

East of Toronto and north of Port Hope and Cobourg are the Kawartha Lakes. These lakes, about

75 in number, with the city of Peterborough at the hub, form the main part of the Trent Waterway system, connecting Lake Ontario to Georgian Bay, along the route traveled by the Indians centuries ago. At Rice Lake, Young's Point, Burleigh Falls, Fenelon Falls, Bobcaygeon, there's good fishing for bass, and further south is Port Perry, on Lake Scugog, also good for bass.

Southwestern Ontario

If an angler enters Ontario at Niagara Falls or Fort Erie, the fine bass fishing along the reefs off Nanticoke, Port Dover, Port Ryerse, and other such towns is within easy reach. Long Point, St. Williams, Turkey Point, and Port Rowan offer accommodations. Even commercial fishermen will take anglers out to sure-fire spots. Entering from Detroit, the same situation is encountered. Highway 3, along the north shore of Lake Erie, passes more good bass territory. At Rondeau Provincial Park, a beautiful forest area and game preserve, an angler can camp. In Rondeau Park there is the usual good bass fishing associated with the Lake Erie region, as at Erieau Beach.

Northern Ontario

Northern Ontario begins at a line drawn across the narrow waistline of Ontario from Mattawa to Georgian Bay. On this line in Lake Nipissing district there are plenty of bass, especially the west arm of Nipissing, Trout Lake, and the French River. Eastward from North Bay the waters connecting Lake Nipissing and the Ottawa River combine bass fishing with historic interest, for this is the time-honored route of Indians and *voyageurs*, the path Champlain took on his first trip into the northland.

Westward from North Bay is Sudbury and such surrounding lakes as Aiginawassi, Wanapitei, Ashigami, Kookagaming, Metagamasine, Oden, Thor, and Ivanhoe . . . all of them containing bass. Farther north, getting into the famous Chapleau District, lakes Onaping, Metagama, Biscotasing are other important names. To the southwest, on the road to Manitoulin Island, lies Lake Penage, famous for bass as well as pike, pickerel, and lake trout.

Manitoulin Island is the largest fresh-water island in the world. It is entirely surrounded by the bright blue waters of Lake Huron, complete with excellent bass fishing all summer long. That's also true of the North Channel, Manitowaning Bay, South Bay, Honora Bay, Bayfield Sound, Meldrum Bay, and adjacent waters. On the island itself are many inland bass lakes such as Manitou, Whitefish, and Mindemoya. Bass and Silver lakes will give you plenty of sport.

To get to the island, take King's Highway No. 17 from Sudbury or the Sault—there's a new highway bridge now, side by side with the railroad from the mainland to Little Current; or you can take the ferry from either Owen Sound or Tobermory. Cars travel on the ferry too.

From Manitoulin Island, north and westward, the fisherman is in his very own territory. This is Algoma . . . and you can start fishing the moment you see water. Massey, Walford, Spragge, and Algoma Mills contain bass. North of Blind River are other good waters. It's interesting to try every road and fish every lake that branches northward off the main Sudbury-to-Soo highway. But this is primitive country, so be sure to locate with an organized camp or guide.

Northwestern Ontario

This is the area from east of Lake Nipigon right to the Manitoba border.

Farthest west is Lake of the Woods, a tremendous lake with thousands of miles of irregular shore line, making it ideal for fishing camps. In Lake of the Woods you are almost sure to have good bass fishing, as indeed is the case from here all the way south to Fort Frances and Rainy River, for this is really good bass territory.

North of Kenora, on one of the transcontinental railways, lies the Minaki district, where sumptuous accommodations and excellent fishing opportunities combine.

Lying between Rainy River and the Canadian Lakehead, Quetico Park forms part of the border between Minnesota and Ontario. Many lakes of this wonderful wilderness area abound in all bass—small-mouths and largemouths. It's really primitive, though, and to get into it means a canoe trip.

Aside from Quetico, however, even though northwestern Ontario offers the peak of wilderness scenery and fishing, this area is well provided with comfortable wilderness resorts, and even in fairly remote parts north of Dryden and Sioux Lookout there are first-rate fishing camps.

There are actually thousands of bass waters in Ontario and to list them all is out of the question. Instead, here is a list, by districts, of the lakes which annually provide some of the best fishing—lakes which are most highly considered by serious bass fishermen. The list was compiled by W. J. K. Harkness, Chief of the Fish & Wildlife Division, Ontario Department of Lands and Forests.

Trolling for smallmouths along rocky shoreline of Trout Lake near North Bay, Ontario.

Erie District: for smallmouths, Mitchell's Bay and Long Point Bay; for largemouths, Long Point Bay.

Huron District: for smallmouths, Clam, Silver, and Puslinch lakes; for largemouths, Clam and Silver lakes.

Simcoe District: for smallmouths, Lake Simcoe, Georgian Bay, and Severn River; for largemouths, Lake Scugog.

Lindsay District: for smallmouths, Pigeon, Stony, and Salmon lakes; for largemouths, Scugog Lake, Pigeon River, Buckhorn Lake.

Tweed District: for both largemouths and smallmouths, Bobs, Gull, and Calabogie lakes.

Kemptville District: for smallmouths, Rideau Lake, Christie Lake, and St. Lawrence River; for largemouths, Newborough and Centre lakes, Rideau River.

Pembroke District: for smallmouths, Madawaska River, Carson and Muskrat lakes; for largemouths, Golden, Greenbough, and Jenkins lakes.

Parry Sound District: for smallmouths, Georgian Bay, French River, Muskoka Lake; for largemouths, Muskoka Lake, Kahshe and Rainy lakes.

North Bay District: for smallmouths, Tomika and Trout lakes, French and Ottawa rivers.

Timiskaming District: for smallmouths, Victoria, Bear, and Labyrinth lakes.

Sault Ste. Marie District: for smallmouths, Wakomata, Stuart, and Matinenda lakes.

Sudbury District: for smallmouths and largemouths, Windy, Kukagami, and Ashigami lakes.

Port Arthur District: for smallmouths, Shebandowan, Muskrat, and Lac des Milles Lacs lakes.

Fort Frances District: for largemouths and smallmouths, Rainy and Pipestone lakes, Sebaskong Bay.

Sioux Lookout District: for smallmouths, Big Vermillion and Little Vermillion lakes.

New Brunswick

Smallmouth bass aren't widely spread through New Brunswick, but in those waters in which the fish have become established the fishing is excellent. These waters are confined to the southwestern part of the province, along or close to the Maine border. They include waters of the Chiputneticook Chain, the beautiful St. Croix River (float tripping is a good possibility here), Lake Utopia, Palfrey Lake, Magaguadavic and Little Magaguadavic lakes.

The greatest fishing of all occurs in early June when smallmouths are in very shallow water. At that time the bass bugging is unbelievably good. Often it is good, but briefly, in September too.

Quebec

Because of widespread stocking in recent decades, smallmouth bass have been established in countless Quebec waters, a large percentage of which are closed to public fishing. Quebec has a strange and unfortunate policy of allowing "clubs" or companies to control vast areas of bush real estate —in which case only a handful of members or friends are permitted to fish in an entire chain of lakes in an entire season's time. Otherwise, as in Ontario, these same lakes might provide sport and wholesome recreation for thousands of residents and nonresidents alike.

In addition, the province evidently isn't interested in entertaining visiting bass anglers. Repeated requests for information to every conceivable government source produce nothing—not even an answer.

Manitoba

Smallmouths have been stocked in a few Manitoba lakes, but today they only exist in numbers in very few lakes of the southeast part of the province. These include West Hawk Lake, Caddy Lake, Falcon Lake, and the Winnipeg River in the Whiteshell Forest Reserve. Another possibility is Lake Athapapuskow in the Pas-Flin Flon area.

Saskatchewan

There is no important bass fishing in Saskatchewan although smallmouths have been stocked in several places. Some are caught in Prince Albert National Park, principally in Lake Waskesiu, but that's just about the whole story.

Appendix

A Directory of Conservation Bureaus; Tackle, Boat, and Equipment Manufacturers; Tourist Agencies and Suggested Reading Material for Bass Fishermen, Including a Résumé of Small-Boat Regulations.

United States Government Agencies

Director of Information
U. S. Forest Service
Washington 25, D.C.
(For information on fishing or vacations in National Forests)

Regional offices of U. S. Forest Service are as follows:

Region 1, Northern
Federal Bldg., Missoula, Mont.

Region 2, Rocky Mountain
Federal Center, Bldg. 85, Denver 2, Colo.

Region 3, Southwestern
510 N. 2nd, Albuquerque, N.M.

Region 4, Inter-Mountain
Forest Service Bldg., Ogden, Ut.

Region 5, California
630 Sansome St., San Francisco 11, Calif.

Region 6, Pacific Northwest
729 NE Oregon St., Box 4137, Portland 8, Ore.

Region 7, Eastern
Center Bldg., 6816 Market St., Upper Darby, Penn.

Region 8, Southern
50 7th St. NE, Atlanta 5, Ga.

Region 9, North Central
Madison Bldg., Milwaukee 3, Wisc.

Director, Information Service
Soil Conservation Service
Washington 25, D.C.
(For information on farm ponds, fishing, fish management)

Office of Information
U. S. Fish & Wildlife Service
Washington 25, D.C.

(For information on fish, fishing, fishing on U.S.F. & W.S. Refuges)

Commissioner
Bureau of Reclamation
Washington 25, D.C.
(For fishing information on areas under jurisdiction of this bureau—which is concerned with water-resources development in the West)

Office of the Chief
U. S. Corps of Engineers
Washington 25, D.C.
(For information on fish and fishing in large reservoirs under U.S.E.D. jurisdiction)

National Non-Government Organizations

American Camping Assn., Inc.
Bradford Woods, Martinsville, Ind.

American Fisheries Society
Box 429, McClean, Va.

Brotherhood of the Jungle Cock
7 St. Paul St., Baltimore 2, Md.

National Assn. of Angling & Casting Clubs
Box 51, Nashville 2, Tenn.

National Wildlife Federation
232 Carroll St. NW, Washington 12, D.C.

Outboard Boating Club of America
307 N. Michigan Ave.
Chicago 1, Ill.

Sport Fishing Institute
413 Bond Bldg., Washington 5, D.C.

State Conservation Bureaus

(Write these agencies for information on open seasons, lake or stream maps, licenses, fishing regulations, etc.)

Alabama: Division of Game, Fish & Seafoods, Dept. of Conservation, Montgomery 4

Arizona: Game & Fish Commission, Arizona State Bldg., Phoenix

Arkansas: Game & Fish Commission, Little Rock

California: Dept. of Fish & Game, 722 Capitol Ave., Sacramento 14

Colorado: Game & Fish Commission, 1530 Sherman St., Denver 5

Connecticut: Board of Fisheries & Game, State Office Bldg., Hartford 1

Delaware: Board of Game & Fish Commissioners, Dover

Florida: Game & Fresh Water Commission, Tallahassee

Georgia: Game & Fish Commission, 412 State Capitol, Atlanta 3

Idaho: Dept. of Fish & Game, Boise

Illinois: Dept of Conservation, Springfield

Indiana: Div. of Fish & Game, Dept. of Conservation, 311 West Washington St., Indianapolis

Iowa: State Conservation Commission, E. 7th & Court Sts., Des Moines 29

Kansas: Forestry, Fish & Game Commission, Pratt

Kentucky: Dept. of Fish & Wildlife Resources, Frankfort

Louisiana: State Wildlife & Fisheries Commission, 126 Civil Courts Bldg., New Orleans 16

Maine: Dept. of Inland Fisheries & Game, State House, Augusta

Maryland: Game & Inland Fish Commission, 514 Munsey Bldg., Baltimore 2

Massachusetts: Div. of Fisheries & Game, 73 Tremont Street, Boston 8

Michigan: Dept. of Conservation, Lansing 26

Minnesota: Dept. of Conservation, State Office Bldg., St. Paul 1

Mississippi: Game & Fish Commission, P. O. Box 451, Jackson

Missouri: Conservation Commission, Monroe Bldg., Jefferson City

Montana: Dept. of Fish & Game, Helena

Nebraska: Game, Forestation & Parks Commission, Lincoln 9

Nevada: Fish & Game Commission, 51 Grove Street, Reno

New Hampshire: Fish & Game Dept., State House Annex, Concord

New Jersey: Dept. of Conservation & Economic Development, Div. of Fish & Game, 230 W. State St., Trenton 7

New Mexico: Dept. of Game & Fish, Santa Fe

New York: Conservation Dept., Albany 7

North Carolina: Wildlife Resources Commission, Raleigh

North Dakota: Game & Fish Dept., Capitol Bldg., Bismarck

Ohio: Div. of Wildlife, 1500 Dublin Rd., Columbus 12

Oklahoma: Game & Fish Dept., State Capitol Bldg., Room 118, Oklahoma City 5

Oregon: State Game Commission, P. O. Box 4136, Portland 8

Pennsylvania: Pennsylvania Game Commission, Harrisburg

Rhode Island: Div. of Fish & Game, Dept. of Agriculture & Conservation, State House, Providence 2

South Carolina: Wildlife Resources Commission, Columbia

South Dakota: Dept. of Game, Fish & Parks, Pierre

Tennessee: Game & Fish Commission, Cordell Hull Bldg., Sixth Ave. N., Nashville 3

Texas: Game & Fish Commission, Austin

Utah: Fish & Game Commission, 1596 West North Temple, Salt Lake City 16

Vermont: Fish & Game Service, Montpelier

Virginia: Commission of Game & Inland Fisheries, P. O. Box 1642, Richmond 13

Washington: Dept. of Game, 509 Fairview Ave. N., Seattle 9

West Virginia: Conservation Commission of W. Va., Charleston

Wisconsin: Conservation Dept., State Office Bldg., Madison 2

Wyoming: Wyoming Game & Fish Commission, Cheyenne

Hawaii: Fish & Game Commission, Commissioner of Agriculture & Forestry, Honolulu

Puerto Rico: Dept. of Agriculture & Commerce, Div. of Fisheries & Wildlife, San Juan

Copies of Federal laws and regulations affording protection to migratory birds and certain other species of wildlife may be obtained from the following:

Commissioner of Fish & Wildlife, Dept. of the Interior, Washington 25, D.C.

Regional directors of the Fish & Wildlife Service having administrative supervision over Service function in the states indicated:

Region 1 (California, Idaho, Montana, Nevada, Oregon, Washington): 1001 N.E. Lloyd Blvd. (P. O. Box 3737), Portland 14, Ore.

Region 2 (Arizona, Colorado, Kansas, New Mexico, Oklahoma, Texas, Utah, Wyoming): 906 Park Ave., SW (P. O. Box 1306), Albuquerque, N.M.

Region 3 (Illinois, Indiana, Iowa, Michigan, Minnesota, Missouri, Ohio, Nebraska, North Dakota, South Dakota, Wisconsin): 1006 West Lake St., Buzza Bldg., Minneapolis 8, Minn.

Region 4 (Alabama, Arkansas, Florida, Georgia, Kentucky, Louisiana, Maryland, Mississippi, North Carolina, South Carolina, Tennessee, Virginia): Peachtree—Seventh Bldg., Atlanta 23, Ga.

Region 5 (Connecticut, Delaware, Maine, Massachusetts, New Hampshire, New Jersey, New York, Pennsylvania, Rhode Island, Vermont, West Virginia): 59 Temple Place, 1105 Blake Bldg., Boston 11, Mass.

Canada

Canada: Chief, Canadian Wildlife Service, Ottawa

Alberta: Fish and Game Commissioner, Dept. of Lands & Forests, Edmonton

Manitoba: Director of Game & Fisheries Branch, Dept. of Mines & Natural Resources, Winnipeg

New Brunswick: Chief, Fish & Wildlife Branch, Dept. of Lands & Mines, Fredericton

Ontario: Fish & Wildlife Division, Dept. of Lands & Forests, Toronto 2

Province of Quebec: General Superintendent, Dept. of Game & Fish, Quebec

Saskatchewan: Game Commissioner, Dept. of Natural Resources, Saskatchewan Resources Bldg., Regina

Mexico: Secretaria de Agricultura y Ganaderia, Director General Forestal y de Caza, Mexico, D.F.

State Recreation Bureaus

(Write these agencies for information on camping or camp sites, on state parks or on traveling within the states.)

Alabama: Div. of State Parks, Monuments, & Historic Sites, Dept. of Conservation, 7 North Bainbridge St., Montgomery 4

Arizona: No State Park Agency.

Arkansas: Div. of Forestry & Parks, Arkansas Resources & Development Commission, P. O. Box 1940, Little Rock

California: Div. of Beaches & Parks, Dept. of Natural Resources, 721 Capitol Ave., Sacramento 14

Colorado: The State Historical Society of Colorado State Museum, 14th & Sherman Sts., Denver

Connecticut: Park Dept., State Park & Forest Comm., 165 Capitol Ave., Hartford

Delaware: State Highway Dept., Dover

Florida: Florida Park Service, 204 Center Bldg., Tallahassee

Georgia: Dept. of State Parks, 418 State Capitol, Atlanta 3

Idaho: State Board of Land Commissions, Dept. of Public Lands, Boise

Illinois: Div. of Parks & Memorials, Dept. of Conservation, 604 Armory Bldg., Springfield

Indiana: Div. of State Parks, Lands & Waters, Indiana Dept. of Conservation, 311 W. Washington St., Indianapolis 9

Iowa: Div. of Lands & Waters, State Conservation Commission, E. 7th & Court Ave., Des Moines 9

Kansas: Forestry, Fish & Game Commission, Pratt

Kentucky: Div. of State Parks, Dept. of Conservation, 737 New State Office Bldg., Frankfort

Louisiana: State Parks & Recreation Commission, 3170 Florida Ave., Baton Rouge

Maine: State Park Commission, State House, Augusta

Maryland: Dept. of State Forests & Parks, State Office Bldg., Annapolis

Massachusetts: Bureau of Recreation, Div. of Forestry & Parks, Dept. of Natural Resources, 15 Ashburton Place, Boston 8

Michigan: Parks & Recreation Div., Dept. of Conservation, Stevens T. Mason Bldg., Lansing 26

Minnesota: Div. of State Parks, Dept. of Conservation, State Office Building, St. Paul 1

Mississippi: Mississippi Forest & Park Service, P. O. Box 649, Jackson

Missouri: State Park Board, 1206 Jefferson Bldg., P. O. Box 76, Jefferson City

Montana: Div. of State Parks, State Highway Dept., Helena

Nebraska: Land Management Div., Game, Forestation & Parks Commission, Lincoln 9

Nevada: Dept. of Highways, Carson City

New Hampshire: Recreation Div., Forestry & Recreation Dept., Concord

New Jersey: Forestry, Parks & Historic Sites Section, Dept. of Conservation & Economic Development, State House Annex, Trenton

New Mexico: State Park Commission, Route 3, P. O. Box 32, Santa Fe

New York: Div. of Parks, Conservation Dept., 507 Arcade Building, Albany 7

North Carolina: Div. of Forestry and Parks, Dept. of Conservation & Development, P. O. Box 2719, Raleigh

North Dakota: State Historical Society of N. D., Bismarck

Ohio: Div. of Parks, Dept. of Natural Resources, 1101 Ohio Departments Bldg., Columbus 15

Oklahoma: Div. of Recreation & State Parks, Oklahoma Planning & Resources Board, State Capitol, Oklahoma City 5

Oregon: State Parks Dept., Oregon State Highway Commission, Highway Commission Bldg., Salem

Pennsylvania: Div. of Recreation, Dept. of Forests & Waters, Harrisburg

Rhode Island: Div. of Parks & Recreation, Dept. of Public Works, 18 State House, Providence

South Carolina: Div. of State Parks, 506 Calhoun State Office Bldg., Columbia

South Dakota: Div. of Forestry, South Dakota Dept. of Game, Fish & Parks, Pierre

Tennessee: Div. of State Parks, Dept. of Conservation, Nashville 3

Texas: Texas State Parks Board, 106 E. Thirteenth St., Austin

Utah: Utah State Historical Society, State Capitol, Salt Lake City

Vermont: Vermont Forest Service, Montpelier

Virginia: Div. of Parks, Dept. of Conservation & Development, Life Insurance Co. of Virginia Bldg., Richmond 19

Washington: State Parks & Recreation Commission, 100 Dexter Ave., Seattle 9

West Virginia: Div. of State Parks, Conservation Commission, Charleston 5

Wisconsin: Forests & Parks Div., Wisconsin Conservation Department, State Office Bldg., Madison 2

Wyoming: The Historical Landmark Commission of Wyoming, 304 West 3rd Ave., Cheyenne

Travel and Tourist Information Bureaus

(Write these agencies about accommodations, road maps, facilities.)

Alabama: State Publicity Director, State of Alabama, Montgomery

Arizona: Arizona State Development Board, State Capitol, Phoenix

Arkansas: Arkansas Publicity Commission, State Capitol Bldg., Little Rock

California: San Diego City & County Visitors Bureau, 499 W. Broadway, San Diego 1; All Year Club of Southern California, 629 S. Hill St., Los Angeles 14; California Mission Trails Assn., 4015

Wilshire Blvd., Los Angeles 5; Redwood Empire Assn., 85 Post St., San Francisco 4; Shasta-Cascade Wonderland Assn., Inc., Redding; California State Chamber of Commerce, 350 Bush St., San Francisco; and Chamber of Commerce of other cities throughout the state.

Colorado: Colorado Advertising & Publicity Dept., State of Colorado, 224 Capitol Bldg., Denver

Connecticut: Connecticut Development Commission, State Office Bldg., Hartford

Delaware: Delaware State Development Dept., Legislative Hall, Dover

Florida: Florida State Advertising Commission, Caldwell Building, Tallahassee

Georgia: Georgia Advertising Commission, State of Georgia, State Capitol, Atlanta

Idaho: State Advertising Commission, State Capitol, Boise

Illinois: Div. of Department Reports, State of Illinois, State Capitol, Springfield

Indiana: Dept. of Commerce & Public Relations, 333 State House, Indianapolis 4

Iowa: Iowa Development Commission, 708 Central National Bldg., Des Moines 9

Kansas: Kansas Industrial Development Commission, 903 Harrison Street, Topeka

Kentucky: Kentucky Div. of Publicity, Dept. of Conservation, Frankfort

Louisiana: Louisiana Dept. of Commerce & Industry, Baton Rouge 4

Maine: Maine Development Commission, State House, Augusta

Maryland: Maryland Dept. of Information, P. O. Box 706, Annapolis

Massachusetts: Massachusetts Dept. of Commerce, Development Div., Boston

Michigan: Michigan Tourist Council, Lansing 1

Minnesota: Minnesota Dept. of Business Development, State Capitol, St. Paul 1

Mississippi: Mississippi Agricultural & Industrial Board, State Office Bldg., Jackson

Missouri: Missouri Dept. of Resources & Development, State Building, Jefferson City

Montana: Travel & Advertising Dept., Montana State Highway Commission, Helena

Nebraska: Nebraska Resources Foundation, P. O. Box 138, State House, Lincoln

Nevada: State Highway Engineer, Nevada Dept. of Highways, Carson City

New Hampshire: New Hampshire State Planning & Development Commission, Concord

New Jersey: New Jersey Dept. of Conservation & Economic Development, 520 E. State St., Trenton

New Mexico: New Mexico State Tourist Bureau, Santa Fe

New York: Travel Bureau, New York State Dept. of Commerce, 112 State St., Albany

North Carolina: North Carolina State Tourist Bureau, Raleigh

North Dakota: North Dakota State Highway Commission, Bismarck

Ohio: Ohio Development & Publicity Commission, 707 Wyandotte Bldg., Columbus 15

Oklahoma: Oklahoma Planning & Resources Board, 533 State Capitol, Oklahoma City

Oregon: Travel Information Dept., Oregon State Highway Commission, Salem

Pennsylvania: Vacation & Recreation Bureau, Pa. State Dept. of Commerce, Harrisburg

Rhode Island: Recreation Dept., Rhode Island Development Council, Providence 2

South Carolina: South Carolina Research, Planning & Development Board, P. O. Box 927, Columbia

South Dakota: South Dakota State Highway Commission, Pierre

Tennessee: Div. of State Information, 115 State Office Bldg., Nashville 3

Texas: Information Service, Texas Highway Dept., Austin

Utah: Tourist & Publicity Council, Room 210, State Capitol Bldg., Salt Lake City

Vermont: Publicity Director, Vermont Development Commission, Montpelier

Virginia: Div. of Publicity & Advertising, Dept. of Conservation & Development, State of Virginia, Richmond

Washington: Washington State Advertising Committee, P. O. Box 546, Olympia

West Virginia: West Virginia Industrial & Publicity Commission, State Capitol, Charleston 5

Wisconsin: Wisconsin Conservation Dept., State Office Bldg., Madison

Wyoming: Wyoming Commerce & Industry Commission, 213 Capitol Building, Cheyenne

Hawaii: Hawaii Visitors Bureau, 2051 Kalakaua Ave., Honolulu

Puerto Rico: Puerto Rico Visitors Bureau, San Juan & Puerto Rico Visitors Bureau, 600 Fifth Ave., New York 20

Outboard Motor Manufacturers

Champion Motors Co.
1325 N. E. Quincy
Minneapolis 13, Minn.

McCulloch Corp.
Marine Products Division
2901 East Hennepin Avenue
Minneapolis 13, Minn.

Oliver Outboard Motors
The Oliver Corp.
108 South McCamly
Battle Creek, Mich.

Outboard Marine Corp.
(Johnson, Gale, Evinrude)
Waukegan, Ill.

West Bend Aluminum Co.
West Bend, Wisc.

Kiekhaefer Corp.
(Mercury)
Fond du Lac, Wisc.

Manufacturers of Boats for Bass Fishing

Aero-Craft Boats
(Harwill, Inc.)
St. Charles, Mich.

Albright Boat and Marine Co.
P. O. Box 3745
Charlotte 3, N.C.

Aluma Craft Boat Co.
1515 Central, N.E.
Minneapolis 13, Minn.

Angler Boat Co., Inc.
Penn Yan, N.Y.

Bemidji Boat Co., Inc.
Bemidji, Minn.

Blue Manufacturing Co., Inc.
2221 North Main St.
Miami, Okla.

Otis C. Borum Boats, Inc.
P. O. Box 1164
Jacksonville, Fla.

Bowman Manufacturers, Inc.
P. O. Box 427
Lake Providence, La.

Bronson Boatbuilding Co.
4301 South Union Ave.
Tacoma 9, Wash.

Bryant's Marina, Inc.
1117 East Northlake Ave.
Seattle 5, Wash.

Carter Craft Corp.
General Delivery
Panama City, Fla.

Century Boat Co.
Sixth Ave.
Manistee, Mich.

Chetek Boat Corp.
Chetek, Wisc.

Core Craft, Inc.
Jamestown, N.D.

Correct Craft, Inc.
Orlando, Fla.

Courtaulds Moulded Products of Canada, Ltd.
Cornwall, Ont.
Canada

Crestliner
Little Falls, Minn.

Crosby Aeromarine Co.
Grabill, Ind.

Cruise-Craft, Inc.
1315 West Belmont Ave.
Chicago 13, Ill.

Cruisers, Inc.
Oconto, Wisc.

Custom Craft Marine
1700 Niagara St.
Buffalo 7, N.Y.

Dorsett Plastics Corp.
1955 LaFayette St.
Santa Clara, Calif.

Dunphy Boat Corp.
Broad and Parkway
Oshkosh, Wisc.

Duracraft Boats, Inc.
Route 202
Peekskill, N.Y.

Feather Craft, Inc.
450 Bishop St., N.W.
Atlanta 13, Ga.

The Fitts Industries, Inc.
P. O. Box 9068
Tuscaloosa, Ala.

Fleetform Corp.
P. O. Box 4106
Fort Worth 6, Tex.

General Boat Corp.
P. O. Box 97
Grand Prairie, Tex.

Glass Magic, Inc.
2751 Ludelle St.
Fort Worth 5, Tex.

Glasspar Co.
19101 Newport Ave.
Santa Ana, Calif.

Glastron Boats
P. O. Box 9211
Austin, Tex.

Jayhawk Marine, Inc.
P. O. Box 243
Parsons, Kans.

Larson Boat Works
Little Falls, Minn.

Larson Boats of California
(Southern Calif. Aircraft Corp.)
Ontario International Airport
Ontario, Calif.

Lone Star Boat Co.
P. O. Box 698
Grand Prairie, Tex.

Luger Industries, Inc.
9200 Access Rd.
Minneapolis 20, Minn.

Lund Metalcraft, Inc.
New York Mills, Minn.

Lunn Laminates
Huntington Station
New York, N.Y.

Lyman Boat Works, Inc.
1615 First St.
Sandusky, O.

Magnolia Boat Mfg. Co.
P. O. Box 1044
Vicksburg, Miss.

Marlin Sales, Inc.
607 South Washington
Owosso, Mich.

Mirro Aluminum Co.
Manitowoc, Wisc.

Mitchell Boat Division
Consolidated Metal Products, Inc.
P. O. Box 63
Elkhart, Ind.

National Marine Plastics Co.
215 North Detroit
Tulsa, Okla.

North American Marine
Warsaw, Ind.

Pabst Boats, Inc.
1648 Liberty St.
La Crosse, Wisc.

Parsons Corp.
Lake 'N Sea Div.
P. O. Box 112
Traverse City, Mich.

Penn Yan Boats, Inc.
Penn Yan, N.Y.

Polar Kraft Mfg. Co.
1237 North Watkins
Memphis, Tenn.

St. Cloud Marine Mfg. Co.
1111 Massachusetts Ave.
St. Cloud, Fla.

Sea Sled Industries, Inc.
P. O. Box 8
Beardstown, Ill.

Shell Lake Boat Co.
Shell Lake, Wisc.

Skagit Plastics, Inc.
La Conner, Wash.

Southwest Mfg. Co., Inc.
P. O. Box 2501
Little Rock, Ark.

Sprayline Boats
P. O. Box 960
Bristow, Okla.

Squires Manufacturing Co.
County St. & Wabash Railroad
Milan, Mich.

Starcraft Boat Co.
516 East Madison St.
Goshen, Ind.

Switzer-Craft, Inc.
P. O. Box 145
Crystal Lake, Ill.

Thompson Boat Co. of New York, Inc.
126 Elm St.
Cortland, N.Y.

Thompson Bros. Boat Mfg. Co.
Peshtigo, Wisc.

Thompson Royal-Craft, Inc.
126 Elm St.
Cortland, N.Y.

Tollycraft Corp.
First at Lincoln, West
Kelso, Wash.

Tomahawk Boat Mfg. Corp.
East Somo Ave.
Tomahawk, Wisc.

Topper Boat Co.
5816 Ritchie Highway
Baltimore 25, Md.

Totem Foldable Boats, Inc.
235 15th St.
San Francisco 3, Calif.

Tri-Star Boats Division
Wolverine Aviation Co.
Detroit City Airport
Detroit 13, Mich.

Wagemaker Co.
566 Market Street, S.W.
Grand Rapids 2, Mich.

Western Oil Tool & Mfg. Co., Inc.
P. O. Box 260
Casper, Wyo.

Winner Mfg. Co.
P. O. Box 266
West Trenton, N.J.

Wizard Boats, Inc.
2075 Harbor Blvd.
Costa Mesa, Calif.

Yellow Jacket Boat Co., Inc.
P. O. Box 264
Denison, Tex.

Yellow Jacket Industries, Inc.
P. O. Box 56
Denison, Tex.

Boat-Trailer Manufacturers

Ajax Boat Trailer Co., Inc.
21942 Dequindre Rd.
Hazel Park, Mich.

Alloy Marine Products, Inc.
4618 Pte. Tremble Rd.
Algonac, Mich.

American Trailer & Mfg. Co.
12222 South Woodruff
Downey, Calif.

Balko, Inc.
P. O. Box 309
Ladysmith, Wisc.

Caldwell Load King Trailers
3204 Agnes St.
Corpus Christi, Tex.

Electric Wheel Co.
Quincy, Ill.

Hilltop Boat Trailer Co.
314 West Chestnut St.
Wauseon, O.

Holsclaw Brothers, Inc.
408 North Willow Rd.
Evansville, Ind.

Little Dude Trailer Co., Inc.
P. O. Box 4513
Fort Worth, Tex.

Lone Star Boat Co.
P. O. Box 698
Grand Prairie, Tex.

Mastercraft Trailers, Inc.
Subsidiary Cadre Industries Corp.
Middlefield St.
Middletown, Conn.

Moody Manufacturing Co.
Maben, Miss.

North American Marine
Warsaw, Ind.

Peterson Brothers, Inc.
P. O. Box 51, Sta. G.
Jacksonville, Fla.

Ramsey Trailers
P. O. Box 147
Sharptown, Md.

Sterling Boat Trailers
P. O. Box 84
Salem, O.

Tee Nee Trailer Co.
215 East Indianola Ave.
Youngstown 5, O.

Tennessee Trailers, Inc.
1311 East Main St.
Chattanooga, Tenn.

Wilmapeg Industries Corp.
Morenci, Mich.

Small-Boat Regulations

Here are the rules you need to know if you fish for bass in waters under U. S. Coast Guard control.

For bass fishermen just getting started in boating, or to brush up on Coast Guard boating-equipment regulations, here is a capsule review of those laws.

These laws, set forth by the Congress in the Motor Boat Act of 1940, are in effect on all Federal waterways.

The act divides boats into four classes: *Class A* includes boats less than 16 feet long; *Class 1* boats 16 feet long or longer but less than 26 feet; *Class 2* boats from 26 feet to less than 40 feet; *Class 3* boats 40 feet to not more than 65 feet.

Equipment requirements are:

Class A

Lifesaving devices: One Coast Guard-approved life preserver, ring buoy, buoyant vest, or buoyant cushion in good condition for each person on board.

Lights: A combination light in the front of the boat showing red to port and green to starboard from straight ahead to two points of the compass behind the beam, visible one mile. A white light in the back of the boat showing all around the horizon for two miles.

Fire extinguisher: Any one of the following types: One-quart vaporizing liquid, 1 1/4-gallon foam, 4-pound CO_2; 4-pound dry chemical. No fire extinguisher is required on pleasure outboards of open construction. (However, you are wise to carry one with you.)

Ventilation: Two or more ventilators with cowls or equivalent capable of removing gases from the bilges in engine and fuel-tank compartments on boats constructed or decked over after April 25, 1940, using gasoline or fuel of a flashpoint less than 110 degrees F. Motorboats so constructed that the greater portion of the bilges under the engine and fuel tanks are open and exposed to air at all times (as most outboards are) do not require ventilators.

Flame arrestor: Carburetors on all engines on motorboats, other than outboards, shall be fitted with an approved device for arresting backfire. Installations made before November 19, 1952, need not meet the detailed requirements of the specifications and may be continued in use so long as they are in good condition.

Class 1

Equipment for *Class 1* is the same as for *Class A*. The only addition is a hand-, mouth-, or power-operated whistle or horn which will produce a blast lasting two seconds and can be heard for a half a mile.

Class 2

Lifesaving devices: Same as *Class 1*. Lights: Individual running lights (not combination lights), red to port and green to starboard that can be seen for at least a mile. Two bright white lights, one in the rear of the boat visible all around the horizon for two miles, and one up front showing right ahead to two points behind the beam on both sides for two miles.

Bell: One which can be heard for some distance.

Horn or whistle: One hand- or power-operated whistle or horn capable of producing a blast at least two seconds long which can be heard for a mile.

Fire extinguisher: Any two of the types described for *Class A*.

Ventilation and flame arrestor: Same as for *Class 1*.

Suggested Equipment

There is no law which says you have to have a rope aboard your boat.

But what boatman would think of operating his craft without line to tie up to the dock?

A boat's equipment needs depend pretty much on the size of the craft and how it is used. A radio-telephone is practically useless on a small lake but next to necessity on big waters.

Here is a list of some of the equipment boatmen should consider:

Smaller craft: Line for tying up, a small anchor, a tool kit (generally furnished by the motor manufacturer), some spare motor parts, a powerful flashlight for running at night in addition to required lights, and fenders to retain the boat's neat appearance.

Larger craft: In addition to the equipment listed for small boats, larger boats would do well to carry an anchor that will hold in a smart wind, a hand-operated bilge pump, and perhaps flare signals and a radiotelephone if operated offshore on the ocean or on large lakes frequently.

Fishing-Tackle and Equipment Manufacturers

Tony Acetta & Son, 932 Ave. E, Riviera Beach, Fla.

A. D. Mfg. Co., 1919 Chouteau Ave., St. Louis, Mo.

Airex Corp., 411 Fourth Ave., New York 16, N.Y.

Fred Arbogast Co., Inc., 313 W. North St., Akron 3, O.

Ashaway Line & Twine Mfg. Co., Ashaway, R.I.

Dan Bailey, Livingston, Mont.

Bomber Bait Co., Gainesville, Tex.

Buck's Baits, P. O. Box 644, Hickory, N.C.

Paul Bunyan Bait Co., 1307 Glenwood Ave., Minneapolis 5, Minn.

Ce-Bet Tackle Co., 2409 Chapel Hill Rd., Durham, N.C.

Conrad Co., P. O. Box 989, Dept. 166, Minneapolis 40, Minn.

Cortland Line Co., Inc., Cortland, N.Y.

Creek Chub Bait Co., Garrett, Ind.

Creme Lure Co., 1414 Piedmont Ave., Arkron 10, O.

DeLong Lures, 4026 Princeton Blvd., Cleveland 21, O.

Denison-Johnson Corp., Mankato, Minn.

E. I. DuPont de Nemours, Wilmington, Del.

Lou J. Eppinger Mfg. Co., 1757 Puritan Ave., Detroit 3, Mich.

The Enterprise Mfg. Co., 110 N. Union St., Akron 9, O.

Glen L. Evans, Inc., Caldwell, Ida.

The Garcia Corp., 268 4th Ave., New York 10, N.Y.

B. F. Gladding & Co., Inc., South Otselic, N.Y.

Gudebrod Bros. Silk Co., 12 S. 12th St., Philadelphia 7, Penn.

Lewis E. Hamel Co. Inc., 24 Browncroft Blvd., Rochester 9, N.Y.

James Heddon's Sons, Dowagiac, Mich.

Horrocks-Ibbotson Co., Utica, N.Y.

Hutt's Tackle House, P. O. Box 1686, Eustis, Fla.

Louis Johnson Co., Highland Park, Ill.

L & S. Bait Co., Bradley, Ill., and Clearwater, Fla.

Langley Corp., 310 Euclid Ave., San Diego 12, Calif.

La Rue Mfg. Co., 3000 Sheridan Rd., Chicago 14, Ill.

Lawrence Tackle Mfg. Corp., 200 Fifth Ave., New York 10, N.Y.

Marathon Bait Co., Wausau, Wisc.

Martin Automatic Fishing Reel Co., Mohawk, N.Y.

Nature Faker Lures, Inc., Windsor, Mo.

Newton Line Co., Inc., Homer, N.Y.

Old Pal, Inc., Lititz, Penn.

Orchard Industries, Inc., Hastings, Mich.

Charles F. Orvis Co., Manchester, Vt.

Parker Lure Co., 821 Florida St., Amarillo, Tex.

Pat's Fishing Tackle, P. O. Box 164, Sheboygan, Wisc.

Pfleuger, Enterprise Mfg. Co., 110 N. Union St., Akron 9, O.

Phillips Fly & Tackle Co., Alexandria, Penn.

Phillipson Rod & Tackle Co., 2705 High St., Denver 5, Colo.

Plano Molding Co., Plano, Ill.

Rockland Tackle Co., Inc., Suffern, N.Y.

Shakespeare Co., Kalamazoo, Mich.

Silaflex, 1919 Placentia Ave., Costa Mesta, Calif.

South Bend Tackle Co., Inc., 625 S. High St., South Bend 23, Ind.

Sportsmens Products Inc., Marion, Ind.

Sunset Fishing Lines, Petaluma, Calif., and Florence, Ala.

True Temper Corp., 1623 Euclid Ave., Cleveland 15, O.

Tycoon/Fin-Nor Corp., 4027 NW 24th St., Miami, Fla.

Uncle Josh Bait Co., Fort Atkinson, Wisc.

Union Hardware, Sealand, Inc., Torrington, Conn.

Bill Upperman's Bucktails, Atlantic City, N.J.

U. S. Line Co., Westfield, Mass.

Wallsten Tackle Co., 5343 W. Diversey Ave., Chicago 39, Ill.

Weber Tackle Co., Stevens Point, Wisc.

Western Fishing Line Co., Dept. W-40, Glendale 4, Calif.

Whopper Stopper Inc., P. O. Box 793, Sherman, Tex.

Williams Gold Refining Co., 2978 Main St., Buffalo 14, N.Y.

Wright and McGill Co., 1400 Yosemite St., Denver 8, Colo.

Zebco Co., 1131 E. Easton St., Tulsa 1, Okla.